# Ethics and education
# for adults

# Ethics and education for adults in a late modern society

## Peter Jarvis

NIACE

THE NATIONAL ORGANISATION
FOR ADULT LEARNING

*Published by the National Institute of Adult Continuing Education*
*(England and Wales)*
*21 De Montfort Street, Leicester, LE1 7GE*
Company registration no. 2603322
Charity registration no. 1002775

*First published 1997*
*©NIACE*

CATALOGUING IN PUBLICATION DATA
• *A CIP record for this title is available from the British Library*
*ISBN 1 86201 015 3 (pbk)*
*ISBN 1 86201 014 5 (hbk)*

*Typeset by Midlands Book Typesetters*
*Text design by Virman Man*
*Cover design by Sue Storey*
*Printed in Great Britain by Biddles Ltd, Guildford*

# Contents

# Dedication

To Seppo Kontiainen
Professor of Adult Education
University of Helsinki

With thanks

# Introduction

This book has been a long time in the writing – about four years. There have been many personal reasons for this which need not be rehearsed here – but education for adults has changed a great deal during this period. Indeed, it has continued to change in the direction that prompted me to want to write the book in the first place, and so it might be the richer for the time that it has taken.

Education for adults has become even more instrumental and a market commodity. Many of the old practices are beginning to disappear and innovative forms of provision come to the fore. I appreciate what is occurring, indeed I have participated in many of them including adult education, distance education. the internationalising of education, etc. In a sense, education has to change with the changing world – but if history is process through time it does not mean that it is always progress. However, it is not the values of postmodernity which are necessarily being analysed here, so much as the values of modernity and the Enlightenment.

The argument of this book is that we can no longer treat moral value as a single entity – there are universal and cultural values. It is strongly argued here that the universal value of the Ego being concerned for the Other can only occur in and through human relationships – which have been been prevalent in education for many years. However, there are cultural goods and they are more relative. Some of these are moral whereas others are non-moral. For instance, a non-moral cultural good is efficiency, and few people would dispute that efficiency is an important value. However, when we juxtapose the universal value with some of the cultural values, we see that they appear sometimes to work in opposition, which indicates something of their ideological nature. But as the ideological cultural values begin to predominate in the educational process the universal value becomes subsumed and begins to disappear.

This process is certainly impoverishing some aspects of teaching and learning but, paradoxically, we do not know if it is actually achieving most efficiently the ends that the cultural values seek to achieve. Hence, this book examines critically some of the processes that are occurring in education for adults. It notes that many of the aspirations that adult educators had for education have been achieved, such as the development of the accreditation of prior experiential learning, but as it becomes incorporated into the system its practice becomes tainted with some of its less worthy values.

The first four chapters of the book lay the foundations for the whole; the following five examine some of the processes of teaching and learning and the final chapters complete the argument.

A few of the chapters have been presented as papers at conferences and have been published separately in journals. For instance, *Education and Training in Late Modern Society: a Question of Ethics* appeared in the *Australian and New Zealand Journal of Vocational Education Research* and *Teachers and Learners in Adult Education: Transaction or Moral Interaction?* and *Power and Personhood in Teaching* have both appeared in *Studies in the Education of Adults*. A paper on the *Philosophy of Mentoring* has also appeared in *Nurse Education Today*. In addition, Chapter 13 is to appear in a Reader entitled *Reconciling the Irreconcilable*, edited by Danny Wildemeersch *et al* and published by Peter Lang.

Thanks must be paid to the National Institute of Adult Continuing Education, notably to Christopher Feeney, for being so patient in awaiting the delivery of the manuscript. Indeed, he had left NIACE before the book was finally completed. All that I can hope is that it has been worth waiting for! I must also acknowledge the time that others have given to me, both in discussing some of the ideas and also, in the case of my family, for encouraging me to undertake this work even though writing is a rather individualistic process. Finally, I want to acknowledge a number of friends and colleagues who have encouraged me to return to scholarship at a time when I was Head of Department and busy with administrative matters. Whilst I feel indebted to many people, the very nature of writing is individualistic, so that nobody else can be faulted for any of the weaknesses that the book might contain.

Peter Jarvis
Guildford
February 1997

# Chapter One

# Education and educational knowledge

The world of education is undergoing rapid change, especially in Western societies. As the Welfare State is being replaced with one which demands self-sufficiency from everyone, it is no longer possible to make the types of claim that were made about it in the 1970s. Bacon and Eltis (1976), for instance, had argued that Britain had far too few wealth producers, and that almost all of its civilised activities were not marketed, *eg*, education and health care, and so these non-wealth producing activities had to be supported by the declining number of wealth producers.

However, in the monetarist economy of the 1980s, when Britain's wealth-producing base was declining fast, services were redefined as potential wealth producers and the market was recognised as being global, so that through the utilisation of modern delivery techniques educational courses and qualifications became marketable and potential wealth producers both at home and abroad. This has helped to change the practice of education. Indeed, it has helped to transform the very nature of education and so any investigation into the ethics of education must first begin with an analysis of the nature of education and the educational.

It is, perhaps, not insignificant to recognise that when RS Peters (1966) wrote his classic book on the ethics of education he, too, was forced to start with an investigation in the nature of education. However, this enquiry assumes a totally different stance to that of Peters, since its main focus is on the education of adults and this raises some different issues to the education of children. In addition, the society in which education is now practised has undergone quite fundamental changes since that time. Even so, many of the points raised here are just as relevant to initial education as they are to the education of adults.

Like ethics, education is very practical so that the first enquiry is into education as a practical activity which is significant for this study, since values are only realised in practice. From there, questions will be raised about the nature of the educational and, finally, in this chapter issues about the nature of educational knowledge will be discussed.

## Education as fields of practice

Education is a social activity and society is complex and fragmented, so that it is hardly surprising to find that the centrifugal and centripetal forces operating within late modern society are also at work in education. The term *late modern* is used here to indicate that contemporary society is still experiencing the consequences of modernity but to avoid entering too deeply into the debate about whether society is now post-modern, even though further reference to this discussion must occur later in this book. Indeed, it reflects the coexistence thesis (Heelas *et al* 1996). Education is no longer a single entity, even if it ever was in the past, and it now assumes a variety of forms each seeking a separate identity and yet each often being embraced by an even larger educational system. Nurse education, for instance, which was independent and separate from other forms of education and located almost entirely within the ambit of the health services, has now been embraced by higher education; but higher education itself is becoming more diverse and unrecognisable from what it was only a few decades previously. Education is by no means static, and educational planners all appear to be involved in the business of trying to predict what forms, or systems, education will assume in the future. Not too long ago, for instance, the National Institute of Adult Continuing Education (McNair, 1993) published a policy discussion paper on an adult higher education but soon afterwards the Centre for Higher Education Studies (Williams and Fry, 1994) published another paper on the longer term prospects for higher education in the United Kingdom. These are now all open to question as the Dearing Committee undertakes its work. It may thus be seen that the fields of practice are in a constant flux and that any description of what is currently occurring will no doubt be dated by the time it is published. Consequently, no attempt is made here to describe the fields of practice, although it is necessary to clarify what is meant here by the idea of a field of practice and to show that there is not just a single field.

In traditional education teachers and students meet in one place and teaching and learning occurs simultaneously (space-time instantiation), but in contemporary society the relationship between space and time has been altered and this has certainly affected education. Traditionally education occurred in a school, college or university, but with the advent of space time distanciation (Giddens, 1990) teachers and learners are separated and a variety of forms of distance education are occurring and learning can now take place long after the teaching materials have been prepared. With space-time compression (Harvey, 1990) a distant teacher can be brought closer through satellite transmission and educational courses are being compressed into very distinct modules. There are, therefore, a variety of forms of education, many of which are not traditional. But even traditional face-to-face education is not all occurring in schools and colleges, etc, but now it is also happening in the workplace, in hotels and in conference centres, etc, and it is not all being provided by traditional educational institutions nor controlled by the government ministry responsible for education. In addition, the emphasis is now not so much on education as on learning.

Consequently, there are many fields of practice and trying to develop criteria by which they can be classified has caused a great deal of difficulty. Apps (1989), for instance, proposed a framework of providers in American adult education in which he suggested that there were: providers which are supported by public taxes and those which functioned for profit; that there are those which are not organised, such as the media; and those which are non-profit making, such as voluntary organisations. Overall, he suggested that there were 31 totally different sets of providers of education for adults in the United States. If initial education is added to this, then it becomes clear that there are indeed many different fields of practice in education. Significantly, many of them occur outside the institutional framework of education and, indeed, many are outside of the control of ministries of education.

It is clear, however, that these fields of practice are not discrete entities but that their boundaries are blurred, as the National Institute policy document on adult higher education indicated; no longer is it possible to separate adult education from higher education, or at least not where they overlap even though it may be easier to do so at the edges where, for example, it is certainly possible to locate Tai Chi in adult education and research in Russian Literature for a higher degree in the higher education sector!

Apps employed the nature of the providers to impart a framework for adult education, although it would also be possible to do so by the nature and level of the subject or even the nature of the qualification to be awarded on successful completion of the study, where one is given. It may thus be seen that even sub-dividing education into its different fields is problematic, but that there are certainly different providers, a variety of types of education and a number of levels of study – all of which constitute criteria by which education might be sub-divided, although it might now be better to regard it as something of a patchwork quilt having a variety of different shaped and coloured patches, all of which are of similar material.

Adults are learners in many of parts of this complex network and for the purpose of this enquiry education refers to any of the fields in which adults learn, and education for, or of, adults is treated as a generic institutional concept. However, the nature of adulthood is a significant question here and it will become more relevant in the later ethical discussion, and there has been considerable debate in adult education literature about this. Some writers refer to the age of the learners as important whilst others suggest that the idea of maturity is a more realistic approach (see Paterson, 1979; Knowles, 1980 for some discussion on this topic). But it was Wiltshire (1966) who highlighted the point which is most significant for this study when he suggested that adult education is not only the education for adults but that 'its content, organisation and conduct is relevant to and to some extent determined by . . . characteristics of adulthood' (cited from Rogers, 1976, p137). For Wiltshire, adulthood is about freedom, maturity and citizenship and in this sense there are ethical issues that need considerable discussion and while, later in this book, it will be argued that ethics are about humanity itself, this qualitative approach of Wiltshire comes close to the position adopted throughout this study. Adulthood is about achieving a social status that the majority of society regards as having left childhood and this may be at 16 years, 18 years or even younger in some societies. It is also about being treated differently to children and expecting different forms of behaviour from adults – issues that are of considerable significance to this study. But it is also about being a human being and this is even more important, and this is why this study is also relevant to those who teach school children. Adulthood is not a plateau, fixed and determined forever. Rather it is a stage in human becoming at which the society in which an individual lives decides to treat that person as an adult human being. This question will be discussed further in the fourth chapter when the natures of ethical and moral conceptual development are examined.

The question that now needs to be asked is, 'what is it that makes all these different fields of "education" in which adults participate education? What is it that is common to them all?'

## The nature of the educational

Peters (1966, p45) wisely tried not to define education but to lay down criteria for it and he specified three:

> i) the transmission of what is worthwhile to those who become committed to it;
> ii) it must involve knowledge and understanding and some kind of cognitive perspective – which are not inert;
> iii) it rules out some procedures of transmission ·because they lack wittingness and voluntariness on the part of the learner.

These criteria have been the subject to considerable debate and it is clear that they do not stand the test of close scrutiny at the present time. Initially, it is difficult to see how they delineate education as a social and institutionalised activity from learning which is subjective and in some sense individual. There are also a number of other criticisms, some of which are noted here, such as the fact that 'worthwhileness' is subjective and while what is learned might well be personal, education cannot be limited to what the individual or even a group of people consider to be worthwhile knowledge; even though it sometimes is regarded in this manner, especially when the dominant elite so define it! Clearly, in these instances it must be ideological and an attempt to transmit knowledge that a powerful individual or group wished to pass on to others. A group of industrialists, for instance, might want to limit worthwhile knowledge to the technical knowledge of industrial society and deny the same claim for the study of ancient myth, while others might wish to embrace all forms of knowledge as worthwhile. In addition, while some emphasis on the cognitive is no doubt correct, might not education also include other senses and aspects of learning, such as skills, attitudes and even values? If the learners are not volunteers to the process does this mean that the process is not educational? It would be possible to debate all of these at length and elsewhere (Jarvis, 1983a) this author embarked upon the task, so that it will not be repeated here. None of these three criteria are basic to the educational process, despite the fact that Peters claimed them to be so.

From a different ·perspective in adult education, Kidd (1973) claimed that the learning transaction has at least five elements: the teacher, the learner, the group, the setting and the subject matter. However, this approach is also open to considerable criticism. For instance, in distance education where the educational material might have been prepared by a team, it is hard to decide on nature of the teacher (see Jarvis, 1995a), or even if there is a teacher. Distance education is often conducted without a group and the learning is certainly not confined to any specific educational setting or situation, so that neither of these elements can be considered to be fundamental to education. Provided distance education is regarded as educational, these criticisms rule out some of Kidd's five basic criteria. This leaves the learner and the subject matter. However, it is possible for the learner to be engaged in a self-directed learning project which is entirely individual and which cannot be classified as any specific form of education, provided education and learning are differentiated. Self-directed learning can be non-institutional and non-social but be focused upon subject matter to be learned, so that subject matter *per se* might not be sufficient as a criterion of education.

At the same time education is a social institution in some way and there needs to be something which is to be learned provided by the educational institution. Educational institutions are, therefore, the providers of learning material in one form or another, either through face-to-face tuition or through a variety of technological media. At the same time, it might be argued that certain forms of experiential learning in the workplace do not actually have prepared learning material since the workplace itself sets the agenda. While this is recognised here, it must be pointed out that there is usually a hidden curriculum of some form in this type of learning.

Clearly there can be no education without some form of institutional provision of learning material, but institutionalisation does not mean that it is formal education since non-formal education might still be institutionalised. Additionally, there can be no education without the learner, or learners, so that it is claimed here that education has only three basic criteria – institutional provision, subject matter to be learned and the learner(s).

It is clear that the concept of education, when limited in this way, does not inherently contain a value, which raises questions about Paulo Freire's, among others, claim that education is never neutral. Freire is, of course, correct at one level, but not at the conceptual one. The concept of education is neutral, since education can be provided by any institution for a variety of purposes, but at the practical level, it always has a purpose and it is here that it is not neutral. At every point of practice there are values involved although those values are not actually inherent in the activity itself but ascribed to it by others. For instance, providing learning opportunities for the poor and under-privileged, as Freire did, has always been regarded by most people as a good and worthwhile thing to do, but it was a dubious activity for the few who were threatened by it. For the many, then, the value placed on the activity is that it was good but the few assigned another value upon it, possibly even that it was a bad activity (see Berger, 1977, p136). The fact that they disagree indicates that the value is not inherent in the activity but lies with those who view it or participate in it, etc. Value, like beauty, is to be found in the experience of the beholder – it is nearly always subjective and social. Naturally, this discussion will be pursued in greater depth in the next chapters, but for the present it may be seen that conceptually education may be regarded here as amoral, but in practice it is recognised that it will always have values ascribed to it.

Education, then, consists of a variety of fields of practice, all interlocked and overlapping, in which there are only three basic criteria – institutionalised provision, learning materials and the learner(s). However, these fields of practice are also studied and so bodies of knowledge, skills and attitudes, *etc*, evolve about them – some of these comprise educational knowledge – but this is a more difficult concept than it appears to be on the surface.

## The nature of educational knowledge

It will have become apparent from the distinction drawn above between the concept and the practice that educational knowledge is a problematic concept. Obviously it also embodies the problems of theory and practice since education is a practical activity, and it is also a field of study and while this is not an area of study that has been well developed in much of the English-speaking world, it is one that has been much more fully developed elsewhere since didactics and pedagogics have constituted the separate fields of study (see Svec, 1990). However, it is suggested here that this discussion can be treated in four separate parts: practice, practical knowledge, theoretical knowledge and metatheoretical knowledge. Each of these are now discussed in greater detail. (This discussion is an extension and revision of a piece written earlier, see Jarvis, 1991.)

### Practice

Education is practised in a variety of fields, as has already been pointed out. It is an institutional provision and in certain circumstances it is also a practical activity, such as teaching and programme designing, and in these latter instances it is a skill. Brookfield (1990) rightly emphasised this in the title of his book *The Skillful Teacher* where he referred to some of the practical skills that the teacher requires. Elsewhere, Jarvis (1995a) has outlined a wide variety of different methods with which teachers should be familiar if they are to be considered skilful teachers. Little more needs to be written at this point, except to note that since ethics is a practical activity the practice of education is always ethical and the relationship between educational skilful practice and morality will be discussed at considerable length later in this book. Heller (1988) actually argued that since social regulation exists in all societies, norms and rules of behaviour are ethical, although it will be argued later that she is actually discussing cultural value as opposed to absolute value. Value is always manifest in action and its moral worth is assessed from either a cultural or an absolute perspective. However, practice is also related to theory, although it is by no means the application of it, and so it is necessary now to explore the epistemological issues that emerge when the fields of practice are studied.

## Practical knowledge

Ryle (1963, pp40–41) made the point that knowing how to play chess does not mean that the player has to be able to articulate the rules, only to observe them during the game. He suggested, in rather the same way as did Argyris and Schon (1974) about theory in use, that so long as the player observes the rules and so long as the chess player is seen to obey them, onlookers are aware that the player knows how to play the game. In a similar manner, Nyiri (1988, p19) discussed the knowledge necessary to know how to ride a bicycle. He pointed out that this ability is learned, not through knowing the theories of a physical and mathematical nature underlying the riding of a bicycle, but rather by trial and error. Practical knowledge is that knowledge that the practitioner has, either as a result of being taught or through learning on the job.

How then is it learned? Nyiri (1988, pp20–21) writes:

> One becomes an expert not simply by absorbing explicit knowledge found in textbooks, but through experience, that is through repeated trials, failing, succeeding, wasting time and effort . . . getting a feel for a problem, learning when to go by the book and when to break the rules. Human experts thereby gradually absorb a repertory of working rules of thumb, or 'heuristics', that, combined with book knowledge, make them experts.

Consequently, it is necessary to ask what relationship exists between the actual performance of an action and the knowledge in the mind, that is – what makes it practical knowledge? This is a much more difficult question to answer because the chess player might, or might not, be able to articulate the rules of chess and the cycle rider might not know the scientific rules that enables the balance to maintained and the bicycle ridden. Is it merely the ability and the confidence to perform the correct actions, because they have become habitualised and memorised, or is it something else? Clearly it is more than this and a chess player may possess the ability to articulate many of the rules. However, even when the rules cannot be clearly stated the chess player knows when they are being broken and the cyclist knows when someone else has not got the confidence to ride the bike. Naturally, this gives rise to the idea that some practical knowledge is tacit, or even that it is merely a matter of confidence that the skill performance is correct, and so no actual thought need go into why it is correct until such time as an action actually breaks the rules. Then the actor has to consider it and devise some new approaches to the performance. If they work, then they can be memorised and the precise formulation forgotten, since practical knowledge is fundamentally pragmatic and, once internalised, possession of it enables the actor to presume upon the world and act accordingly. It is certainly clear that in the provision of education, teachers and others might well act in precisely this manner.

This practical knowledge is personal and resides in the practitioner, and it might not be systematically organised in the practitioner's mind. It is rather like everyday knowledge, that is the knowledge of how to live in everyday, ordinary life. In everyday life people do not think about how they are going to behave, for a great deal of behaviour in social life has been habitualised, and then consciously decide which bit of philosophy and which bit of psychology, or ethics, *etc*, they are going to use in that situation, even though analysis of their actions might suggest that this is what they do. There may be times, however, when individuals are aware that they are acting in a philosophical or a psychological manner, *etc*, or even that that is underlying their behaviour, but it would be unwise to claim that actors are not always aware of the bits of knowledge that make up their everyday practical knowledge. The point is that everyday practical knowledge is integrated and internalised knowledge. (See Heller, 1984, pp185–215 for a discussion of everyday knowledge.) Practical educational knowledge is precisely the same: it is subjective, sometimes tacit, and a unique constellation of utilisable knowledge that falls within the ambit of the other disciplines. It is only independent in as much as it relates to the fields of practice.

However, everyday behaviour has a moral dimension and, in precisely the same manner, educational practical knowledge also has one. Consequently, it might be assumed that behaving in a specific manner is the right way for a teacher to behave, *etc*, even though an ethical analysis might never have been conducted about it. There is a sense in which the ethical dimension to everyday knowledge is tacit but it might well relate to the moral maturity and ideology of the practitioners and the extent to which personal and professional morality coincide is a contentious question for the welfare professions.

Practical knowledge, therefore, is *knowledge how* to act – which is both conscious and tacit. It is not the same as having the ability to act in specific situations, although it is close to it. *Knowledge how* and skill are close but not synonymous and the relationship between them is pragmatic; that is, for as long as the practitioner can presume to act in certain ways then the *knowledge how* remains undisturbed, but once actions can not longer be presumed then new learning has to occur and now *knowledge how* acquired. (The relationship between learning and action has been fully discussed elsewhere – see Jarvis, 1992.)

Knowledge how must also involve a number of other aspects; for instance, in order to do something well practitioners need to know the alternatives, so that practical knowledge also includes *knowledge that* (Ryle, 1963) and also *knowledge why* (Jarvis and Gibson, 1987) and *knowledge when*, etc. Many of these elements of practical knowledge might not be articulated in the normal run of events and might, consequently, become the tacit knowledge of practice. This integrated, practical knowledge can, however, be articulated and recorded so that it forms the basis of theoretical knowledge. It is these latter aspects of theoretical knowledge that indicate that practitioners have understood reasons for their professional actions.

## Theoretical knowledge

It is possible to observe behaviour, research it and gather together a body of knowledge about the practice of education (for adults) which might be called a body of educational knowledge, or even a body of knowledge about education for adults, etc. This body of knowledge can be systematised, recorded and taught to others; it is a body of theoretical knowledge. It is possible to have slightly different bodies of theoretical knowledge for each of the different fields of practice, but as the educational processes are similar the bodies of knowledge about the educational processes are similar whatever the field of practice. Indeed, this body of knowledge is driven by practice and if the mode of practice changes, then the body of knowledge adjusts accordingly. Clearly there is a larger gap between the practice and the body of theoretical knowledge than there is between practice and practical knowledge.

Does this, therefore, mean that education is an academic discipline, like other disciplines? Response to such a question must be negative for a number of reasons. In the first instance, it is possible and meaningful to talk about a sociology of adult education or a philosophy of continuing education – but it is hardly meaningful to refer to an education of economics, etc. Education is a practical activity and the body of knowledge gathered together in this way is a body of utilisable, knowledge which is theoretical and frequently drawn from the social and human sciences, such as sociology, psychology and philosophy. This is the body of theoretical knowledge and it has, as its base, the integrated practical knowledge that has been discussed above.

But, often, when this body of knowledge is taught, it is also sub-divided into academic discipline bases, such as educational psychology and educational sociology, etc. In this way, educational knowledge takes the form of an academic discipline, although there is a utility about it, since each section is still practice-driven rather than discipline-driven. There has, however, been a considerable debate amongst educationalists about the nature of these subjects and how they relate to the psychology of, and the sociology, of education, etc. Further reference to this will be made in the next section of this chapter.

This body of theoretical knowledge of education is a unique mixture of knowledge that can be utilised in practice, and like practical knowledge it is frequently integrated, although it can be sub-divided into the human and social sciences, as mentioned above. It is this body of knowledge that can be called a subject, or subjects, and taught in universities or colleges, but it is not a discipline. Among those disciplines that constitute this body of educational knowledge is some ethical knowledge – about how to act in a moral manner in educational practice. This body of knowledge contains the strictures, procedures and instructions about how things should be performed and what the likely outcomes are. Codes of ethics and the normative rules of practice, which were referred to above in relation to Heller's (1988) analysis, are also contained within this body of educational knowledge. One study of ethics in adult education has been written which falls into this category (Brockett, 1988), and further reference will be made to it later in this study. It was also often claimed that the formulation of a code of ethics was one of the marks indicating that an occupation had achieved professional status (see, for instance, Greenwood, 1957 *inter alia*). To some extent these formulations of codes of ethics are what professional philosophers might call 'lay ethics', but the are also practical in nature and tend to fall within this category.

## Metatheoretical knowledge

Education comprises many fields of practice situated in, and affected by, the wider society. Thus far the basis of the knowledge that has been discussed has been practice, rather than the wider society or the broader fields of intellectual enquiry. Consequently the educational knowledge base, as discussed until this point, is limited and unable to provide a wider rationale for its discussions; what is lacking is a *knowledge* about the field and its contexts.

The fields of education can be studied by economists, historians, philosophers, political theorists, psychologists, sociologists, and moral philosophers, etc, and their studies are not driven by practice but by the intellectual framework of their own discipline, so that they can produce sociologies of education, economics of continuing education, *etc*. Herein lies the difference between sociology of education and educational sociology, for instance; the former is driven by the demands of the academic discipline while the latter is driven by those of practice. At one level the latter is more useful than the former and clearly relates more closely to practice than the former. However, the former provides opportunity to locate educational knowledge within a wider intellectual framework and to offer a *knowledge* about it.

Continental scholars use the term 'science of education' (see Pastuović, 1995, for instance) to relate educational knowledge to the academic disciplines. While this approach tries to bring together educational knowledge within a single structure, it is perhaps not as helpful as it first appears because it does not account for the different types of knowledge or their differing relationships to practice.

Metatheoretical knowledge of educational practice, for the purposes of this study, refers to that knowledge located within specific academic disciplines or sub-diciplines and driven by the demands of those disciplines. However, it has to be recognised that these disciplines are not discrete, so that it is possible to have social philosophy, social psychology, etc. Even so, in order to analyse moral behaviour it is necessary to have some knowledge of ethics, as a discipline, or, as it is also called, moral philosophy.

Moral behaviour, however, might be regarded as a field of practice, just like education – but it is clearer to see it as occurring in all fields of practice, but the above discussion about the relationship between educational skills and knowledge, *etc*, is just as applicable to moral behaviour as it is to education. This demonstrates something of the complexity of the type of analyses which need to be undertaken if practice is going to be understood in a reasonably comprehensive manner.

Ethics, or moral philosophy, is a theoretical study and may be defined as 'an investigation into the fundamental principles and basic concepts that are or ought to be found in a given field of human thought and activity' (Speake, 1979). Underlying educational practice is an ethical dimension which may be analysed from a moral philosophical theoretical perspective, so that there is an ethics of education in the same way as there is a sociology of education, *etc*.

Clearly the relationship between ethical issues in education and an ethics of education depends to a considerable extent upon the philosophical sophistication of the proponents of the former. The distinction between a 'lay study' and one by a professional philosopher may be too broad to be useful, but the extent to which the study is driven by the demands of philosophy as an academic discipline is much more meaningful.

## Conclusion

This book is not being written by a professional philosopher, but by an educationalist. At the same time it does endeavour to utilise philosophical knowledge so that it will come closer to a metatheoretical study than to a theoretical one, but the issues with which it deals reflect a keen concern with events that are occurring in education, especially education for adults, in this late modern Western European society.

Having begun to point to the nature of ethical study, it is now necessary to pursue this quest even further and the second chapter explores some relevant issues in ethics for the study of education and continues to lay the foundations for the study.

# Chapter Two

# The nature of ethics

Ethics is concerned with analysing moral values and seeking to understand what people consider to be good, right, just, etc. It is also about what individuals consider, or feel, that they ought to do and about the actual way in which they behave, so that it is both cognitive and action-orientated. Despite some claims, these questions are hardly self-evident and people are not born with innate values which they recognise in some instinctive manner. If they were, there would probably be little debate about the nature of goodness, or of value in general. Values are learned by individuals as a result of living in society and in this one sense they are cultural, as Heller (1988) suggested. This raises a number of quite major questions about the nature of what might be considered to be good – if goodness is a cultural phenomenon, does it change with cultural revolutions in society? Are values relative, or are there values which are always considered to be good by everybody? By what criteria may values be judged to be good? Or what ought people to do in specific circumstances? Are values objective, social or subjective, or is there another possibility? To what extent are ethical values related to the process of maturation and adulthood? These are all questions that need to be posed in an analysis of ethics and education for adults.

   Some of these issues are explored in this chapter, while others are discussed in the next. The general thesis of this book is that there is one universal moral good, which consists of being concerned for the Other, and that this is the underlying principle of all morally good actions, and it is especially important when considering the practice of education. It will be argued that this approach combines both the cognitive and the action perspectives of ethics. It will also be argued that there are other morally good values which find their origins in culture but that these are not universal. In addition, non-morally good values are implicit in the traditions of social behaviour, and they occupy an important place in education for adults. Consequently, it is important to analyse the difference between universal and cultural good, as well as between moral and non-moral good. In order to explore and expand upon this thesis, this chapter has two sub-divisions: moral and non-moral goodness and a brief but critical examination of some of the arguments for moral goodness. The following chapter examines an existentialist argument for one universal moral good, how this is to be distinguished from cultural moral values and the application of this position to the wider society. In so far as it is possible, examples will be drawn from fields of education in order to illustrate these discussions.

## Moral and non-moral goodness

The word *good* is used in a variety of ways as the above introductory discussion illustrates and, as Hare (1956) points out, there are always difficulties in using it, especially in relation to whether it is used morally or non-morally. There are a variety of reasons for this, such as the difference between moral and non-moral is not always being clear and that there are few universally-agreed criteria for any form of goodness. Additionally, many phenomena, objects or actions, to which values of goodness or badness are ascribed are not capable of precise measurement, so that they can only be regarded as good or bad if there is some form of agreement about them, and as agreement is not always easy to reach this becomes problematic. Another issue surrounding the socially accepted values of goodness is the extent to which they have been affected by those who exercise power or influence in a society, since it is a well-known sociological phenomenon that dominant discourses reflect the dominant ideologies in society. Consequently the norms of behaviour operate to the advantage of the most powerful in society, *eg*, the so-called free market always operates to the advantage of the successful business companies, etc, so that the politicians' desire 'to leave it to the market' is actually an action in favour of those who control business and commerce.

Additionally, the word 'good' is often used in a subjective manner indicating something of the perspective of the speaker, or speakers. For instance, if students say that it was a good examination paper, they invariably mean that they found it easy or, perhaps, they thought that it was fair; if examiners say that an examination paper was good, then this might mean that the paper was fair, tested the whole syllabus, was clearly written, without catch questions, etc. At the same time, other students sitting the same paper might have said that it was a horrid paper, since they found the questions difficult to answer, or some examiners might disagree over their assessment of the paper. Good, in these cases, reflects the biases of the speakers which, in turn, relates to their position in the educational system. But it also indicates that words like this have little or no empirical base but reflect a meaning perspective, or even an ideological bias. For instance, a teacher might say to another about a student, 'She's a good student' and this might mean that the first teacher likes the student, or that the student is quiet and hard working in the class, or that the student is extremely intelligent and willing to participate fully in the class activities, etc. Whatever the reason, the point is that people use the word in a subjective, and sometimes individualistic, manner although the speakers may have their own criteria for it. Sometimes, however, there is a degree of agreement between them about what they regard as good or bad and in this case there is an apparent objectivity about the value of goodness, which might be regarded as being objectified, or inter-subjective, but it is still not objective.

Perhaps the only word – besides good – in the above paragraph that carries any moral overtones is 'fair', conveying something that is generally regarded as moral. This indicates that in everyday speech moral and non-moral evaluative statements are sometimes combined and are rarely distinguished from each other, and that the word 'good' is used to connote both. However, this is not always the case and frequently the word 'good' is used in a totally non-moral manner, for if a student were to say that he had a good car, he might mean that it is fast, modern with all the latest gadgets, etc. An elderly lecturer might also say that she has a good car and imply that it is reliable, economical and comfortable. However, these two statements could be reversed and the elderly lecturer like the fast modern car! In both of these instances, however, the word 'good' is used evaluatively to convey that the relevant car's performance according to specific criteria of goodness, but in neither case are those criteria moral. In a social sense, when we discuss the efficiency of the market, as if it were good, we are using it in a non-moral manner.

Similarly, from my own experience in training examiners, the assessment of an essay as good by one teacher does not necessarily mean that another teacher will view it in the same manner, even when there is an agreed marking scheme. Assessment is necessarily subjective in many instances, although attempts have been made to devise schemes that subjugate the subjective to more objective approaches. Nevertheless, non-moral goodness relates in some way to criteria of excellence that are specified by the users of the word, but in these cases it refers to inanimate phenomena, since they can never be moral. Additionally, the evaluation of the cars might change if one of them fails to achieve the same level of performance on some future occasion, and the essay assessment might be different if the same examiner marked it a few months later. This indicates that the goodness is not intrinsic to the car or essay concerned, but that it resides in the evaluators – who are themselves social human beings – and is ascribed for as long as the phenomena meet the expectations of the assessors or evaluators at the time when they are making the assessment. It must also be pointed out here that while the criteria of goodness are subjective, it does not mean that there are not differences in objective performances, so that there is a potential confusion between objectivity and subjectivity at this point. Additionally, since criteria for excellence change over time, questions about the relativity of values must be raised and this is a topic to which further reference will be made in subsequent discussions.

The above examples illustrate what Hare (1952) called descriptive or evaluative standards which he wanted to distinguish from those ethical values which prescribed what people should do. For him, therefore, ethics is about what people do, or should do, in given circumstances.

To return to the examination paper, then, it may be asked whether the actual paper was fair or was it that those who set the questions were behaving fairly to the examination candidates? It is impossible for an inanimate object, such as an examination paper, to make judgments of fairness, so that it must be concluded that fairness lies in the examiners, and that this use of language is shorthand for a longer but more correct sentence. At the same time the structure of the sentence, 'That was a fair examination paper', gives the same impression of objectivity as do the claims that 'this is a good car', 'the market if efficient' or that 'this is an excellent essay', which is a fallacy created by sloppy use of language. It would be more correct to say, 'I think that the examiners were being fair to the candidates in setting that examination paper'. Assessing the examiners as being fair suggests that morality is something that guides people's behaviour when their actions impinge another (see Hare, 1956); in other words, this is what individuals think that they ought to do. In this instance fairness refers to the behaviour of the people who devised the examination paper in respect to the candidates, and while it implies that they acted morally, it does not specify the criteria for fairness, or even justify why fairness should be regarded as a moral concept. It does, however, suggest that the examiners behaved according to a set of principles that allowed the candidates to make such an evaluation. While the principles were not necessarily articulated, there might have been a tacit agreement among them about their nature. Moral goodness, therefore, relates to people's behaviour, especially when that behaviour affects others.

However, the description of the student as a good student did not really convey a moral message about the student and unless something more of the values and expectations of the teacher who commended the student are known, it is impossible to decipher what the word 'good' means in this context. Certainly, it may relate to the manner in which she fitted into the classroom. Hare (1956, pp146–7) uses an illustration about two Indian army majors of the old school describing a new arrival in the officers' mess as 'an awfully good man', and he goes on to suggest that they the word was being used in a sense of conforming to the standards set for an officer in that position – plays polo well, *etc*. The new arrival's actions do impinge upon the behaviour of others but it is not necessarily moral, only conforming to the expectations of the establishment, so that these two illustrations demonstrate that moral goodness does not refer to all behaviour impinging upon others. Indeed, conformity might well be immoral! Consider a teacher conforming to the expectations of Apartheid in South Africa a few years ago and refusing to educate black South Africans – this would rightly be regarded as immoral by most people in most circumstances. Again, if two workers for a non-governmental organisation were to make the same claim that 'she's a good woman' about a new women recruit to the organisation for which they worked, then people's perceptions of the woman might well be that she spends much of her time performing charitable and other acts which might well be considered moral, so that conformity to the prevailing culture need not always be immoral. Therefore, only certain forms of behaviour might be considered moral and further discussion on this point will occur in the first section of the next chapter.

From the above discussion it is possible to conclude that moral good refers only to certain forms of human action that impinge upon the Other, although this requires further discussion. On the other hand, non-moral good refers both to all forms of goodness ascribed to non-human phenomena and to some non-behavioural assessments of people, *eg*, she's a good student.

Good, therefore, is an evaluative word, whether it is used morally or non-morally, for which there are usually criteria for its usage. Agreeing upon criteria, or even on the form of argument for goodness or badness, is a much more difficult process, as the history of moral philosophy indicates.

## A brief review of some major approaches to the analysis of goodness

In order to make out a case for the existentialist position about moral goodness that will be produced in the next chapter, it is now necessary to review some of the dominant theories of goodness that have been espoused in moral philosophy in the past. There have been many introductory books written about these theories (see, for instance, Atkinson, 1969; Frankena, 1963; Mabbott, 1966; Sprigge, 1988; Urmson, 1968; Williams, 1985; *inter alia*) and so it is not intended to provide a full review here. However, the deontological, teleological, intuitionist and emotive theories and, finally, discourse ethics are discussed below. While the theories are separated in moral philosophy generally for the sake of analysis, in most situations people combine them as they try to decide on what to do or on whether the behaviour that they are evaluating is good or bad, *etc.*

### Deontological theories

Deontological theories are based upon the idea that the basis of moral action is the fulfilment of duty, irrespective of the consequences of the act, and are especially associated with the work of Immanual Kant. Obedience to a set of rules, such as the Old Testament statement of 'The Ten Commandments' (Exodus 20), constitute the basis of this position which specifies that the moral rules must always be kept, whatever the circumstances or the consequences. The Church of Rome bases much of its teaching upon obedience to Natural and Canon Law in precisely this manner. Obedience to laws has a number of strengths at first sight, for example, actions do not depend on individual beliefs or motives and that the actor does not have to take the likely outcomes into consideration. It might be argued that Codes of Professional Ethics almost fall into this category, where the expectation of the profession is that all its members will follow this code and that they can be disciplined if they break it. (See Chapter Three for a more complete discussion of this.) Additionally, bureaucratic procedures might be viewed in precisely the same manner and the good bureaucrat is the one who follows the procedures of the organisation rigorously. However, potential conflict arises when the manager of the educational institution expects adherence to the rules and procedures of the organisation while the lecturer puts her students first, since the organisational and professional ethics might conflict in such circumstances – and so what constitutes a good teacher, and for whom?

Consequently, the position has a number of crucial weaknesses including the fact that the laws have to be decided and propounded by someone or some group, and they will invariably reflect the interests of that person, group or organisation. This argument can also be levelled at professional ethics, even though the ethic of service underlies a great deal of professional practice, since the profession does tend to protect itself. In addition, following a code of ethics in such a manner might result in the actors not relying on their own beliefs or motives but on the beliefs and motives of others. This might diminish their own sense of responsibility for their own actions. At the same time, it must be pointed out that in a world where clients and, perhaps, students are seeking litigation for perceived professional failures, a careful adherence to such procedures is a protection for the practitioner – at considerable cost sometimes to professional judgment and expertise.

Additionally, long-term outcomes might be more beneficial than short-term obedience of the law. Consider, for instance, the situation where an educator of adults marks the first essay of an adult returner who has not written a piece of academic work for many years. A truly critical assessment of that piece and a truthful statement about how poor it is might well destroy the adult returner's fragile confidence and put him off studying for the remainder of his life. Consequently, it would be wrong to tell the truth about the piece of work, even if he asks, and telling an untruth and uttering encouraging words might be a much more beneficial act both for the person now and for the person's potential achievements in the longer term. Hence, the untruth might not only be the better educational practice, but also the better moral one! But, consider the opposite outcome and the student does not prove to be a success, he can then claim that he was not given correct information at the start of his course and the encouragement provided acted as an incentive for him to continue and, as it now appears, waste his precious time and money on something in which he was unlikely to succeed. The teacher can be accused of being culpable of providing false information and of bad practice. Nobody can predict the long-term outcome that the untruth will help generate, whether it is success or failure, but it is much more certain that the truth, in this situation, would not only hurt, it might also destroy the confidence of the student and his motivation to continue. Hence, the adult educator should consider the outcomes of an action, but even more, the personhood of the student must be taken into account in teaching situations.

It can also be argued that in this complex world of late modernity there is not a simple, single law that can be applied to many different situations, so that the law has to be amended to respond to the specific situation. However, this is a slippery slope because once the law has been modified, it can be further ameliorated many times over, so that the original law disappears under a welter of qualifications. By contrast there may be a variety of possible responses to a situation and the simple application of a law might both be too simple to be meaningful and so destroy its own credibility. The existence of a law might also remove something of the freedom of individuals to act in a manner that they consider most appropriate and responsible in such a complex world, so that the idea that morality is undergirded by a law of almost any form is questionable.

While deontological approaches appear to have strengths in overcoming the idiosyncrasies of actors, they run into insurmountable difficulties when it comes to putting them into everyday practice. Indeed, it might be noted that such practitioners sometimes, but by no means always, appear to be inflexible and lack compassion and understanding in complex situations of contemporary society.

This approach also appears paradoxical from an educational perspective since education should help individuals think and act in a reasonable and responsible manner. Overall, this position seems to detract from the responsible humanity of individual actors to be accountable for their own actions, or even to plan their own actions in the light of possible consequences. Additionally, the approach is unacceptable because it is impossible to advance laws relevant to every situation and to take every possible outcome into consideration, so that it is now necessary to examine the theories that are more concerned with the outcomes of actions.

## Teleological theories

Teleological theories are the complete opposite of deontological ones with their strengths being the weaknesses of the deontological, and *vice versa*. The most well-known statement of this position is Bentham's (1822) utilitarianism (see Mill, 1962, pp33–77). Basically this position states that acts are morally right if they can produce the greatest balance of good over bad. In its most extreme form it might appear that an individual can do what she likes in order to produce a greater balance of good over evil. Crudely, the end justifies the means – but obviously the position is not always as crude as this, as Frankena (1963, p30) shows when he distinguishes between two forms of utilitarianism – act utilitarianism and rule utilitarianism. Act utilitarians appeal directly to the outcomes of the act and acts are treated as good if they are utilitarian. Rule utilitarianism, in contrast, asks which rule will produce the greatest amount of good rather than which act will. Nozick (1993) prefers to discuss principles rather than rules in his approach to teleology, and perhaps this overcomes some of the problems of the use of rules discussed in the previous section. Even so, it is clear that the principle of utility has been quite central to a great deal of ethical thought since the Enlightenment and its underlying instrumental rationality might now be seen to be amongst its greatest weaknesses.

Clearly, however, the end might not justify the means in education or in any other aspect of social living as the following two illustrations demonstrate. It might be possible to get achieve a one hundred percentage pass in an examination by ensuring that the weak students are forced to leave the course before they sit the examination. Forcing students from courses, or preventing them sitting the examinations, may not be common practice, but it is a means to obtaining high levels of passes for the record to be published in the Government's league tables! It is also possible to specify certain ends in behavioural approaches to education (behavioural objectives), but the teaching methods by which they are attained might have been indoctrinational, the students' learning experience might not be very rich and their comprehension of what they have learned may be very limited indeed. Behaviourism, as a whole, in education is open to ethical scrutiny and certain aspects of it will be discussed later in this study.

However, it is more likely that the outcome of an act cannot be specified, or even controlled. Often unforeseen circumstances happen which prevent the desired ends occurring. But much more significantly, it has to be asked what are the ends of an act – the immediate, the short-term or the long-term? Time does not stop at any one point and allow the consequences of an act to be measured; nor is it reasonable to declare that circumstances thereafter are not the result of the aforesaid action. How often, for instance, have adult educators discussed educational problems with adults who refer to some incident in their initial schooling that has put them off education? How often has the fear of asking questions in the group been generated by some situation many years previously when a parent or a teacher mocked the questioner, or tried to silence her because she was being awkward, *etc*? In this latter instance it is possible to see that in achieving the short-term goals there are long-term, often unforeseen, consequences that are extremely detrimental to the recipients of the initial act.

There are at least three other major criticisms of this position. The first refers to the impossibility of deciding upon the morality of an act until its consequences have occurred, especially as the actor might have no control over the events that generate those consequences. The morality of an act cannot, therefore, lie in its repercussions. Hence, it has to lie with the actor in some way rather than the uncontrolled outcomes of the action, although the motive of the actor in seeking to produce desirable outcomes might be a significant factor in assessing the morality of an act.

The second major criticism lies in the taken-for-granted rationalism of utilitarianism. This is the instrumental rationality of the Enlightenment and the question has to be asked as to what extent this is a fully rational approach at all? In *Paradoxes of Learning*, (1992, pp191–2) I used an earlier version of the following example. A junior manager attends vocational education to learn how to be a successful manager in a large technological capitalist corporation during the day and in the evening she attends an evening class on how to self-actualise, thinking that both courses would be useful preparation for the management role. On the surface this might well be true since both appear to be logical courses of action. But what happens when the manager learns in the first course that in order to succeed as a manager in the company she has to comply with company policy regardless of whether or not it is consistent with her own ideals? In other words, if the day-time course is to achieve its ends, she must learn that self-actualisation is not always a good thing; or that the purposeful activity of both courses calls for one set of purposeful activity to displace the other. The aspiring manager is confronted with a choice: which approach should be adopted? The choice is no longer merely one of purposeful rationality, for both alternatives are instrumentally rational. It is an ideological choice, but an ideological choice of instrumental rationalities! The instrumental rationality of Modernity might also be an ideological statement of the Age restricting instrumental rationality to too narrow boundaries, so that it is now necessary to recognise that this apparently taken-for-granted common sense idea might actually need to be broadened (Nozick, 1993, pp133–9).

Indeed, there are other elements of rationality, as Weber (1947) pointed out when he suggested that there are the rationalities of tradition, value and affect as well as instrumentality. Traditional rationality is the underlying rationality of practical knowledge, which was discussed in the previous chapter, but it has also to be recognised that there is an element of instrumental rationality even here since the objective is to continue to perform well in practice. Hence the rationality underlying practical knowledge is both instrumental and traditional.

In addition, there is a third problem, one which Moore (1903) called the naturalistic fallacy. Producing pleasure in other people might have been an intended outcome of an action and regarded as a good act, as many utilitarians claim, but if the teacher is a clown and gets the class to laugh, thereby producing pleasure, yet teaches them nothing, it is neither good teaching nor a good act. Producing pleasure is not necessarily good in itself and, even if it were, to claim that the production of pleasure is itself good is to confuse two different concepts since the production of pleasure cannot be the same as goodness itself – good is good and the production of pleasure is the production of pleasure – but good is not the production of pleasure and the production of pleasure is not goodness itself. A similar argument might be levelled at Aristotle's *Nicomachean Ethics* in which he claims that happiness is goodness.

But, it might be asked, is not producing the greatest amount of happiness a moral act? The answer to this is not a simple affirmative or denial as the illustration about the teacher clowning and producing pleasure illustrates, since happiness might be a short-term outcome while long-term disappointment is to follow for many. Additionally, an act might not be performed for the most altruistic of motives but produce good short- and long-term consequences – is this a good or a bad act in utilitarian terms? Clearly it appears to be good but common sense would almost certainly suggest it to have been less than good. In addition, good motives might not produce a good outcome since unforeseen circumstances might intervene and the outcome of the action be unfortunate – was it, therefore, a bad act even though the intention was good? Consideration of likely outcomes must be a factor in moral action, for it is certainly one of the basic tenets of a rational and responsible person, but it is certainly not the only basis for morality. Consequently, this point needs more discussion later in this chapter.

## Intuitionism

If goodness is not located in the rules or in the outcomes of action, then it is necessary to examine the actors themselves. One such theoretical perspective is intuitionism which specifies that people make ethical judgments intuitively, or as if the answers to the ethical questions are self-evident, so that they do not need any further justification. As Frankena (1963, p86) suggests, they regard goodness as indefinable and that the actions are undertaken as self-evident in their context. One of the criticisms of the teleological arguments was that pleasure does not equate to goodness, because good is good. Intuitionism was the position espoused by Moore (1903), which was prevalent among moral philosophers for a considerable period of time earlier in the twentieth century, and while this may answer one of the problems posed by the discussion above about goodness being goodness, it actually raises more questions than it answers. (See Sprigge, 1988, pp28–49). Still, it is clearly possible to combine an intuitionist perspective with a utilitarian or a deontological one, as Ross tried to do (Sprigge, 1988, pp49–53).

However, intuitionism does raise problems about rationality and responsibility – for how can it be argued that an intuitive response is both reasoned and reliable (Nozick, 1993, p64) and if it is neither, can it be regarded as responsible? The fact that goodness is hard to define is no reason for claiming that actions do not have to be rational and responsible. Additionally, it is hard to sustain that because the response to a situation appears self-evident to one person, that it is necessarily good – especially when others in similar situations disagree with that specific response. It is possible to imagine a situation in which two self-evident but diametrically opposed responses occur to different people in the same situation, each claiming to know the right action. If there is no underlying reasoning, it is impossible to decide which is the better on their own merits.

Frankena (1963, p87) also points out that the intuitionist has no motivation for acting at all. Just because an individual has an intuition that this is the right thing to do in these circumstances, why should he do it? The response might be claimed that he should do it just because he has an intuition that this is the correct thing to do – but does he also have to have an intuition that it is right for him to act in the way that he intuits that he should?

Intuitions are almost certainly learned responses from previous experiences, unless they are innate knowledge – which is not a sustainable position, and the knowledge learned from one experience may not be right in another since no two situations are necessarily the same. Obviously, there may be occasions when individuals learn from one situation and use that experience in another one, but if that knowledge is used unthinkingly it might not actually provide a good response to a difficult situation.

Consequently, it may be seen that intuitionism is not sustainable as a basis of morality, especially when those ethical theories have to be applicable to education. However, there is another major theory that recognises the problems of defining goodness, and that is emotivism.

## Emotivism

This theory of ethics emerged, according to Urmson (1968, p19) as a result of epistemological despair, since there was 'no account of the meaning of ethical utterances hitherto proposed which (was) epistemologically acceptable'. In other words, ethical words do not convey any sense of meaning, as Ayer claimed (1971, p146) when he wrote that

> Thus if I say to someone, 'You acted wrongly in stealing that money,'
> I am not stating anything more than if I simply said, 'You stole that
> money.'

Ayer regarded the moral phrase as superfluous in respect of cognitive meaning. For him, it is both an expression of feeling and a calculated attempt to arouse emotion and consequently to motivate action. In a sense, emotivism seeks to overcome the problem of having no reason to act and, at the same time, to be consistent with linguistic philosophy. One of its most full statements occurs in Stevenson's (1944) *Ethics and Language*. Emotivism seeks to relate reason and the affect and provide emotive meaning. In addition, it is based on the idea that the affect is aroused prior to reasoned consideration and that the latter in some way operates to bring the desired end to fulfilment. While there is a certain logic to the emotivist position, and we shall return to this in the final chapter of this study, there are occasions when it is not really sustainable as the following examples demonstrate.

In a sense, the illustration used above of a teacher commending a student to another teacher by saying 'She's a good student' might only be saying, according to the emotive position, 'I like this student and you ought to like her as well'. The communication does not relate to anything other than a feeling of approval that the one teacher seeks to convey to the other, but significantly the speaker might actually be trying to use the second teacher by influencing his attitudes; this is what Habermas (1990, p58) calls strategic action rather than communicative action. In a sense, if emotivist statements are expressions of interest, they may also be a subtle manner of influencing other people to act in accordance with the desires or affections of the speaker.

In addition, there are situations where the someone might know that she does not like what she feels that she has to do and she knows that others will not like it either – but she thinks that it is right. By articulating this sentiment to herself she is not trying to convince anybody of anything, even herself, and at the same time she does not equate the desire with what she believes to be right. However, it is clear from this situation that morality still lies in the person and not in the situation – but also not in the language of the situation either.

Urmson (1968) also notes that the emotivist theory tends to confuse emotion and attitudes in an unhelpful manner and that it leads to the view that evaluation is based on a non-rational element in human behaviour.

The four theories examined thus far each try to locate the moral in different aspects of human behaviour: the first in rules, the second in consequences, the third in intuition and self-evident responses and the final one in language and communication. None offer a satisfactory set of answers to the problems of moral behaviour but other theorists, *eg*, MacIntyre and Habermas, actually locate the whole of this moral discussion within the framework of the question of Modernity and the Enlightenment project, which the former claimed had to fail in respect to morality. Habermas' theory of discourse ethics, by contrast, is an attempt to overcome some of the problems discussed above and still locate the moral discussion within the framework of modernity.

## Discourse ethics

Habermas' (1990, 1993) work on ethics emerged naturally from his theory of communicative action and he has adopted a Kantian position of deontology, although he maintains that 'none of the competing ethical traditions can claim *prima facie* general validity any longer' (Dews, 1986, p248). Additionally, Habermas has endeavoured to relate his work to that of Kohlberg's moral development, which will be discussed in the fourth chapter. However, he has a profoundly different approach to that discussed earlier in the chapter. He is more concerned to produce a cognitive argument that enables the norms of practice to be evaluated as moral, and in this he differentiates between morality and ethics. He contends, that ethical understanding can only be undertaken through argumentation so that the consensus reached represents a universal agreement and conviction, and that the moral norms can be regarded as good for everyone. For him argumentation is not a decision procedure which results in resolutions but a procedure which leads to convictions (Dews, 1986, p255). This principle of argumentation is quite central to Habermas' position in as much as he (1990, p67) suggests that Kant's categorical imperative needs to be reformulated so that the principles of universality come from discourse:

> Rather than ascribing as valid to all others any maxim that I can will
> to be a universal law, I must submit my maxim to all others for
> purposes of discursively testing its claim to universality.

Habermas is, therefore, seeking universal agreement to truths that can be regarded as normative rules. He is concerned with producing a procedure which tests their validity rather than discussing values themselves – his only normative statement is the principle of universalisation, following Kant. Hence, his position is one of discourse rather than language and the affect – it is this approach that he calls discourse ethics.

Unlike the existentialist position discussed in the following chapter, this is a position which is to be located directly within the framework of modernity, so that Habermas is forced into defending the modernity project against those who see it undergoing profound change. Consequently, his position is open to a number of criticisms. Habermas argues, for instance, that norms are valid when they are determined by rational consensus but, as Benhabib (see Rasmussen, 1990, p67) suggests: rational discussion about norms usually occurs when they are endangered and not when they are taken for granted. Indeed, it might be questioned as to whether discourse is actually the method through which a universalisable ethic can be presented and Rasmussen (1990, p73) sums up the problem thus:

> can one sustain the claim that basic assumptions regarding the com-
> municative resolution of truth and validity, are given in the language
> as discourse?

Ultimately, it appears that Habermas' ethical position is totally dependent upon his views of communicative action and the ideal speech act. The ideal may point to a utopian society in which everybody interacts without a strategic interest but it is far removed from the actual world of everyday practicalities. While his emphasis upon communicative relationship is important to the position adopted here, the rational endeavour that he has undertaken separates his discussion from the conditions of the actual world in which people endeavour to act morally, or otherwise.

While Habermas tries to defend the Enlightenment project, MacIntyre, among others, concludes that Western society is moving beyond it. MacIntyre considers that the early Enlightenment thinkers shared very similar views about human nature and about moral beliefs, but he argues that there is an ineradicable discrepancy between the two (1985, p52). He suggests that the thinkers regarded morality as a matter of human beings fulfilling their roles in society – a deontological position – but with the development of modernity and the complexity of the ensuing society a great many alternative actions in any given situation emerged. A variety of different role possibilities resulted and so the individual was invented (p61), and this changed the nature of moral thought since

> the self had been liberated from outmoded forms of social organization which had imprisoned it simultaneously within a belief in a theistic and teleological world order and within those hierarchical structures which attempted to legitimate themselves as part of such a world order (p60).

As a result of the changes, moral experience has a paradoxical character, as both an autonomous individual and as a member of social organisations which results in an incoherent set of moral attitudes because a new open, loose and rather unco-ordinated social system had arisen (p68). Now there were no simple moral rules and so emotivism emerged, which has now been seen to have failed. MacIntyre's argument is one which is naturally disputed by Habermas, among others, but supported by those who consider that Western civilisation has reached a stage where at least the Enlightenment can be questioned.

From a different type of analysis Baudrillard reached very similar conclusions, summarised thus:

> The glorious march of modernity has not led to the transformation of all values, as we once dreamed that it would, but instead to a dispersal and involution of value whose upshot is total confusion – the impossibility of apprehending any dominating principle, whether of an aesthetic, a sexual or a political kind.
>
> (Baudrillard 1993, p10)

For him, there is a total confusion and no anticipation of a future and no possibility of a radical critique of society. While his apparent pessimism about society might reflect the concerns of the post-modernist, this does not negate the possibility of a moral stance about it – indeed, implicitly Baudrillard seems to hold one!

Additionally, Bauman (1993, pp247–8) has argued a similar case about the future of morality and, like MacIntyre, he does not feel that morality is safe in the hands of the type of reason that has dominated modernity, although he is not quite as pessimistic about morality as Baudrillard. Bauman suggests:

> Morality is not safe in the hands of reason, though this is exactly what the spokesmen for reason promise. Reason cannot help the moral self without depriving the self of what makes the self moral; that unfounded, non-rational, un-arguable, no-excuses given and non-calculable urge to stretch towards the other, to caress, to be for, to live

for, happen what may. Reason is about making correct decisions, while moral responsibility precedes all thinking about decisions as it does not, and cannot, care about any logic which would allow the approval of an action as correct. . .

More recently, Giddens (1994) has begun to point to non-cultural values as being important to the good society, and he has returned to the Aristotelian position that happiness is the most important value. While his position is not accepted here, it is significant that he goes beyond the values of Modernity in search of universal values for the good society. It is also important to note how he also separates human values from positions in the social structure.

## Conclusion

This chapter has presented a critical overview of the main theoretical positions in moral philosophy. Many of the values which underlie these positions must, consequently, be regarded as non-moral goods rather than moral ones. Significantly, many relate to modernity, or to specific cultural values, and they will be referred to hereafter as cultural goods, but they are not universal good. Towards the end of the chapter another, more recent adaptation which is not based in the rationality of modernity is beginning to emerge. Indeed, Bauman's position is similar to the one adopted in the following chapter, since it points to the self reaching out to the Other in a sense of self-giving.

# Chapter Three

# An existentialist position

MacIntyre, Baudrillard and Bauman all locate the debates about ethics within the wider framework of current thinking about the questionable state of modernity. Significantly, Giddens (1991) argued that the discussion about late modernity has created a situation where existentialism has emerged as a major philosophical force within which individuals seek to understand themselves and the meaning of their own existence, although the use of power in society hardly enters that discussion. In precisely the same way, it is argued here that existentialism provides a theoretical understanding for the contemporary debate about moral questions, although it is recognised that there is a potential weakness in this position in relation to the misuse of power in society (Adorno, 1973).

Underlying a great deal of the morality of the modern world are the twin ideas of individualism and the resulting self-interest. These stem from the Enlightenment and from the morality implicit in the division of labour and, consequently, in the market place. Fundamental to the division of labour is the idea that human beings produce different commodities, which they then seek to offer in the market place in exchange for others that they also need. Clearly this is an efficient method of production and one which has been generally accepted in modern society. In 1759, Adam Smith, in *The Theory of Moral Sentiments*, developed the idea of self-interest which was applied in a more narrow economic fashion in *The Wealth of Nations* in 1776 (Brown, 1992), where he recognised the moral significance of the division of labour and suggested that the exchange in the market is based upon the philosophy of self-interest, *ie,* 'give me what I want and I will give you what you want'. This outworking of self-interest, it was claimed, functions for the social good, and society seems to function efficiently as a result – as if an 'invisible hand' has guided its transactions.

## Existentialism and individual relationships

As a consequence of this approach to social life, instrumental rationality has become widely equated with rationality itself, and it is regarded as quite natural for people to act in such a manner in order to further their own self-interest in a market situation. Imagine a transaction where two people are bartering over the sale and purchase of a commodity; it is regarded as quite natural that both should be concentrating on getting the best deal for themselves. The outcome of this might well be amicable agreement in which the social good results. But this market approach also means if the actors are unable to reach agreement then the more powerful usually get their way and the less powerful become even more dominated, so that while there is social cohesion as a result of the power relationship it does not mean that the good of all the actors in the transaction has been achieved. (See Poole, 1990 for a full discussion of relationship between modernity and morality.) This power relation might also have immoral implications, as was implied in the introduction to this chapter. Taylor (1991, p17) states quite specifically that 'some forms of life are indeed *higher* than others, and the culture of tolerance for individual self-fulfilment shies away from these claims' (*italics* in original).

If these approaches are applied to the teaching and learning transaction, the following two scenarios can be drawn. In the first, both students and teachers act in self-interest. Students might approach the transaction with their needs and with the intention of satisfying these, but by doing as little work as possible in order to gain the best qualification for themselves. The qualification is the sign of ownership of the commodity which has been provided by the teacher. Teachers are all aware of, and have often experienced, this instrumental approach to education by some students. Teachers, on the other hand, bring their own knowledge and skills to the transaction, but what if they were also to approach it in such a manner as to see how they can satisfy their needs and get the best out of the transaction for themselves, while still trying to get the greater majority of students through their examinations? They might seek to save time, do as little preparation as possible, provide as little of the necessary knowledge as possible, see the students as infrequently as possible, and even encourage self-directed learning, and so on.

It might be argued that if the learners actually gain their qualifications then the conservation of energy and time to use on other activities is perfectly acceptable, both sets of actions are perfectly rational and that the actions of the role players are right. But what if, in the long term, the teachers have not really kept abreast with developments in their discipline and their students begin to fail examinations and courses? Then the students will not achieve their qualifications and they will become dissatisfied with the provision and might well look elsewhere for their education. The logic of this position, therefore, is false. It is not really possible for both teachers and learners to try to get the best deal for themselves all the time and to produce the instrumental outcomes that they seek from participating in the educational process. Indeed, this suggests that high quality of education can only be maintained by less instrumental orientations by the participants.

Almost as an aside from this, if educational institutions, or governments, try to overload teachers, then it is not the teachers who are trying to get more for themselves but the employing organisations, and the same outcome is inevitable. In this instance, it is the language of efficiency that prevails, not the language of needs.

But it is significant that the language of needs has been used and this is because some of the philosophy underlying ideas commonly used in the education of adults is problematic. Maslow's (1968) hierarchy of needs, for instance, places self-actualisation at the apex of human development, but this is an individualistic perspective which can easily be used to justify individuals striving to self-fulfil or to actualise their own self-interest at the expense of others. It can easily become a legitimating ideology for this bartering transaction, so that Maslow's position apparently implicitly reflects something of the same set of values as the market discourse – a point to which further reference will be made in subsequent chapters – although he probably would not have viewed it in this light.

In the second scenario, teachers might use their position to dominate the learners and get the best out of the situation for themselves. One way in which this occurs is when teachers impose their will on the class and use the teaching and learning situation as an opportunity for self-aggrandisement, while their students are forced to be the recipients of the tutors' performance, eloquence, wit, etc. When education is so teacher-centred that the teaching and learning transaction is a process which the teachers control for their own personal or psychological benefit, then the students are given no encouragement to grow or develop. Teaching, or the teachers' performance, is the end-product of the process and the students' learning is almost incidental. The teachers might come away from such a class claiming that it has been a 'good session' and untrained observers might also regard it as an excellent lesson. The students, also, might have enjoyed the performance, but the outcome of the session might be that they might have learned very little. Indeed, this approach to education is in accord with the thesis of Bourdieu and Passeron (1977, p5) that all 'pedagogic action. . . is objectively, symbolic violence insofar as it is the imposition of a cultural arbitrary by an arbitrary power'. In this instance, teachers use their dominant position for their own self-interest; a form of teaching has occurred but educators might question whether education has actually happened. Indeed, Buber (1961, p120) suggested that the educator is not ' "the man (*sic*) with the will to power," but he was the bearer of assured values'. This scenario will be discussed in greater detail in a later chapter.

Neither of these approaches have what most people would regard as the underlying philosophy of teaching and learning in any form of education, let alone adult education. Indeed, their very individualism is part of the problem, as MacIntyre pointed out. Society is not an agglomeration of individuals but, amongst other things, it is a set of interpersonal relations. It is necessary, therefore, to examine a philosophy of human interaction, as an ethical basis of social living, even though, or because, society is itself becoming more impersonal. This is also a point that Habermas sees clearly in his concern for communicative action and the ideal speech act.

Perhaps the crucial idea in social living lies in the word 'relationship'. This is also true for certain forms of education, although not in all forms of distance education, since it involves a relationship between the teacher and the learner. Some philosophers have concentrated their analyses on 'relationship'; of these, perhaps the most well known in adult education is Martin Buber, after whom the adult education institute of the Hebrew University in Jerusalem in named, although there are many other eminent philosophers whose work is important to this discussion.

Buber, in a number of major works, explored the idea of relationship, especially in *I and Thou* and *Between Man and Man*. In *I and Thou* he (1959) explored the idea of personal relationship, as opposed to I-It relationships. He might also have, but did not, postulate a third form of relationship, I-Group relationship, since there are many occasions, especially in education, where individuals are confronted with a group, or an agglomeration of individuals. While such interaction might be regarded as impersonal, it is not the same as trying to interact with a tree, so that it must be seen as a form of personal relationship. However, the fundamental issue in Buber's analysis is that there can be no *I* without *Thou*, because it is only through living being in relationship that either can exist as separate beings.

For Buber, the personal relationship is conducted at three levels – with living being, with individual persons and with spiritual beings; each of which could be expanded upon here but the second of these is most relevant to the present discussion, although the first needs some initial comment. People can enter some form of relationship with animals, especially household pets, and it would certainly be regarded by most people as wrong to disregard the basic needs of animals, so that it might be argued that relationship with living beings other than human beings is the basis of morality. However, there is a major problem here in as much as at what point in the hierarchy of living beings does one argue it is not possible to enter relationship – perhaps that would be when living being changes from the animal to the insect world, or the vegetable one, *etc*? While the ethical problems surrounding living being are acknowledged here they lie beyond the scope of this study and the core of the following argument relates to the person-hood of the Other, and for no other reason than that the Other is a living being.

People enter personal relationships through direct experience, usually because they share the same space at the same time and through so doing they have opportunity to interact with each other during which time they share a mutual bond. Before a relationship is formed, I exist in my world and the Other is a stranger, a significant idea since the stranger is free (Levinas, 1991, p39) over whom I have no power. When I enter into relationship with the Other it is usually through the medium of language in the first instance, although relationship is more than an exchange of words. Levinas (1991, p66) suggests that 'Discourse is . . . an original relation with exterior being'. When I and the Other are face to face, the distance between the Stranger and Ego recedes and some form of bond begins to be created, but the very formation of that bond impinges upon the freedom which is the prerogative of the Other. At the same time, my own freedom in respect to the Other is curtailed. The bond's existence, however weak, signifies that I am prepared freely to forego some of my freedom in order to enter a relation-ship. This relationship may be only for a brief period of time, although there is potentiality for it to continue beyond the first interaction.

Bauman (1993, p124) suggests that:

> (m)oral behaviour is triggered off by the mere presence of the Other as a *face*: that is, an authority *without* force. The Other demands without *threatening* to punish, or promising rewards. The Other cannot do anything to me, neither punish nor reward: it is precisely that weakness of the Other that lays bare my strength, my ability to act, as responsibility.

But sometimes the Other can harm me and does have power over me, but it is not the power possessed by the Other that triggers off the moral response, it is the very presence of the Other, the face, which signifies the presence of the one with whom I can enter into relationship. Even so, it has to be recognised that I might not have the immediate possibility of entering into a personal relationship with the Other since I might not experience the Other directly. The relationship between space and time has been changed by modern technology and I might become aware of the presence of the other through means of technology – I do not directly experience the Other as one starving in Ethiopia – but I do so indirectly through space-time compression and I am still able to communicate with, and feel responsible for, the Other. The presence of the Other, even on the television screen, does not threaten me and has no power over me, but that presence demands my response. If I were there, then I might feel the desire to enter a personal relationship with the Other whom I experience through the wonders of modern communications technology, but if I ignore that presence then the Other remains a Stranger. Herein lie two important features to which we shall return later in this book. The first is the distinction between the desire to enter such a relationship and the feeling of moral duty that I ought to enter such a relationship because I have a responsibility to do so. The second is that modern communications have made me more aware of the needs of the Other and, consequently, placed more moral demands upon me – but distance education might also be considered to fall within the ambit of this discussion, a point to which reference will be made later.

Additionally, relationship with the Other is mediated to me indirectly through the structures of society. Harvey (1993, p106) points out that:

> Relationships between individuals get mediated to me through market functions and state powers, and we have to define conceptions of justice capable of operating across and through these multiple mediations.

I do have impersonal and indirect relations with the Other mediated to me through all the social processes of society and it is not the relationship which demands my moral response, but the potentiality of entering a relationship with a fellow human being wherever she is, but the impersonal and indirect calls into play the idea of social justice, to which further reference will be made in the final section of this chapter.

I am able to enter such a relationship with the Other for whatever period of time it exists because of our common humanity. Where there is no humanity, the relationship is of necessity an I-It one. Relationships with a group, because all its members are human beings, share many of the same characteristics as with the Other, but they tend to develop the bonds of community rather than those of the more exclusive personal relationship. The exclusive personal relationship always puts at risk the community since it has the power to fragment the group. The potentiality of individual personal relationships always exists in the educational situation, and this is one of its problems. Herein lies a fundamental truth, when the I-Thou relationship is formed the Stranger, or the group member, becomes a person with whom I, as a person, can share a human bond. My personhood can only be realised in relationship with another person – or as Buber (1959, p18) put it, 'In the beginning is relationship', and MacMurray (1961, p17) suggested 'the Self is constituted by its relation to the Other'. Elsewhere, MacMurray (1961, p24) claimed that 'the idea of an isolated Agent is self-contradictory. Any Agent is necessarily in relation to Other. Apart from this essential relationship he does not exist.'

As the relationship becomes established, certain patterns of interaction begin to appear and it is these which curtail freedom. Sociologists call these norms and mores and some scholars, such as Heller (1988), wrongly regard these as the foundation of ethics, although it must be recognised that values, both moral and immoral, are manifest within norms and mores. Indeed, norms and mores may reflect the cultural and the non-moral goods of a society. Like the case studies, norms may not reflect the morality of the interaction for a number of reasons, including the fact that the norms of modernity were shown above to be morally flawed in certain situations. Additionally, if there is an unequal power between the actors the patterns of interaction may reflect the selfish desires of the more powerful actor even though they may not be presented to the less powerful, or even to the general public, in this manner. Hence, it appears that the actual location of morality lies with the intention of the actors rather than with the behaviour itself. One of the problems with this, as is demonstrated in the above discussion on teleological theories, is that individuals can claim that they had good intentions, even though their actions had unfortunate outcomes and, in other situations, bad intentions can produce good outcomes – but in these latter situations the morality underlying the action has to be questioned. Consequently, ethics is not an empirical science! It is not one of the sciences of modernity, neither does it reflect the characteristics espoused by many scholars of the Enlightenment. It is grounded in human intention, wherein the morality of action lies. In order for individuals to understand the Other's actions it is necessary to understand what it meant to the Other, and this is a hermeneutical exercise. Gadamer (1976, p15) points out that 'avoiding misunderstanding can be regarded as the specific task of hermeneutics'.

It is in a common humanity that the foundations of arguments for ethics lies and in the formation of the relationship in which personhood may be realised rests the practicalities of ethics. Indeed, Levinas (1991, p43) argues that ethics arise when an individual's spontaneity is inhibited by the presence of Other, which is before the relationship is actually formed. It will be seen from the above discussion that this position is too narrow and yet he captures a great deal of the understanding of the moral relationship which is regarded here as imperative in contemporary society. Levinas actually regards the bond that is established between the Self and the Other, the I-Thou relationship, as religion and MacMurray develops his discussion in a similar manner in relation to the celebration of communion, although this point will not be developed further here. However, it is clear that in the potentiality of personal relationship itself lies a fundamental basis of any discussion of the nature of ethical value. MacMurray (1959, p116) would agree with this analysis and he claimed that the 'moral rightness of an action . . . has its grounds in the relation of persons'. In other words the intention to act out of concern for the Other's advantage, whatever the actual outcome, is the moral ought of social living.

The moral good is concern, or care, or what is regarded in Christian theology as 'agape'. Frankena (1963, pp42–45) actually refers to this position as agapism and he then discusses whether it can take the form of Act-Agapism or Rule-Agapism, which means in the former instant that the actor seeks to act out of concern for the other irrespective of rules whereas in the latter that the actor chooses the rules which further the cause of concern for the Other. He also recognises a third possibility which he (1963, p44) summarises thus: 'it is a twofold principle, telling us to be benevolent to all and to be equally so in all cases'. However, his analysis does not emerge from an existentialist position and is not really grounded in the ideas of relationship, although it will be necessary to return to the principles by which social action is judged in the final section of this chapter. But concern for the Other can only emerge if the possibility of relationship between the Other and me exists.

It is significant that whatever the relationship, whoever the people and whatever the historical time, this argument still applies. It is for these reasons that it can be claimed that the basis of moral value is that it is universalisable. It may thus be seen why Kant claimed that values had to be generalisable in this manner, which is implicit in MacMurray's (1961, p122) claim that;

> To act rightly is . . . to act for the sake of the Other and not of oneself. The Other . . .always remains fully personal; consequently its objectives must be the maintaining of positive personal relations between all agents as the bond of community.

The underlying point here is that it is the intention behind the action – some form of care, or concern, for the Other – that creates the type of community that he espouses. It is doubtful, however, if people living in tightly-knit communities would see freedom to respond to the Other as a basis of their community, since there is a sense of compulsion to conform to the expectations of the group, so that MacMurray might really be desribing the idea of communitas rather than community.

This intention for the Other is, as Bauman (1993, p90) specifies, something that must precede knowledge, since it is the presence of the Other and not knowledge of the Other that creates it. It is the desire to enter a relationship and be with the Other because the Other is and to be concerned for the Other that is the beginning of morality. However, the manner in which that concern is worked out that involves knowledge and planning, *ie*, the 'What should I do?' *etc* that involves knowledge – since it must be in a very thoughtful manner and mistakes might be made for a variety of reasons as the outcomes might later demonstrate. But, as it was argued in the previous chapter, the outcomes cannot be the criteria by which the morality of an act is judged. Moral actions are not mindless nor antinomian, nor are they contrary to careful reasoned thought, but they are guided by love or concern for the Other. That people are in different positions in the social structure, have different perceptions of the situation and are fundamentally different means that the manner in which that concern is manifest through action will be different. It is not the action that is universalisable, but the universalisable morality lies in the concern towards the Other because the Other is, which is demonstrated through the action.

It is maintained that such an intention is never wrong in itself, although there are at least two situations which demand further discussion. Firstly, if the intention does not actually result in any action at all, then the concern is not demonstrated – although it must be acknowledged that there are occasions when the concern is best demonstrated through no observable action, *eg*, when a teacher watches a learner struggle with a problem but does not immediately provide assistance because that act might have damaged the other's self-image, *etc*. Competency is not always apparent nor measurable! In this instance, the morality lies in the fact that the teacher is with the learner and available if needed, rather than in any outward act. Secondly, the desire to care for one other may put many others at risk, which illustrates the distinction between the I-Thou and the I-Group relationship. Clearly in this latter instance, there is a major ethical problem about putting one's loved ones before unknown others, or the teacher devoting more effort to favoured learners or to those who have special needs than to the class as a whole. Teachers must be concerned for all those with whom they work and act for their own sake rather than the teacher's own self-interest or the interests of the few. At the same time teachers interact with all the class individually, so that there is both an I-Group interaction and a potential I-Thou relationship with each individual member of the class.

However, the position adopted here is that concern for the Other in relationship constitutes the basis of moral behaviour, and that the one moral good is the loving care for the Other. This does not inhibit the individual actor from acting freely within the context of the action, although she has to develop her own praxis between the intention to be concerned for the Other and actually caring for the Other and that her concern is manifest through informed and reasoned behaviour orientated to bring about the further well-being of the Other. But, it might well be asked, does this position not consider the actor's self at all? Clearly this is a legitimate question in as much as the individual has been privatised in many ways in contemporary society. Naturally, there are individual concerns in this position, although it does leave the individual more free than certain deontological statements of ethics do. Indeed, it can be argued that people are often more able to be themselves when they are supported by another, so that it is a false premise to suppose that relationship is, in itself, always going to inhibit individual autonomy. However, an individual should do nothing to himself that would in any way be construed as not being concerned for the Other, which places certain moral restrictions upon the self. Apart from this it has to be recognised that in relationship the Other is concerned for the Ego, so that the Ego is free to be as concerned for himself as the Other would be for him. Indeed, it is recognised psychologically that individuals only learn to love themselves, indeed be themselves, when others love them and are in relationship with them. Hence, there is a sense in which he has to be concerned for himself as the Other would love him, since this form of concern can only be manifest in human relationship. It is in this relationship of mutual concern that the moral ideal is realised – it is an ideal, although one capable of realisation.

It is recognised, however, that within contemporary impersonal society the potentiality of relationship is lessened and its nature changed. This will constitute the basis for the discussion in the final section of this chapter.

## Implications of the existentialist position within the wider social context

The above position suggests that morality resides in persons in seeking to develop a relationship; but the point of significance for the following discussion is that the actual morality lies in the intention to be in a caring relationship with the Other. It is now necessary to discuss this in the light of the wider society which appears to be antithetical to personal relationship, since it is impersonal, organisational and global. Relationship occurs where individuals' lives intersect in both time and space, but both the nature of relationship and the relationship of time and space has been altered in this global village; the world has been apparently depersonalised by its bureaucratic and technological infrastructures, and people paradoxically appear to have both more freedom but to be removed further from the ambit of decision making. All of these issues need to be addressed here and elsewhere in this study, so that this section has four sub-sections: the change in the nature of relationship; trusting in abstract and expert systems; professionalism and professional ethics; social justice.

### The changing nature of relationships

As long ago as the work of Toennies (1957) on community and association it was recognised that the nature of human relationships was changing and clearly as modernity developed individualisation came to the forefront, as Simmel (1903) showed, human relationships have become fragmented. Giddens (1990, pp117–9) illustrates how human relationships have altered as a result of social change and while a friend might now be an acquaintance, *etc*, it is important to point out that the ethic of concern for the Other can be practised irrespective of whether Ego actually likes the Other, or whether the relationship occurs in a communal setting or in a society which has become fragmented as a result of the rapid changes that are currently occurring. In addition, and this is much more significant for our purposes, the concern can be demonstrated even if the relationship is formalised, or contractualised (a point to which we shall return below), or only potential. Indeed, it is also possible to enter a relationship of concern when the speech is transmitted through technological media and the face appears on the television screen. The position adopted in the previous section was that the point at which the potentiality for relationship exists is the beginning of ethics, so that the type of relationship does not affect the ethical argument at all. Even so, it is recognised that in a hierarchical world some people seek to exert power over the others, and power is always problematic when the basis of ethical relationship is mutual concern. Significantly, in the traditional educational setting, the teacher is always in a situation where the potentiality for human relationships exists. But teachers also control the space within which they teach, so that while teaching is always a moral interaction, it is one within which power might be exercised by the teacher in an immoral manner.

The situation when individuals are concerned for the Other in relationships of mutuality without rules and regulations gives rise to a major problem in society at large, since it is almost impossible to consider life in society without rules and regulations. Indeed, it might be claimed by some that this could only happen in utopian society while others would claim that this would be anarchic (see Jarvis, 1993 for a discussion on this). But the word 'anarchy' comes from the Greek meaning no laws and this might well be utopian if people were sufficiently morally developed always to endeavour to live in relationships of mutual concern. Unfortunately, we are not! Consequently, it is necessary for society to have rules and regulations in order to provide a structure within which people may act and the structures actually allow a level of freedom to be achieved that would not otherwise be possible.

Society always precedes and succeeds the individual – the paradox of society is that it creates the individuals who maintain it – but the social structures are essential for freedom to be exercised safely. This is not, however, claiming that the principles underlying the existing social and legal structure of any society are themselves necessarily moral or based on moral precepts. Neither is it claiming that individuals cannot act out of concern for the Other if they live in a society which has no systematic structure or in structures that are antithetical to the exercise of care and concern – it is only claiming that such structures facilitate opportunities for people to live in relationships of mutual concern. This does leave unanswered questions about how these rules arise and what are the underlying principles that guided their framing. But it has to be recognised that this problem reflects something of the paradox of society itself; people, especially those who exercise power in society, make the rules into which the succeeding generations are socialised. Like the law, cultural morality is a socially constructed process and the moral self is both mediated and mediating. (Aboulafia, 1986, cited in Wolfe, 1989, p220) As Wolfe (1989, p220) writes:

> We make the moral rules that make us: we are, in a word, what we do, and what we do is done together with others. We create our moral rules as we link our individual needs with the understanding we obtain from other people of what the consequences of our actions are likely to be.

Thus, it may be argued that the cultural values of morality are learned, like any other aspect of our social and cultural existence. But it must be noted that the actual laws of any society may not be universally accepted as being moral, since they are usually enacted in the interests of those who have the power to make and enforce them. Consequently, the law is sometimes an ass in the eyes of others in society, or even in the eyes of those who frame it when it is applied to situations for which it was not originally intended. But at least the laws provide a stable social situation within which people may be able to act morally, so that the question that the remainder of this section investigates is the relationship between what the underlying principles of the social structure should be if it is to be consistent with the existential moral position adopted here.

## Abstract and expert systems

One of the main elements of entering into personal relationships is that a sense of trust develops between the participants, which occurs because of the human interaction. The trust is in people, but in modern society large organisations emerge which are much more impersonal. Hence, there is the need to change the locus of this trust to abstract principles and procedures, which exacerbates the feeling of risk that people experience in daily living (Beck, 1992; Giddens, 1990). Many of the managers of these organisations have recognised this problem and have endeavoured to give their organisations a 'Face', by naming personnel with whom the general public can enter into discussion about their business – the Open University counsellor might be regarded in this light! Regretably, the Open University is being forced by financial constraint to lose local counselling, and it is losing some of its local face. Certainly the Open University regional full-time staff try to put a face on the large bureaucratic educational organisation, and they succeed to a considerable extent.

Even so, organisations have to earn that trust, however good at public relations the individual employees happen to be, which places certain constraints upon the organisations themselves. They have to demonstrate that same concern for individuals who enter into relationship with them, either as employees or clients, and herein lies a major difficulty. Being concerned for the Other may be costly both in time and money, but most contemporary organisations function in an advanced capitalist society where neither of these are limitless. This is one of the major problems of the capitalist market because, however well-intentioned the managers of such institutions concerned might be, the exercise of concern cannot add too much to the basic cost of commodity production since every company has to compete with other organisations providing a similar commodity. The competitive market has no room for concern for persons, only for profit!

Organisations have developed their own quality procedures in both production and service, so that the commodity manufactured and sold will normally meet the clients' expectations. By so doing, the organisation seeks to earn the trust of its clients. It might also be argued that these procedures have been developed in order to ensure that the market can operate freely and without intervention from politicians or consumer pressure groups – but the market itself does not generate the conditions whereby individuals can interact with the Other out of concern. Indeed, the market favours the strong and the successful but, as Bauman (1991, p264) reminded us, 'the quality of society is to be measured by the welfare of its weakest member'.

It is significant that as education has become a marketable commodity the quality assessment and quality control procedures have become more significant in course production and delivery. But the fundamental question underlying this must be whether the reason for so doing is concern for the Other, or whether it is to allay the potentiality of discontent with the product that would redound unfavourably upon the supplier of the commodity. Naturally, this is not a simple either-or problem, but these alternatives do illustrate the two extremes of the complexity of organisational intentions.

Since employees are at risk in this type of situation they also need some form of support against employers who might seek to cut production costs by exploiting them. This is a function that Trades Unions should serve – which puts attacks on the Trades Unions into perspective in a monetarist economy. It is often claimed that management accusations about the Unions are ideological protestations rather than accusations based upon firm foundations and it is important to be aware that discourse also carries ideological overtones.

However, the question remains – can the principle of agape, concern, be applied to the abstract and expert systems in wider society? If so, with what consequences? Clearly the answer must be in the affirmative, not because of the principles of benevolence which Frankena suggested, but because of the principles of relationship in which concern for persons should arise in whatever type of society that they occur. At the risk of over-simplifying the discussion, it must be pointed out that whatever form of society that emerges, human interaction, in one form or another, will always occur, and consequently, the moral basis of human behaviour is unchanged.

Very few organisations function in such an impersonal manner so as to exclude personal relationships. Wolfe (1989, p229), for instance, points out that even 'securities markets which are supposed to be anonymous and so hurried that they allow little time for personal relations, operate chiefly because social patterns and ties develop that enable the participants to conduct their business because they know and trust one another.' Few educational organisations function as impersonally as the securities markets, so that it is clear that the patterns that emerge will reflect those relationships. Whether the principles underlying these will reflect the concern of the one for the Other may depend upon the management style of the organisation concerned and the way that the participants exercise their own interest – but even if the patterns are not quite ideal, they do provide a structure within which the moral self can operate. Indeed, the self who acts in such a manner provides a moral critique of the behaviour of others who do not show the same concern for the Other – actions do indeed speak louder than words, although words are sometimes necessary!

Organisations and abstract systems operate in a market system and so their initial obligations are to their owners and shareholders, which means that they have less obligation to be concerned for their clients. Thus, it might be argued that such organisations need to be controlled in some way to ensure that they do not exploit their clients for the sake of profit. As Wolfe (1989, p75) points out:

> Privatization is an important trend because it raises the implicit question of whether people have any common stake in the provision of the services that define their society. If they do not, then the term used to describe this activity, *deregulation,* is an appropriate one, for regulation is at the heart of the social fabric. If deregulation is carried to its logical extreme, it is difficult to imagine exactly what aspects of civil society would remain.

Wolfe goes on the argue that it is necessary for people to be aware of this process and be active in protecting the common society of the people. Obviously deregulation is a major danger since abstract and expert systems can so easily exploit their clients because of the latter's ignorance. This is extremely important for educators, as education itself is apparently becoming deregulated and privatised. The place of the pressure group, often one having an educational role, becomes obvious and extremely urgent in a deregulated society in order to highlight the processes that are occurring, and so it is necessary to translate the ethical idea of the moral self to a social principle upon which pressure groups might act.

## Professionalism, professional ethics and the customers' charter

The 1960s were a time when many occupations began to seek professional status and it was during this time that many of them prepared their statements of professional ethics. By contrast the 1990s has been a time of the market when many organisations have been forced to issue customers' charters, *eg*, the students' charter. Both of these relate in some way to this discussion of existentialist ethics, although the relationships have not really been expounded.

As occupations began to professionalise, one of the accepted symbols of their professional status was an ethical statement: indeed, many scholars during this period regarded this as an essential feature of the professionalisation process, *eg*, Caplow (1954), Greenwood (1957), *inter alia*. Caplow, for instance, suggested that a code of ethics

> asserts the social utility of the occupation, sets up public welfare rationale, and develops rules which serve as further criteria to eliminate the unqualified and unscrupulous. The adoption of a code of ethics, despite certain hypocrisies imposes a real and permanent limitation on internal competition.
>
> (cited from Vollmer and Mills 1966, p21)

It should be noted that the rationale for the code of ethics is utilitarian: it is necessary because this is what it will produce and while the concern for the client is implicit throughout, it does not specify this as the major reason for having such a code. When professional groups actually agree a Code of Ethics, it then becomes a deontological statement of professional behaviour, *ie*, this is what members of this or that profession are expected to do in order to be a respected member. As more clients have gone to litigation over malpractice of professionals such a code can serve as a protective mechanism for the professional, but it does not encapsulate the ethics of concern for the Other discussed above.

Clearly, however, one of the major bases of professionalism has been concern for others as one of the earliest definitions of profession suggest. Carr-Saunders (1928, cited in Vollmer and Mills 1966, p4) claims that a profession 'may perhaps be defined as an occupation based upon specialized intellectual study and training, the purpose of which is to supply a skilled service or advice to others for a definite fee or salary'. Here the element of service is clear, although by 1972 others were defining professions in terms of the control of bodies of expert knowledge (Elliott, 1972, p11). The paradox of service is that it so easily becomes a route to power and control and there is a real sense in which power is the antithesis of service – a point to which further reference will be made in a later chapter.

Consequently, it is argued here that professional ethics, as such, are statements of cultural good rather than universal good, reflecting a variety of concerns of which the care and concern for the Other who crosses my path is but one. Nevertheless, this does not mean that professionalism does not necessarily embody a universal moral good. Certain professionals can and do exercise that moral value in their own practice, so that the intention to serve might actually relate much more closely to the values underlying an individual's practice rather than to the code of ethics which seeks to encapsulate the occupational group as a whole.

There can be no code of ethics for educators of adults until such time as there is a single occupation or professional association and since none exists at present, no code has yet been formulated although there was a movement with the Commission of Professors in the United States towards creating one during the 1980s.

By contrast, the clients' charters of the 1990s reflects the level of service which clients should expect to receive from organisations as well as from professional practitioners. Perhaps the most famous one in the United Kingdom is the Patients' Charter, specifying the level of service a patient should expect to receive from the emasculated public health service in the United Kingdom. While education has not yet adopted a charter for adult learners of quite this nature, a parents' charter exists and a students' charter also exists in some places. These charters are concerned with ensuring customer satisfaction and, implicitly, with the standards that different producers are maintaining in the market place of competition.

Education for adults has, however, begun to adopt a similar approach, although in this instance – The Bill of Rights for the Adult Learner – was published by educational organisations as a propaganda weapon, similar to codes of professional ethics, rather than a government imposed charter. On 21 February 1991, the board of directors of the Coalition of Adult Education Associations (26 national adult education associations in the USA) published a Bill of Rights for the Adult Learner, which states:

A democratic nation is made possible through the efforts of a knowledgable populace actively committed to the general welfare and alert to the opportunities for personal growth and development. Essential for realising this commitment is the wide variety of adult and continuing education opportunities. The institutions and agencies of a democratic society will strive to assure that the following rights are possessed by all who have adult responsibilities and who seek to learn in any setting.

- The right to learn regardless of age, gender, colour, ethnic or linguistic background, marital status, the presence of dependants, or of financial circumstances

- The right of equal opportunity to relevant learning opportunities throughout life

- The right to educational leave from employment for general as well as vocational or professional education

- The right to financial aid and educational services at levels comparable to those provided for younger or full-time learners

- The right to encouragement and support in learning subject matter that the learner believes will lead to growth and self-actualisation

- The right to a learning environment suitable for adults to include appropriate instructional materials, media and facilities

- The right to have relevant prior experiential learning evaluated and, where appropriate, recognised for academic credit toward a degree or credential

- The right to participate or be appropriately represented in planning or selecting learning activities in which the learner is engaged

- The right to be taught by qualified and competent instructors who possess appropriate subject matter qualifications, as well as knowledge and skill relating to the instructional needs of adults

- The right to academic support resources, including instructional technology, that can make self-directed learning or distance learning possible

- The right to dependant care and related structures of social support

- The right to individualized information and guidance leading toward further study

(Cited from *Adults Learning* Vol 3 No 4 1991, p106)

Clearly this is not quite the same as a patients' charter, since it is an idealised statement from a number of pressure groups. The fact that there are a number of groups co-operating demonstrates that competitive market forces do not operate between them, as they are beginning to in the United Kingdom, so that a charter for learners might not yet be appropriate. The only rationale provided for this Bill of Rights is that it will hopefully lead to a more democratic society and individual growth. Each of these may be regarded as good, but they are cultural and non-moral goods in the sense that the terms are used here. They are teleological in formulation and still reflect the values of modernity.

The difference between the universal moral good in education and the wider cultural values and non-moral goods of society is clearly demonstrated in this section, since the formulation of the code of ethics or the charter reflects the power positions in society of the proponents, whereas moral good bears no direct relationship to power and is concerned only with concern for the Other.

## The principle of social justice

The idea that all people should be concerned for the Other in relationship smacks of utopian and unrealistic ideas. Indeed, throughout history there have been many thinkers who have longed for such a utopian society. For instance, Jesus Christ taught about the Kingdom of God on earth and early Christians longed for the millennium; Marx postulated the classless society; Morris' utopia was depicted in *News from Nowhere*; the idea that society should be truly democratic has also been espoused by many utopian thinkers. But humankind cannot build utopia, that was the message of the fall of the Berlin Wall, and so is utopia a myth? Do utopian thoughts not have some functions? Levitas (1990, p196) suggests that:

The function of utopia . . . reverts from that of goal and catalyst of change to one of criticism, and the education of desire . . .

And so, it might be argued that while utopian thinking may be unrealisable in practice, the moral principle of the individual seeking always to enter relationship and be act in a concerned manner towards the Other is a utopian ideal by which it is possible to critique contemporary society's norms and laws – pointing to a better world without seeking to regulate for it or for human behaviour in general. Indeed, any laws that were formulated would inhibit the differences in people from being manifest in various responses to social situations and would, consequently, fall short of being utopian for them. Morality does not lie in society's rules but in the intentions of the people who comprise society. Society itself must be sufficiently free to allow the manifestation of difference and individuality while having some principles by which to evaluate behaviour morally since not every difference is necessarily good in itself. Utopia must always lie beyond the bounds of space and time, but are the principles upon which (it has been argued here) morality is based applicable to society as a whole in such a manner as to constitute a just society? This must be the final question posed in this chapter but it is one which numerous writers have tried to answer in recent years (Rawls, 1971; Phillips, 1986; Heller, 1987; MacIntyre, 1988; Wolfe, 1989; Peffer, 1990; Harvey, 1993, *inter alia*).

It will be seen from these many references that it is not possible to explore in depth all of the recent debate on this subject, but a number of conclusions may be drawn from the discussion in this chapter which is related to some of the current debate about social justice.

It was pointed out earlier that the basis of morality is the potentiality firstly of relationship with the Other regardless of how my experience of the Other is mediated to me, and secondly of my intention to be with the Other for the Other's benefit. This, it was argued, is a universal good, and while many postmodern thinkers have argued, that there can be no universals, Harvey has (1993, p112) also argued that 'universals are necessary and that some form of epistemology (unspecified) is needed to establish when, how and where difference and heterogeneity are significant.' It was pointed out that it is not possible to formulate rules that are universal since they do not recognise difference, and they are usually formulated in order to further the interests of those who construct them. Consequently, MacIntyre's (1988) question 'Whose Justice?' is recognised as being very relevant to this position. The moral principle does indeed enable interests underlying the rule to be demonstrated!

Therefore, the only principle that is adopted here is that of mutual concern, whatever the colour, creed or gender of the persons in the relationship – be it personal and direct or impersonal and indirect. This, then, is the only universal and it is incapable of being made into a law. Even so, it was pointed out that there are times when the interests of the Other have to constrained, *eg*, those of the serial killer: since the serial killer does not act for the benefit of those others with whom he relates, his interests must be curtailed, so that the universality principle is not rejected here but pursued more rigorously since it is literally applied to all possible social encounters.

Fundamentally it has been argued here that morality is about the potentiality of human relationships and it is this which constitutes society. While some postmodernists (and some politicians) might argue that there is no such thing as society, this proposition is rejected here. The nature of that society has changed, has become more fragmented and complex, but it has not been destroyed. Society has changed from community-type relationships to associational-type relationships, and now to a greater concentration on the individual and the freedom to be oneself. While society has changed, it still exists and we function within it, with all our differences and our similarities, and we are learning to respect both more than ever before. Perhaps the fact that we have taken these and social living for granted has been to our detriment, for Wolfe (1989, p261) reminds us that it is a gift.

> When we recognize society as a gift, we realize that we are free because our preferences can change through interaction with others, not because they are constant. We are free because we can give meaning to the way our situations are defined. We are free because we recognize that the condition of being modern sets internal limits on free-ridership, even if there are no external obstacles to impede us. We are free because we elevate loyalty over exit and voice, because we have strong intimate relations that enable us to resist mass society's pressure to conform. We are free to fulfil our obligations to society because we want to, not because government does it for us . . . We are free only when others are also free, and they are free only when we are.

It is into society that we are born and grow and develop and learn to become our individual selves. Because of our differences and our complexities, it is impossible to universalise laws and rules but it is not impossible to universalise the concern of the One for the Other as the basis of a moral relationship. Utopia will never exist within the bounds of time and space but the phenomenon of creating human relationship is universally essential and so the possibility of being concerned for people always exists. Consequently the possibility of creating a more just society always exists.

## Conclusion

We are born into this society and in it we learn to become ourselves, as moral human beings. However, it is important now to distinguish more carefully between the universal moral good of caring for the Other and the cultural values espoused by society which are themselves regarded as moral values, such as personal autonomy, *etc*. It is not denied that they are values, although it is denied that they are always good and so, for the purposes of this study, they are treated as cultural goods, as relative values rather than universal ones. The distinction between the moral and non-moral good is also maintained and this is between goodness and social value. The fifth chapter will explore this distinction further and it will be argued that the values of modernity actually exclude this form of moral goodness. Universal goodness, or love, cannot be codified or legislated for, so that it is always an intention underlying human action; it is universal and unchanging although the manner in which it is put into practice differs with each person. It is, therefore, a principle by which the relative cultural values can be judged but it is not a law and none can be formulated to encapsulate it. Social values are relative to the societies that espouse them and their taken-for-grantedness gives them the appearance of both objectivity and unchangeableness but, as we have seen, they are neither, and in that sense neither do they form the only basis for morality.

It is now important that we investigate how individuals learn this moral principle of concern, something that is pre-knowledge according to Bauman (1993), but which forms the basis of moral understanding and action. Learning is crucial to this process. But, as we argued in the first chapter, the learner is also one of the essential features of the educational, and so the next chapter leads us through the ideas of learning about morality into the discussions of social value and the education of adults.

# Chapter Four

# Learning to be a moral agent

Thus far the fields of education for adults and an introductory discussion about morality have been undertaken. It was also argued that the only universal moral good is care/concern for the Other which can only be demonstrated in human relationships. It was maintained in the third chapter that morality lies in the intention of the actor as evidenced in the ensuing action rather than in any other aspect of human action. Hence care or concern for the Other will be referred to throughout the remainder of the book as the universal moral good. However, the individual's actions, or decisions about how to demonstrate that concern, are based on knowledge and an understanding of the values of a given culture and, henceforth, these will be referred to as cultural moral goods which are relative, subjective and are not necessarily entirely based on concern for the Other. It is now necessary to explore the basis of social values and what constitutes socially accepted behaviour.

This will be undertaken during the process of this chapter in which it is intended to argue that we learn the universal moral good pre-consciously and that initially it is pre-knowledge. But as we develop as human beings, we acquire and develop the cultural moral goods, a set of values which are socially accepted and which enable us to play a role as social human beings within society. The cultural moral good will differ between people according to their cultural background and socialisation, so that there may well be sub-cultural variations, as well as a broad cultural form that in Western Europe and North American culture generally reflects those values embodied in modernity. As modernity is being called into question, so are many of the values of this cultural moral good being questioned.

Giddens (1994, p151) highlights the significance of this discussion when he points out that underlying the risk society, in which we live, 'stands nothing less than the whole weight of Enlightenment philosophy. For the idea of risk is integral to the endeavour to control the future and to harness history to human purposes'. He goes on to make the point that the notion of risk, and its unintended outcome – accident – imply the need for an ethic. It is this ethic which is bound up with the cultural moral goods.

However, it can be seen how the cultural moral goods can easily become predominant over the universal moral good, since they can be articulated and argued within the framework of the contemporary culture which they actually reflect and out of which they have arisen. Indeed, the very nature of the universal moral good is that it does not prescribe the forms of behaviour that responsible love for the Other should take, so that it is easy to see how it becomes embodied within, and confused with, the cultural moral goods, or even completely overlooked. Nevertheless, it was shown in the second chapter that there are flaws in the arguments for cultural moral goodness which is a reason why the universal moral good is being rediscovered at the present time, although it will often be articulated in different terms to those employed here.

However, becoming a moral agent is not just a matter of being concerned for the Other bcause the Other exists; it is a matter of behaving in a manner that we consider to be moral and, where appropriate, conforming to patterns of morality which are culturally accepted. Morality, however, does not always lead to conformity and many a moral person has been attacked by those in authority because of their stance on certain issues! Becoming a moral agent is, therefore, a very complex operation and involves a variety of learning processes, and the purpose of this chapter is to try to unravel some of the elements in this development. This chapter has three sections: the first propounds a theory about how the universal good, the morality of responsible caring for the Other, is learned by experience in relationships during childhood and precedes knowledge. Additionally, the initial culture of ethical behaviour in society is also learned in the family and, although social in origin, it is subjective rather than objective. The second explores the manner in which humans mature in their understanding of values. This is cognitive development, incorporating the work of Kohlberg, in which it is suggested that this conscious moral knowledge of what is right, the cultural moral good, overlays the pre-conscious learning of the universal good developed in very early childhood. The final section examines the relationship between the intention to act and becoming a moral agent, which results in a discussion about practical moral knowledge. This, in turn, leads to a brief concluding discussion about the autonomy of the moral agent.

## Learning and experiencing loving care

The thesis propounded here is that the universal moral good is pre-knowledge and learned pre-consciously through experience. In addition, children are socialised into the value system of the family or the initial group in which they are nurtured and much of this learning is initially preconscious, but it also develops in a more conscious and cognitive manner through both socialisation and education. However, it is doubtful whether many people actually develop a sophisticated and coherent code of ethics although they do learn to behave in a manner which is socially and morally acceptable, according to the cultural moral good. The argument rests upon three perspectives: the phenomenological position of GH Mead in which he argues that both the mind and the self are social constructs, the idea of preconscious learning that I (1987, 1992) have explored in a number of writings about human learning and Bauman's assertion that morality is pre-knowledge.

## The emerging mind and self

While it is essential to look back to Mead, it is also important to recognise that recent thinking has raised issues fundamental to this debate, so that I am drawing initially on my own treatment of Mead from an earlier work (Jarvis, 1987, pp37–62) and, thereafter, examining this in the light of some more recent writings.

Until very recently the concept of person hardly entered the debate for many educators of adults, but it is a topic to which return will be made in the next chapter. Paterson, however, was one exception to this, and he (1979, p32) wrote:

> The concept of 'person', however, is an open-ended concept. It is conscious selves who evolve as persons, and as a conscious self a man is always conscious of himself over and against his present circumstances, behaviour and identity; as a conscious self, he is always capable of surpassing his present level of personal existence and of transcending himself. We can never say that of a man that he has exhausted his potentialities as a person, or that he has fully and finally realized in himself a perfect completeness of personal being. Thus we can never say that a man's education is complete.

Paterson did not extend his analysis of personhood into a discussion of how the person emerged or of its constituent elements, even though Mead's work was widely known at the time when he wrote. For Mead, the emergence of both mind and self are the result of social processes which occur in early childhood. Children are born with very few sense experiences stored in their brains, so that the mind, (ie, the store of memories of experiences which guide further thought and action) is still a human potential rather than a reality. Indeed, he regarded the social act as a precondition of consciousness. Interacting with significant others, the baby becomes conscious of the other, and through the language and gesture of the significant other the child acquires linguistic knowledge and develops the ability to think. Since that interaction is social the language which the young child acquires is already a social construct and a reflection of the social milieu into which the child has been born. Mead argues that 'out of language emerges the field of mind' (Mead in Strauss 1977, p195). He (p195) goes on to suggest that:

> We must regard mind, then, as arising and developing within the social process, within the empirical matrix of social interactions. We must, that is, get an inner individual experience from the standpoint of social acts which include the experiences of separate individuals in a social context wherein individuals interact . . . Mind arises in the social process only when that process as a whole enters into, or is present in, the experience of any one of the individuals in the social process.

Since Mead's basic concern was with language and the cognitive, his concept of mind is of a cognitive and rationalistic nature. Mind emerges as a result of a very small child learning through experience and interacting with significant others.

Mead concentrated on language as a vehicle through which the infant learned the knowledge which formed the basis of both thought and the mind as a whole.

While Mead is correct in his analysis, it is necessary to extend it since language is not the total content of the child's experience or learning. Mead's insight into the significant other is also most important, since it is in relationship with the significant other that the experiences occur from which the child learns. The fact that has been missed is the relationship itself. The significant other with whom the child has this momentous relationship is usually the mother, or a mother figure, and its content comprises more than just language and cognition – it is the love and care that the significant other lavishes upon the infant. This is often not expressed in words. At the same time, in order to articulate that experience, language must be utilised.

The significance of this relationship was implicitly emphasised by Bruner (1968) when he discussed the idea of reciprocity; he (p125) wrote that the will to learn 'involves a deep human need to respond to others and to operate jointly with them toward an objective'. In other words the need for relationship had itself already been learned preconsciously in the very early experiences of life. Reciprocity is recognised as a necessity for survival and the value of love is experienced.

## Pre-conscious learning

All learning comes from experience and there are basically two forms of experience: primary experience is direct contact with other persons, things, *etc*; while secondary experience is mediated experience. In this latter form we experience a great deal of the world through people telling us about their experiences of the world; our experience of the world is also mediated through technology and the reporting skills, or deficiencies, of journalists. It is from experience that learning begins and while a great deal of secondary experience is mediated through language, much primary experience is not linguistic. It is, in one sense, pre-knowledge.

While the small child cannot necessarily articulate every aspect of the experience from which it learns, it learns preconsciously of what it means to be loved and cared for. I (1987, p31) described this form of learning as something 'that occurs to every person as a result of having experiences in daily living that are not really thought about but merely experienced.' Other writers have used different terms to describe similar forms of learning, Reischmann (1986) called it 'learning en passant' and Marsick and Watkins (1990) as 'incidental learning'. Reischmann describes this form of learning as 'the forgotten dimension' and this is a most apt description when it comes to understanding how the universal moral good is learned. While MacMurray (1961) based a great deal of his argument for the development of the personal on the mother-child relationship, and recognised the significance of experiencing love in that relationship, he did not pursue his argument far enough and conclude that it is in this relationship with a mother that an infant child preconsciously learns about love, which becomes the basis of its own future feelings about morality. The fact that this is an almost universal experience of a caring relationship enables the idea of caring for others to be regarded as a universal moral value, or as it has been suggested here it is the universal moral good.

This relationship is continued throughout childhood and so the process of living in the family means that two important elements of morality are learned in the family: firstly, the relationship and care itself are both continually experienced and so socialisation reinforces this early preconscious learning. At the same time, social values are also learned through socialisation in both a preconscious, and later, a more conscious, manner so that the beginnings of a code of cultural ethics or moral 'oughts' are learned. Hence, through experience a child learns about both 'the universal moral good' and the cultural moral 'ought', or the socially regarded right behaviour.

The value of this relationship is, therefore, quite fundamental to the development of moral values in human beings, as Habermas (1990, p114) argues:

> I will defend a thesis that does not sit well with the spirit of the times: that anyone who has grown up in a reasonably functional family, who has formed his identity in relations of mutual recognition, who maintains himself in a network of reciprocal expectations and perspectives built into the pragmatics of the speech situation and communicative action, cannot fail to have acquired moral intuitions . . .

This aspect of Habermas' argument is fully accepted here; the emphasis that he places on the family is very important because the initial very early experiential learning is the foundation upon which all of us acquire both the universal and the cultural good. For these reasons, we do well to heed Wolfe's (1989, p60) warning that: 'when ties in the intimate realm weaken, ties in the somewhat more distant community can be expected to weaken as well'. Here then is the symbiosis of the family and the society: for so long as the significant other/child relationship is maintained and fostered, then there will always be a heart of concern in society, but if the relationship is destroyed, then the universality of inter-personal care and concern may become less prevalent and other moral values will not have been learned in quite the same manner.

## Pre-knowledge

Thus it may be seen that values, both the universal good and aspects of the cultural moral good, are learned pre-consciously, and that they are not all in the cognitive domain. They are experienced in social relationship, and as Bauman (1993) has maintained, they are are learned before the development of language and are implanted in the emerging mind as a result of having learned them from experience: they are pre-knowledge.

This does not mean that they are irrational or that they are not capable of being defended intellectually, but it does ask fundamental questions about the nature of rationality itself. For the most part rationality has been regarded in modern society as cognitive, instrumental or technical, and implies that it is a means-and-ends phenomenon. The teleological arguments discussed in the previous chapters are instrumentally rational, but they were rejected as a firm basis of morality. Being concerned for the Other is rational in itself. It is a form of value rationality which has a different basis from that of instrumentality but, nonetheless, it is rational. Indeed, it might also be argued that the rationality of caring is fundamental to Being itself; there can be no human being without caring since the human species is incapable of survival without the long period of care required by the human infant.

Additionally, it was demonstrated in the previous chapter that the position can be sustained in an intellectual form and so it is necessary to recognise that the learning process is much wider than merely the cognitive. Even so, it is important to recognise that the experience of being cared for in early childhood is translated into a knowledge domain as the infant grows up, which might then be described as a form of tacit knowledge (Polanyi, 1967), and also that there is an additonal layer of cultural moral knowledge learned though other experiences that are added to the child's moral understanding. This is a combination of the universal and the cultural. It is important here to recognise the distinction being drawn: the universal moral good is learned pre-consciously through the experience of being loved as a baby, while the cultural moral good reflects the cultural and is learned both consciously and pre-consciously through both education and socialisation. Most thinkers who have examined the process of acquiring moral values, *etc*, have concentrated upon the cultural to the detriment of the universal. Freud, however, did point to the significance of the relationship in the development of the super-ego. Bocock (1976, p49) writes of Freud:

> The ego-ideal of the young child is based on those closest to them, usually the parents, and later on other educators and youth workers who have some resemblance to the parents.

Elsewhere, Bocock (1976, p120) suggests that the 'process of building up the super-ego starts with the relationship between the child and an external authority, usually a parent'. It is in relationship that the conscience develops and Freud illustrates how this happens. Freud actually describes this developmental process in terms of a relationship by using such expressions as 'He is waiting for me to go now' and 'He thinks that I should do such and such' (Bocock, 1976, p49). Freud certainly equates the conscience with the super-ego and in a sense this is the second phase in the development of morality – the first being the experience of being cared for and the second beginning to accept some form of authority provided by the significant other as a reason for acting in a specific manner. Now it must be clearly recognised that the value of the good experienced in the relationship of loving care need not be the same as the moral values learned cognitively by the child during that socialisation in the family and which constitute part of the conscience.

By this time, the process of acquiring culturally accepted moral knowledge has begun and the significance of relationship, as opposed to individuality, has been emphasised. In the next section it is important to see how this cognitive process develops with the emergence of the individual self, since this plays an important part in giving meaning to experiences which form the basis from which all future learning occurs.

## The developing cultural sense of morality

Children do not suddenly acquire a fully-fledged ability to articulate morality, nor have all adults actually developed one, and so it is now necessary to explore the way through which this ability is learned. It must be emphasised here that learning to conceptualise and articulate moral ideas is a different form of learning to that which has already been discussed and in a sense it is subsidiary to the preconscious learning which occurs first. Piaget's work clearly indicated the way in which this occurs (see, for instance, Piaget, 1929), although he did not place any emphasis on pre-conscious learning, but he did suggest that there are five stages in a child's cognitive development, which is summarised from Jarvis (1972, p23):

| Period | Age (in years) | Characteristics |
| --- | --- | --- |
| Sensori-Motor | 0–2 | Infant learns to differentiate between self and objects of the external world |
| Pre-Operational Thought | | |
| Pre-Operational | 2–4 | Child ego-centric, but classifies objects by single salient features |
| Intuitive | 4–7 | child thinks in classificatory terms but may be unaware of the classifications |
| Concrete Operations | 7–11 | Child able to use logical operations as reversability, classification and serialisation |
| Formal Operations | 11–15 | Trial steps towards abstract conceptualisation occurs. |

**Table 3.1 Piaget's Stages of Cognitive Development**

What can be seen in this progession is the fact that initially children deal with experiences directly, that is that most of their learning comes from primary experience, and it is only as they grow and develop that they can deal with secondary experience and learn from this. It is important to recognise, however, that preconscious learning tends to be from primary experiences rather than secondary ones where the external world is focused upon in a more objective sense.

Piaget, however, was criticised for his lack of systematic sampling and Bruner (1968, p27) claimed that

mental growth is not a gradual accretion . . . It appears more like a staircase with rather sharp risers, more a matter of spurts and rests. The spurts ahead in growth seem to be touched off when certain

capacities begin to develop. And some capacities must be matured
and nurtured before others can be called into being.

Kohlberg also demonstrated that the stages of development were not so clearly
demarcated as Piaget had suggested, although his own work was based upon
Piaget's pioneering studies, especially *The Moral Judgment of the Child*.
Underlying Kohlberg's work is the following thesis: that there is a universally
valid form of rational moral thought process which all persons can articulate
assuming social and cultural conditions that are suitable for cognitive-moral stage
development. He goes on to claim that the ontogenesis toward this form of
rational moral thinking occurs in all cultures in the same stepwise, invariant stage
sequence.

While I am unable to subscribe to this thesis in quite such a categorical
form, since the socio-cultural milieu into which a child is born might emphasise
other virtues which undermine the sequence for which he argues, I do consider
that moral growth and development occurs as a result of learning from experience, and that his researchers demonstrate considerable validity in contemporary
western societies. However, socialisation is social, and as individuals are exposed
to a more complex respresentation of social reality in their early childhood
through the pressures of the mass media, their understanding of the world
becomes more complex and individuated.

Significantly, Kohlberg's work was on the development of moral judgment
(Hirsch *et al*, 1979, pp45–8). Not only was Kohlberg concerned about moral judgment, he also recognised that this development occurs as a result of relationships,
or about relationships, and moral judgments are made with reference to the
performance of roles and the ability to take the role of another person (Kohlberg,
1969).

Kohlberg was concerned to develop his research beyond the childhood studies of Piaget and as a result he (1976, pp34–5) formulated a six-stage lifespan
model, which is summarised in Table 3.2.

Kohlberg's terminology has differed in various publications (see for instance,
Kohlberg 1987, p228 when he utilised a 1973 formulation) although the general
principles of the stages remain largely the same. It will be noted that the universal
moral good accepted in this study study fits into Kohlberg's final stage, since
there is a universal principle but the actors have to act in accord with that principle
at whatever cost. However, it is argued here that since the universal moral good is
pre-knowledge individuals do not have to reach the highest stage in Kohlberg's
hierarchy in order to practise it, although they may have to reach this level in
order to defend it intellectually!

Additionally, it is clear from his research that people's approach to moral
judgment does not always mean that they exhibit the same level each time or that
all adults actually achieve the highest levels of development, as he (1987, p229)
writes:

. . . over 50% of late adolescents and adults are capable of full formal

**Level 1 – Pre-conventional:**

Stage 1

*Heteronomous morality*
  – sticks by the rules in order to avoid punishment and has an egocentric point of view

Stage 2

*Individualism, instrumental purpose and exchange*
  – right is what is fair, individuals only follow rules when they are in self-interest in order to serve needs of self, concrete individualism and aware that people's interests conflict

**Level 2 – Conventional:**

Stage 3

*Mutual interpersonal expectations, relationships and interpersonal conformity*
  – lives up to what others expect in order to be a good person in the eyes of self and others, puts oneself in the other person's shoes

Stage 4

*Social system and conscience*
  – fulfilling agreed duties and contributing to society in order to keep the system going. Considers individual relationships in terms of place in the social system

**Level 3 – Post-conventional: (Principled)**

Stage 5

*Social contract, utility and individual's rights*
  – upholds relative rules in the interest of impartiality, abides by the rules for the welfare of all and in order to protect people's rights since the actor is a rational individual aware of values and rights.

Stage 6

*Universal ethical principles*
  – following self-chosen ethical principles even when they conflict with laws, because they are committed to those principles and because the actors recognise that this is the nature of morality and that people are ends in themselves and should be treated as such.

**Table 3.2  Kohlberg's Model of Moral Development**

reasoning, but only 10% of these adults (all formal operational) display principled (Stages 5 and 6) moral reasoning.

Since Kohlberg's work has been replicated in western Europe, it is recognised that this aspect of moral development provides a firm basis for discussion, although the basis of moral behaviour is regarded here as distinct from the ability to conceptualise morality. At the same time, it has to be re-emphasised that Kohlberg did not discuss the issue of care and concern that is itself experienced in relationship pre-consciously and which is regarded here as the universal moral good. However, a number of other aspects need to be drawn from this which relate to previous points raised in this study, and to which further reference will be made throughout the remainder of this book.

The first is to note that, since education has become a commodity that is being sold on the market, the market requires only a Stage 2 level of moral development in order to function. Hence, criticisms of the market will occur throughout this study, since individuals with a more developed sense of morality ought to be able to rise above the morality of the marketplace. Secondly, it is seen that following rules that are regarded as being of a universal nature is also of a rather low level of development, but that recognising that rules are themselves relative is an attribute that individuals of a higher level of moral development can accept. Thirdly, the highest level of moral development involves distinguishing between law and principle, and accepting that some of the actions utilised by a moral person in response to that principle are themselves relative. For instance, the principle of love or care and concern for the Other, the sole universal good and an expression of Kohlberg's highest stage of development, requires cultural responses in action and these may be relative. There are no rules of practice.

It is firmly maintained here that the universal moral good itself is not relative. At the same time, where the principle is exercised without the cognitive ability to defend it, it may require courage rather than intellectual ability to act morally, and in this sense there need be no relationship between good behaviour and intellectual learning. Finally, moral maturity does not equate to physical development, so that educators of adults should not assume that the adults with whom they are working automatically have well-developed moral senses.

However, it needs to be emphasised that the position adopted in the previous chapter argued for a universality, although not a universality of law. Being concerned for the Other is never wrong but the ways in which that care is demonstrated are relative. Kohlberg, himself, used the following example in his work – the inventor of a drug is selling it at ten times the cost of producing it and is unwilling to lower the price to the husband of a dying woman who could be saved by it, but cannot afford to purchase it. The question asked is: what should the husband do? The dilemma poses questions about abiding by the law, stealing the drug, *etc*, and was used by Kohlberg to investigate the structures of moral reasoning by the respondents. However, most would probably have agreed that to be concerned for the dying woman was a moral ought, even though ideas about how that concern ought to be demonstrated in action might have differed considerably. Hence, two things emerge from this – that the pre-knowledge value of the good differs from the actual structures of moral thought about what is right thereafter, and that moral knowledge might itself differ from moral actions. Despite the fact that people grow up in families, their lifeworlds are individualistic and the patterns of their actions are their own. In other words – they can own their own actions.

## Becoming a moral agent

It has been pointed out already that having the knowledge is not sufficient reason for action, and Argyis and Schon have (1974, pp6–7) clearly shown that theories in use are different from those espoused theories to which a person gives allegiance. Consequently, it is not to be expected that even those individuals who achieve the highest levels in Kohlberg's moral development research would necessarily act in accordance with their principles and, as it was pointed out above, those whose awareness of the Other impels them to act without the intellectual ability to defend their position require courage not knowledge. Nevertheless, Kohlberg (1987, p231) does report some research that he and Richard Krebs undertook in which they discovered that:

> only 15% of students showing some principled thinking cheated as compared to 55% of convential subjects and 70% of preconventional subjects. Nevertheless, some 15% of principled subjects did cheat, suggesting that factors additional to moral judgment are necessary for principled moral reasoning to be translated into "moral action".

He goes on to suggest that these factors include situational pressures, motives and emotions and the strength of their will. He (p231) notes that Krebs discovered that only 26% of strong-willed subjects cheated as opposed to 74% of the weak-willed ones. There is, therefore, a sense in which it takes courage to behave in a moral manner. Kohlberg asks if moral reasoning is only one factor in moral action, why should so much emphasis be placed upon it? He points out that moral reasoning is the single most effective factor thus far discovered in moral action although it has to be pointed out that this is open to considerably more research since moral behaviour lies in intentionality to care for the Other rather than anything else and it is pre-knowledge. Indeed, it is in the intention to act that the espoused theory and the theory in use come together. Moral knowledge is not the only unique factor in moral action, and moral judgment is more consistent and developmental so that it is less likely to change with situations. Nevertheless, becoming a moral agent is about action rather than education and so it is necessary to explore this distinction a little further here.

This is a familiar problem: it is the distinction between theory and practice. In this case, however, the moral reasoning is cognitive knowledge and the moral action is the practice. Freire (1972, p60) regards this as a form of praxis – a congruency of reflection and action. For Freire, moral agents enter a dialogue with the world which must be political as well as educational, since reflection and action offer the opportunity to produce circumstances from which change emerges. Hence, moral action points to the possibility of radicalism and encourages those forms of learning in others that demand a willingness to be changed. But dialogue with the world also involves entering relationships, which lies at the heart of the position being argued here – it is only in relationship that moral human values can be manifest, and only if the social situation cannot be improved should moral action not demand some form of change as part of the response to it.

This problem of the relationship between moral theory and moral action is no new one, Aristotle introduced us to the concept of practical wisdom in his *Nicomachean Ethics*, which he defined as the virtue of being able 'to act with regard to the things that are good or bad for man' through reason (p142). This definition has to be qualified in the light of the earlier discussion in order to recognise that the good or bad for individuals in relationship is underpinned by the care or concern that is the beginning of ethics, so that practical moral wisdom must begin with care and concern for the Other, rather than a more general practical knowledge like that discussed in the opening chapter, or even that which relates to the achievement of the culturally good. However, this care does not mean that individuals have no choice, for they should always be free to choose how to demonstrate their concern for each other, and this will assume a cultural form.

Fundamentally, a distinction is maintained here between the universal moral good which might lie in the intention to act and the actions themselves which might, or might not, be regarded as good by other people. In order to care for the Other we have to act within our socio-cultural milieu, since intentions without actions cannot be moral. This, then is a form of rationality and in this I agree with Williams (1985, p56) who argues that 'we know that we do not live in a magical world, where wanting an outcome can make it so', so that we have to plan and act in order to produce these better conditions. Habermas (1993, pp122–3), however, criticises Williams at this point for being too Aristotelean in seeking to secure a cognitive basis for this form of practical reasoning which is different from scientific rationality, without explaining its basis. No such criticism can be made of the position adopted here, since underlying rationality is that of a pre-knowledge, non-cognitive concern for the Other.

While the moral action may not always coincide with the cognitive basis, for a variety of reasons, it is still important to demonstrate that there is a firm moral basis for both guiding and evaluating action.

## Concluding discussion

If people learn the universal good preconsciously and retain it tacitly, then the question might legitimately be asked whether their autonomy has been removed from them. But clearly this point was raised in the previous chapter – when my spontaneity is inhibited by the presence of the Other, that is the beginning of ethics. As a moral agent I voluntarily forego some of my freedom and this might actually involve acts of resolution and bravery, or as Williams (1985, p58) has suggested: 'As rational agents, then, we want . . . freedom, though this does not mean limitless freedom'. At the same time the values which I have learned about what is right should also guide my behaviour but these are values which I myself have espoused quite freely. One of the foundations of moral action is being prepared to forego freedom, although not autonomy, in order to act as a moral agent.

However, I acquire cognitive values through the normal processes of growth and development in a society. Giddens, (1994, p25), for instance, emphasises this position when he points out that '(m)oral truth is intrinsic to the social order and transmitted to the individual through language'. These values are different from that which is learned directly through experience, and which lies at the heart of the thesis of this book.

Having reached a position in which both morality and its basis have been discussed it is now necessary to begin to apply this argument to education and training for adults, so that the next chapter will explore the moral base of learning, education and training and then it becomes necessary to examine teaching and teaching techniques.

Chapter Five

# Learning, education and training

There is a sense in which the crude division between education and training has resulted in education occupying the high moral ground and training the lower, especially since the latter has been equated with indoctrination. While this chapter does not seek a clear demarcation between education and training, it does seek to re-assess the moral overtones implicit in much of this debate, and it does so from a position which questions the very basis of the morality upon which these judgments are made, reflecting the earlier discussion in this book. The chapter itself has three sections: the first examines learning from a moral perspective and argues that learning in itself is amoral. The second argues that both education and training reflect the values of modern society, albeit sometimes different values, and that these are culturally relative and, consequently, in a world in which these values are being questioned it behoves educators and trainers to be aware of the debate. The third section begins to point to another way of examining these values. However, the conclusion to the chapter is that within the framework of our society and its values, we must regard education and training as morally positive but different from a cultural perspective, but be prepared to question the moral foundations of our society itself.

## The amorality of learning

In order to develop this argument it is necessary to recognise that underlying any form of learning is Being itself. Being has occupied the minds of philosophers for centuries. However, this is not the place to explore these profound philosophical debates; for our purposes, it is enough to highlight a few findings that are significant for the study of human learning.

It might be claimed that at birth, children have being – that is, that they exist and are alive – but it would be imprudent to assert that they are fully-fledged social beings. There is a significant difference between the concepts of being and existence. A stone might be said to exist, but it would be harder to claim that it has being. In contrast, it might be demonstrated that an insect has being, albeit in a lowly form, as well as existence. Existence then, would imply some form of occupation of time and space in the world, whereas being implies life. However, this apparently simple distinction is not universally accepted.

Jaspers, for instance, seeks to relate existence to human life. Existence is, he suggests, 'the unreflecting experience of our life in the world' (quoted in

Macquarrie, 1973, p68). This is an important point, since a great deal of learning involves a non-reflective response to both primary and secondary experience, as we have already seen. Jaspers goes on to claim that existence is potential being – that is, that 'I do not have myself but come to myself' (in Macquarrie, 1973, p68). Jaspers is equating existence with being, or human life (or human existence), rather than with the occupation of space and time, but we can still accept his argument that in human living the individual becomes a self through a variety of learning processes in a culturally dominated milieu.

There is an implication here that human being is not something static, but dynamic. Indeed, Macquarrie (1973, p62) makes the point that the word 'existence' formerly meant 'to stand out' or 'to emerge' from nothing. This concept is more closely related to the idea of a living, dynamic phenomenon than to the existence of a stone, for instance. However, the very idea that existence is dynamic immediately makes it difficult to distinguish from the idea of essence. The word 'essence' denotes the fundamental characteristics of an object or a phenomenon that differentiate it from another object or phenomenon. Thus the essence of human-ness is what separates us from other living species. Macquarrie (1973, p71) points out that for Heidegger, the essence of humanity is found in existence, whereas for Sartre, existence precedes essence. The position adopted here more closely resembles that of Sartre than that of Heidegger: human-ness remains a potentiality within human existence until it emerges from it as mind and, eventually, as self or identity. This initially occurs as a result of the learning processes – mostly non-reflective learning – during the course of what sociologists regard as primary socialisation; later it occurs through a combination of non-reflective and reflective learning.

This might appear reminiscent of Cartesian dualism, which posits the existence of a separate mind within a physical body – the position which Ryle (1963) attacked as being a 'ghost in the machine'. But I am arguing for something different. Descartes gave primacy to the mind, as if it preceded and transcends the body. However, I am underscoring the primacy of Being, which is first manifest in the body. Thought processes of all forms follow from human existence. This also implies that there are physical dimensions to learning, as Bohm (1987, p90) suggested: 'modern physics has already shown that matter and energy are two aspects of our reality', so that thought energy and matter are intimately connected.

Children are born into the world, they have existence in space and time, and they have being – life. Fundamentally, they are living human bodies with the potential for human being. Through living and learning, those bodies develop and eventually fully-fledged human beings emerge. Learning, then, results in this process of emerging and becoming a person able to play a socially acceptable role as a human being. The role that the body plays in the learning processes still requires further discussion, although some psychologists, among other scholars, are beginning to explore this area. Philosophers have perhaps paid less attention to it than they might have, and theologians have maintained that from birth the baby has a soul as well as a body, and that personhood is constituted by the fusion of body and soul, although for them the body has rather evil connotations. However, it is not the intention to enter this theological debate since this is a matter of individual faith, and so the concept of soul is neither specifically equated with mind nor is it discussed further here.

The body is an important phenomenon in this discussion but it adds to the complexity of any theory of learning. To have existence implies that there is a living body and that that body is responsive to the social forces that act upon it. However, it also implies that individuals not only have bodies but that they are bodies.

We are both able to receive stimuli from and act on the world because we have physical existence. But what is the relationship between the physical body and the human being? Heidegger (1962, p73) claims that 'physical Being has nothing to be with personal Being' and this is a position that has espoused more recently by Miller (1995), in a study seeking to demonstrate that there is something beyond secular culture. In the light of the previous assertion that energy and matter are inextricably intertwined, the proposition adopted by Heidegger might seem a little sweeping. Others, such as Mead, have explored the process through which the body and self, or existence and essence, become fused in human beings. Mead (cited from Strauss, 1964, p161) writes that 'the body is not a self, as such; it becomes a self only when it has developed a mind within the context of social experience'.

The body is responsive to the social forces that act upon it, certainly from the moment of birth, but possibly even earlier in the womb, although it is not a passive recipient of these since it has its own genetic constitution. The impressions of these encounters are stored in the baby's or the child's brain and become a fund of memories, or a body of knowledge, *etc*, about an individual human life. The living human body learns to become a human being. The title of Edgar Faure's (1972) famous UNESCO report on the future of education – *Learning to Be* – assumes another meaning in the light of the fact that the body actually has to learn to become human. However, that body is not only the passive recipient of experiences; it soon creates a mind that is able to reflect upon them in a creative and critical manner. The human essence is energetic, it is creative, and the results of those acts are also stored in the mind, or learned. Those memories form the foundation on which the human self develops through continued learning.

Learning, then, is a natural process. No human body born into a social environment can avoid learning – it is the basic driving force through which the human essence emerges from the human existent. It is fundamental to Being itself and while there is Being and awareness of the environment in which Being exists, there is the potential for learning. Learning is both natural and individual, but it also requires the presence of the social, the Other – and because it is natural and occurs automatically as a result of being, it cannot be moral! Learning, then, is part of the basic process of living and every individual must do it in order to become a human being, but it leads only to the development of the discrete and separate person. It is the driving force writing every biography – but it is a natural phenomenon and as such it cannot be a moral phenomenon. What is written in the life-story reflects the process and the individual becomes in part what has been learned. Paradoxically learning is about the self but not selfish; individualistic and yet universal. And herein lies its significance, individuals might have grown and developed naturally as free beings, as Rousseau might have wished, were it not for the fact that they always must grow up in society. Had Rousseau's picture been possible, they would have been free individuals but not in relationship with each other – strangers! But they do grow up in society – and, as we shall argue here, it is only in this relationship that values can be manifest and ethics emerge. The fact that it is a social process does not deny the fact that it is still a natural one – which is amoral. Significantly, however, I have argued elsewhere (Jarvis, 1993) that learning is a religious phenomenon, but this does not invalidate the argument that it is amoral in terms of universal value, since religion *per se* is not intrinsically moral.

Nevertheless, the type of person one becomes as a result of the learning is a moral question! It is partly for this reason that our society has tended to place such cultural value on education and training: on education because of the type of person who develops as a result of that teaching and learning process and training because of the utilitarian value the trainee can be to society itself. This viewpoint is being reflected in contemporary attitudes to lifelong learning; for instance, Longworth and Davies (1996, p24) cite Ball with approval, that 'learning civilizes'. It is interesting that I read these words just after having had a discussion with a London taxi driver who had told me how clever he thought some of the criminals were! The learning process is amoral – but the outcome is a moral phenomenon. Significantly, the value of the person is paramount and this is recognised explicitly in the previous chapter because the moment the Other becomes a face – a person – to me, then the ethical relationship is established. Education and training are discussed in the remainder of this chapter, but personhood is discussed in a later chapter.

## Learning, education and training

The argument thus far suggests that learning cannot occur in a vacuum of isolated individualism in the way that some early thinkers postulated. Learning always occurs within a social context (Jarvis, 1987) which has its own culture and its own values. It is from this perspective that it is necessary to develop this argument and we will do so from within the framework of modern society.

Whilst learning is a natural, amoral process, learning within the context of being taught is a social process and, therefore, one which is always open to moral analyses. Both education and training, whatever their definition, are social processes and as such they can be analysed from a moral stance, and they are always intrinsically related to the culture of the society in which they exist. Indeed, Lawton (1973, p21) actually regards the content of any curriculum as a selection from culture. In a similar manner, Pring (1993, p62) relates training to the wider culture. Education, on the one hand, is generally regarded as more cognitive and open-ended while, on the other hand, training is related to the more specific, and tends to be limited to skills. However, the selection from culture is always an act of power, and those who claim the right to define what should be learned exercise power which always contains moral intentions.

Peters (1966) is amongst the most well-known philosophers to try to distinguish between education and training, and for the purposes of this discussion, I will concentrate on his analysis. He is quite specific that education is a normative process in as much as it 'implies that something worth while is being or has been intentionally transmitted in a morally acceptable manner' (Peters, 1966, p25). He specifies that this does not commit the educator to any specific content, only to a commitment to what is thought to be valuable, so that at this point he actually locates the morality in those who have the power to determine the syllabus.

He goes on to point out that education is task-orientated in as much as educators are always seeking to achieve some goal, even though education does not always specify what the goal is. Indeed, we talk of the aims and objectives of education and the objectives of training. However, he is also quite clear that vocational training might also be educational and so, while it is possible to argue that education has broader aims than training, it would also be quite possible in this time of economic stringency to view education as a luxury that we can ill-afford because it is too broad, and training as a necessity because it is specific. Indeed, this is clearly government policy in Western Europe, since it has become recognised that the Welfare State is an expensive luxury that the West no longer wishes to afford. Peters recognised the difference, although he did not draw a hard and fast distinction between education and training at this point, and he certainly did not anticipate government policy moving away from the social reformist position which he adopted, although he was clear that liberal education is the process most likely to free the mind from the constraints of society.

Peters did, therefore, make a distinction between knowledge and skills. For him, being educated is about having knowledge and understanding and it is also about having a different view on life as a result of having gone through this process. Indeed, he (1966, p31) used the term the 'whole man' to describe one who has achieved a sense of wisdom, as opposed to the one who has learned something specific and focused. The educated person is, therefore, able to tackle problems in a more rigorous and systematic manner. Training, by contrast, means that specific skills have been acquired, whether they are the skills of work or those of behaviour – such as controlling the emotions in public – and need not relate in a more profoundly analytical approach to living. For him, training 'suggests the acquisition of appropriate appraisals and habits of response (which are) limited to conventional situations; it lacks the wider cognitive implications of "education"' (Peters, 1966, p33).

Peters was quite clear that education is about 'the transmission of what is of ultimate value' (1966, p29) so that education is a moral process and necessary to the good life. Liberal education is the ultimate expression of this form of education. He writes (1966, p43):

> Traditionally the demand for 'liberal education' has been put forward
> as a protest against confining what has been taught to the service of
> some extrinsic end such as the production of material goods, obtain-
> ing a job, or manning a profession. In other words it has been a plea
> for education rather than vocational training or training of hand or
> brain for utilitarian purposes.

For Hirst (1974, p43), similarly, 'liberal education remains basic to the freeing of
human conduct from wrong' since he assumes that rational knowledge is the
basis of behaviour and, therefore, a liberal education is essential for the good life.

It is quite clear from this discussion of Peters, and also from reading Hirst's
work, that he sees a continuum with liberal education at the one end and with
other forms of education being closer to that end of the spectrum, whilst at the
other end he sees some forms of restriction upon the learning, such as training
and, even worse, indoctrination – although his discussion on indoctrination is
not extensive. (See Hollins, 1964, Snook, 1972 for more thorough analyses.) He
ruled out indoctrination as an educational activity because it restricts the freedom
of the learners in a variety of ways. Nevertheless, many sociologists (*eg*, Bourdieu
and Passeron, 1977 *inter alia*) have viewed all forms of education as a reproduc-
tive process both socially and culturally and since few, if any, changes in society
have occurred as a direct result of education their position is extremely credible.
Indeed, it is clear that the introduction of mass education has not necessarily
produced a good society in terms of social concern for the Other, although the
'good life', in terms of the standard of living, has been introduced into Western
society for a great many people – but by no means all!

Peters represented a tradition prominent in the philosophy of education in
Western Europe and the United States in the 1960s and 1970s and clearly conditions have changed in society since then. Indeed, there have been recent attempts
to reconcile the liberal tradition with these changing conditions. Pring's (1993,
p65) excellent contrast between liberal education and vocational preparation
highlights the distinction between the two nicely: 'The liberal programme is a
process, an engagement; the vocational specifies the product (an "output"
compared with "input")'. However, Pring's intention is to set a agenda to reconcile
the differences and he suggests an agenda around four areas: aims and values to
be pursued; structure and content of the knowledge to be acquired; the respective
virtues and dispositions to be fostered; and the authorities to be obeyed. He is
relatively optimistic that this is not an impossible task, a position with which I
agree since they are being combined within the current practice of continuing
education. Indeed, the more clearly they are seen as having similarities, the more
obvious it is that they both emerged within a similar culture, having similar norms
and values. These are the values of modernity and capitalism which have been
embedded in contemporary Western culture for the past two centuries, or so.

The emergence of modernity in the West was a fairly complex phenomenon,
starting perhaps before the Protestant Reformation but finding its fulfilment in
the period, or movement, known as the Enlightenment. The Enlightenment itself

occurred over a period of more than a hundred years, in three broad tranches, in which a whole set of ideas about human beings, their social world and their relationship to the natural world came together. A number of dominant thinkers typified the main ideas that were to become taken-for-granted in society in the subsequent years, such as: Voltaire, Montesquieu, Rousseau and Diderot in France; Locke and Newton in England; Hume, Adam Smith and Ferguson in Scotland; Kant in Germany. The period during which they lived began in the mid-seventeenth and ended in the early nineteenth century. It would be wrong to call this a concerted movement, although the period was certainly one which laid the foundations of modernity. Smart (1990, pp 15–18) illustrates the complexity of meaning given to the terms, modernity and modern, but for the purposes of this study modernity is used to refer to both the period and the culture that emerged in Western society as a result of the overall period of the Enlightenment.

Perhaps the most comprehensive list of the social values that emerged with the Enlightenment is contained in a useful summary by Hamilton (1992, pp21–2), who suggests that most philosophers at the time of the Enlightenment would have agreed on the following ten points:

- *Reason* – this is both reason and rationality as ways of organising knowledge, tempered by experience and experiment.

- *Empiricism* – thought and knowledge about the natural world is based upon empirical facts, apprehended through the sense organs.

- *Science* – the key way of expanding human knowledge is through the experimental method.

- *Universalism* – reason and science can be applied to every situation.

- *Progress* – the natural and social condition of humanity can be improved by the application of science and reason.

- *Individualism* – the individual is the starting point for all knowledge and individual reason cannot be subjected to a higher authority. Society is the product of the thought and action of a large number of individuals.

- *Toleration* – all individuals are essentially the same.

- *Freedom* – all individuals should be free from the social constraints that have traditionally bound them.

- *Uniformity of human nature* – principal characteristics of human nature are always the same.

- *Secularism* – knowledge should be free from religious orthodoxies.

Within these ten points we see many of the values that are to be found in both education and training: the equation of reason with instrumental rationality; the belief in the supremacy of science and a scientific approach to empirical knowledge; an emphasis on individuality and freedom in a secular world; the idea of progress which can be achieved through rational planning.

Naturally enough, Hamilton did not discuss the slightly later movement which might be regarded as a product of the Enlightenment or, perhaps more correctly, an epiphenomenon of it – entrepreneurial industrial capitalism. Both have a similar historical origin in the Calvinistic Protestantism that came to the fore as a result of the Reformation. Capitalism obviously embraced many similar values to those underlying the Enlightenment, such as individualism and progress, although some were emphasised more than others, while some, such as secularism, were assumed. However, it also introduced two other values to contemporary society – the competitive market, reflecting the ideas of the invisible hand and, later, of Darwinism and the survival of the fittest, and later still consumerism. Capitalism became one of the carriers of the values of modernity and Berger, Berger and Kellner (1974, pp102–3) argued that modern consciousness emerges from the world of employment which has the following six characteristics:

- *Rationality* – functional rationality of everyday life;

- *Componentiality* – reality is apprehended as being fragmented, each component relating to others through structures of causality, time and space;

- *Multi-relationality* – relationships are varied, complex and always undergoing change;

- *Makeability* – life is viewed as an on-going problem-solving exercise

- *Plurality* – there are a variety of realities;

- *Progressivity* – things can always be improved.

They go on to demonstrate that modernity is a depersonalising and individuating phenomenon, creating ideologies of individualism, *etc.* In addition, it is possible to see some later effects of the rational implementation of some of the values implicit in the first, *eg*, componentiality is the logical outcome of the rational implementation of the division of labour, *etc*, which is also epitomised in the specific focus of training.

Few would dispute the fact that some of these values are generally regarded as desirable, and that they should be found in various forms of education and training, although it is clear that there is not a total congruence between them. As individuals are educated or trained they should acquire some of these characteristics, especially those which relate to reason and rationality, to knowledge and planning, *etc.* In our culture, we would certainly want to question the values implicit in either education or training if they did not emphasise the value of the individual, rational thought, science and empirical knowledge, *etc.* We also assume that being able to think clearly enables people to play a more significant role in democratic society. These are the same characteristics that Peters emphasised throughout his writings. The cultural values of Western Europe are contained within these processes and it is widely agreed that they should be preserved, since they are regarded as valuable. Education and training are, therefore, products of our time and through their practice the good things in our society are transmitted to others.

No set of values in any society goes uncriticised, however, and while liberal education has been an implicit criticism of those forms of teaching and learning which are more restrictive, radical adult education and other movements in education, such as self-directed learning, have contained implicit criticisms of liberal adult education. Radical adult education theorists, for instance, have criticised the values of the dominant culture in Western society and highlighted their ideological nature, *eg*, those of capitalism, while self-directed learning has implicitly spotlighted the total encapsulation of teaching and learning within a process that inhibits some of the values of Western culture, such as autonomy, being fully practised. In a sense they have also begun to imply that these values are perhaps no more than ideological manifestations, reflecting the types of value those in power desire to be embedded in culture. We live in a cultural world which is completely engulfing and from which we are unable to escape, like a cultural solipsism, something which Levinas (1991) calls 'Totality', for even the criticisms of this process are encapsulated within the same framework.

Modernity tends to treat its values as absolute and so its cultural values were regarded as 'good' and most desirable. After all, Western culture was regarded as the most progressive society of all time and it gained its confidence of identity as it judged itself against traditional, pre-modern societies whose values it did not really understand – but now the West is beginning to recognise that there are other systems which can utilise its values and other value systems also exist that have legitimacy, so that its values are not necessarily correct nor unchanging – but I must emphasise that although I am going to criticise some of these values, I am not being destructively critical of those people who, like myself, entered the world of education and training for altruistic and professional reasons of service to humankind. Indeed, I shall suggest later that in some ways the motivation behind the professional ethic comes close to the universal moral value although is was rarely really practised.

## Towards post-modernity?

One of the elements of the Enlightenment, that of the division of labour, exacerbated the growth of both individualism and pluralism. Once pluralism became an established factor it became harder to view reality as having a single meaning. Multiple realities emerged, a variety of interpretations of reality became a fact and it has become increasingly difficult to regard any single one as being totally correct. The emergence of a plurality of interpretations of reality calls into question the notion of a single 'truth' or a single 'correct-ness' about any phenomenon, which in turn has implications for our way of understanding reality. Indeed, many contemporary thinkers are beginning to question some of the views that have dominated our society for two centuries and so it becomes possible to recognise the emergence of what might be a post-modern era. I regard this as a late modern period because we still live with the consequences of modernity and perhaps there has not yet been a period of discontinuity between the modern and whatever we now live in. Indeed, many of the carriers of modern culture, *eg*, Protestantism, capitalism, technology and consumerism, have not changed although the first is beginning to face considerable problems as Western European culture is changing.

But other aspects of that culture are also undergoing change, such as the nature of knowledge. Knowledge has now become regarded as relative (almost narrative) and its rational basis has changed. When Lyotard (1984) wrote *The Post-Modern Condition* he claimed that all knowledge had become narrative, but later he recognised (1992, p31) that he had over-emphasised his position and he now thinks that different forms of knowledge have to be recognised, even though he still considers some forms of scientific knowledge to be narrative. The point about a great deal of narrative is that it reflects the dominant theories of the day.

The question might well be posed about the extent to which there is unchanging scientific knowledge, and clearly nobody is going to reject the idea that there are some universal and unchanging laws of nature, although it has been recognised that these are much less frequent than was previously claimed. Advances in scientific research do tend to modify prevailing theories and this has also come to be rather taken for granted; new discoveries reveal more about phenomena than was previously known; new technological advances mean that what was impossible a year or two ago now becomes possible and tomorrow becomes the everyday. Scientific knowledge, therefore, has become recognised as relative and its validity can always be questioned, and other evidence produced to refute or recast a current theory.

Now the basis of knowledge is changing. Increasingly it is becoming apparent that many statements about society are ideological rather than empirical, and claims about it seen to be discourse rather than factual. These may still be firmly based in reason although they are less possible to substantiate since empiricism itself is under attack. But there is another basis to knowledge that is now being accepted and this is clearly described by Lyotard (1984, p48), who argues that the knowledge being taught is now only socially legitimated by the criterion of its performability in the social system, so that the teaching and learning process now only has to produce skilled experts since:

> The transmission of knowledge is no longer destined to train an elite
> capable of guiding the nation towards its emancipation, but to supply
> the system with players capable of acceptably fulfilling their roles at
> the pragmatic posts required by the institution.

Knowledge is now based on pragmatism and this is not the same as rational planning. This is not the place to explore the philosophy of pragmatism, but it might be claimed now that knowledge is legitimated by its utility which is quite contrary to the ideas of Peters. If something works, then it can be transmitted to others, so that another new concept has become quite central to the educational system in recent years, continuing education, which is something of a combination of liberal and vocational education, and the validity of continuing education is pragmatic since its value depends on performability. Consequently, the role of academics is changing – now they are interpreters of reality rather than legislators about it (Bauman, 1987). Good education results in a successful qualification and a lucrative occupational position, and the outcome of good training is expert job performance. Education and training are both changing and the values that surround them are changing too.

Now the values of pragmatism, utility, marketability and relativity reign. Once more it is difficult to step outside the values of the culture – they are learned through the social processes, just like the earlier values were learned. Indeed, this is still a *Totality* within which people are encapsulated and from which they cannot escape. Now the values that dominate society – the values that the dominant elite wish to perpetrate – are taught through the processes of continuing education. They are still regarded as good and essential for the survival of our society, and even for our civilisation. And still the radical critique stands, not quite so firmly as it has in previous generations, and offers another interpretation, although it is also located within the same cultural framework and remains part of the totality, although I think it contains a clue to universal value.

But it is not only the basis of knowledge that is being questioned. Many people, especially those from a social reformist background, have believed that the provision of education will automatically produce better people able to make a better world. But this position has already been demonstrated to be false. Indeed, Bauman (1992, pp166–72) makes the point that rational planning in Eastern Europe did not lead to the good society, and the fall of the Berlin Wall is a symbol that rational planning, another Enlightenment feature, does not work. There has also been an increase in narratives about what society should be like, rather than what it is – more ethical studies and even a return to utopian thought (*eg,* Kumar, 1987; Levitas, 1990).

Consequently, it might be seen that the amount of learning is going to affect the growth and development of the individual, so that the greater the amount of cognitive learning the more knowledgeable a person becomes, the more skills that are learned the more skilful the individual grows, the more attitudes or beliefs are learned the more one knows about them, the more one experiences the senses or the emotions the more one retains memories of them, *etc.* Significantly, more knowledge does not make one a better person or the more one learns about values does not mean that an individual is going to behave in a more moral manner. The social reformist's position that holds that the more education that people receive, the better persons they will become can be seen to be an illogical argument. There is no logical connection between learning *per se* and behaving in a morally accepted manner.

The argument being presented here is that learning is an amoral process and in itself it does not produce people who naturally behave better. Nor does the existence of mass education or training produce a more just society. Rather it reproduces values relative to the social milieu in which it is practised. Does this mean that there are no values in education and training? I think that it means that both are the products of, and encapsulate the values of, the age of modernity. But it is perhaps more important for this argument to make a distinction between cultural value and universal moral value and in the concluding discussion I will return to this.

## Conclusion

We have seen that education and training both reflect the values of society; clearly education is seen as being broader and more cognitively orientated, and training more focused and skills-orientated – but they are not mutually exclusive. Neither are wrong and we have witnessed a major shift since the 1960s when knowledge was regarded as more important than skill whereas now the combination of both is regarded as important. We need both knowledge and skills in our society, both are necessary and neither are wrong. The way that we view them fluctuates with the values of society and our evaluation of them varies accordingly. These are cultural values and they are relative.

But clearly there is more to education and training than this – there is a process in which teachers and taught meet and relate – except in certain forms of distance education. There have been times when adult educators especially have suggested that teaching itself is wrong, but this is also a relative claim since it is in relationships that universal values are to be discovered. Levinas (1991, p51) suggested:

> To approach the Other in conversation is to welcome his expression, in which at each instant he overflows the idea a thought would carry away from it. It is therefore to *receive* from the Other beyond the capacity of the I, which means exactly: to have the idea of infinity. But this also means: to be taught. The relation with the other, or Conversation, is a non-allergic relation, an ethical relation; but inasmuch as it is welcomed this conversation is a teaching . . . Teaching is not reducible to maieutics; it comes from the exterior and brings me more than I can contain. In its non-violent transivity the very epiphany of the face is produced.

Here Levinas points to the fact that in relationship with the Other there is the potentiality of experiencing universal moral value. This is not knowledge-based but person-orientated. It is pre-knowledge. It occurs as a we-experience, when individuals are willing to forego their own freedom for the sake of the Other as a person. This is a similar but profoundly different ethic to that of professionalism, for the professionals professed their expertise and offered it as a service to the client. Here an individual enters a relationship with another for no other reason than that the Other is and has impinged upon the individual's freedom. Bauman (1993, p185) claims that:

> If it happens, it will happen only as an accomplishment. There is not

and there will never be any guarantee that it will indeed happen. But it does happen, daily, and repeatedly – each time that people care, love, and bring succour to those who need it.

In all professional relationships, but especially in teaching in both education and training, this potentiality exists. It is in the forging of the relationship that the opportunity to probe the depths of infinity abides and the totality of cultural values is exploded. Universal moral value is not to be discovered in education or training *per se*, whatever they are, but its potentiality lies in the relationship that emerges between persons, and teaching and learning in both education and training affords this possibility. It is, therefore, in the process and not in the systems that infinity is to be explored and, perhaps, universal moral value discovered.

Chapter Six

# Power and personhood in teaching

The last chapter ended with reference to the process of teaching and learning as being the location of universal value rather than in the social institutions of education and training. The purpose of this chapter is to explore the teaching and learning process in some depth in order to examine this assertion.

For a number of years, however, the literature of adult education tended to concentrate on adult learning and it is only recently that teaching has become a focus of attention again (Brookfield, 1990; Galbraith, 1990, 1991). Even in the books edited by Galbraith, the language of adult learning rather than teaching dominates. The reasons for this emphasis on adult learning are clear because the validity of scientific knowledge has begun to be questioned and alternative explanations for many phenomena are being provided (see Lyotard, 1984). Teachers, consequently are no longer regarded as the fount of all wisdom and, indeed, the function of teaching might have changed from that of legislating for what is correct knowledge to that of interpreting diverse explanations about these complex phenomena (Bauman, 1987). Additionally, there has been a tremendous emphasis upon the individual learner and the individual's own rights and autonomy, which has resulted in the emphasis on self-directed learning and the facilitative function of the teacher. Downplaying the place of the teacher led Rogers (1983, p119) to exclaim that 'Teaching . . . is a vastly over-rated function'. He might be right – after all, it is clear that many adults are self-directed learners and many teachers of both adults and children do use facilitative methods, and he has also raised a number of valid points about the way that adults actually learn. But to dismiss teaching as an over-rated function without a full examination of all the issues that has led to the emphasis being placed on learning is perhaps an over-reaction to some of the problematic issues in the teaching and learning process.

Teaching is itself not a single uncontentious concept as the following meanings demonstrate: to give instruction; to cause to learn or understand; to help to learn; to cause someone to suffer unpleasant consequences. The final one of these relates to the idea of 'teaching someone a lesson' in terms of punishing the person. It is interesting that teaching should be used in such a manner, although the origins of the phrase are harder to trace. By contrast, the other three meanings indicate that teaching can be about providing information, providing an opportunity to learn and even assisting in the learning process. These three are not mutually exclusive and so it is obviously a multi-faceted process of enabling learning – but like many service functions this one has assumed a more dominant position than the one it serves and it has become almost taken for granted that the teachers are more important than the learners. Perhaps the current emphasis on the market economy in education is one of the reasons why this assumption is now being questioned. Nevertheless, teachers certainly can and do exercise power over learners, and the morality of this is to be explored in this chapter.

These processes also occur outside of traditional educational institutions and both learning and teaching happen in all types of setting. While there can be learning without a teacher, it is hardly logical to think about teachers without learners. Distance education and the new media, however, have now made it possible for teachers and learners to exist independently of each other, *eg*, as a result of time-space distanciation and the transmission of information through technological media learners might study material that the teachers have provided in another time and place.

Despite Rogers' assertion, however, the re-emergence of books about teaching indicate that teaching, in one form or another, in the classroom has never disappeared nor lost its place in educational practice. Whether this position will continue the in future is another matter and beyond the scope of this book to discuss. Whenever teaching occurs, however, there is a potential for human relationships in which teachers might dominate learners, but in every instance the relationship that potentially exists between teachers and learners must contain a moral dimension. Levinas (1991) argues that whenever the existence of the Other impinges upon Ego's spontaneity ethical situations are created. Teaching and learning in a classroom, or lecture theatre, *etc*, is, therefore, necessarily of ethical consequence. It is also one in which teachers exercise power and authority – sometimes in a rather arbitrary manner – since they control the space in which the teaching occurs, and the exercise of power implies some form of dominance, even the potentiality of violence or coercion. Bourdieu and Passeron (1977, pp5ff) have argued that 'all pedagogic action is . . . symbolic violence'. Their argument is quite compelling especially in relation to child learners and it is one of the purposes of this chapter to explore the power and authority dynamics of the teaching and learning relationship. It is maintained that the morality of teaching lies in the intention of the teachers and that the way teachers utilise their power might impinge upon the personhood of the learners. The thesis of this chapter is that teaching can, but need not, be symbolic violence and that, therefore, the autonomy and authenticity of the person need not be violated – although it frequently is! The chapter itself has four parts: power and authority; teaching style and method; the moral paradox of intentionality; the personhood of the participants.

## Power and authority

Neither power nor authority are simple, unitary concepts: power has at least three dimensions to it (Lukes, 1974) and there are at least four forms of authority. Each of these will be discussed briefly in this section and related to the teaching role.

### Power

At its crudest, power is behavioural since it involves the ability that either systems or persons have to make others conform to a predetermined behaviour pattern and to ensure that they make the types of decision that the power holders desire. This is an *overt* form of power. Underlying this view is the fact that the State should have the only legal power to utilise a country's agencies of ultimate coercion – the military and police forces. Teachers do not have this type of coercive power but there are situations in teaching and learning where this crude understanding of power is appropriate, especially in the realm of children's education where teachers act *in loco parentis* and in former times would administer forms of corporal punishment to children. Even in the education of adults, teachers can insist on students conforming to patterns of behaviour in the class, even egalitarian ones, and even though they do not have recourse to physical power to enforce their will they do have some legal power to have difficult students removed from the classroom.

However, there are more complex ways of viewing power since it is not always behavioural. For instance, if people or institutions can get issues on to an agenda for discussion at vital meetings or in the media, or if they can prevent other discussions emerging, then they exercise a form of *covert* power – this is what Gramsci called hegemony. This power also operates in such a manner as to enable the power holders to control the way in which the issues are discussed, when they are actually on the agenda. In political terms this covert power is probably greater and more effective than the previous form. But this is not far removed from people or institutions having the ability to get subjects included in educational curricula or controlling the manner by which they are taught or discussed. This may be a matter of State interest when national curricula are introduced, or of professional organisations which seek to control the knowledge that new recruits to the occupation should learn but, significantly, it is most frequently teachers who control the manner by which the learning material is taught and learned. For instance, teachers can ensure that certain topics occur in a lesson and that others are omitted.

Even so, these two approaches do not cover all aspects of power in society, for there is another form of power, one that relates to the actual control of the social processes themselves. Everybody is brought up, *ie,* socialised, in a social system and becomes part of its culture. However, the social processes through which individuals pass have not just naturally occurred – they emerge as a result of most people accepting the *status quo* and conforming happily, or otherwise, to society's inequalities. Power to control those institutions that benefit the few and not the many, and more significantly to produce people satisfied with their inequality, is the most covert and insidious of all forms of power. Lukes (1974, reprinted in Anderson and Ricci, 1990, pp127–8) summarised this form of power thus:

> ... is it not the supreme and most insidious exercise of power to prevent people, to whatever degree, from having grievances by shaping their perceptions, cognitions and preferences in such a way that they accept their role in the existing order of things, either because they can see or imagine no alternative to it, or because they see it as natural and unchangeable, or because they value it as divinely ordained and beneficial? To assume that the absence of grievance equals genuine consensus is simply to rule out the possibility of false or manipulated consensus by definitional fiat.

Education, whether it is children's or adult, is clearly part of this power process and, it will be recalled that Althusser (1971, reprinted in Cosin 1972) regarded education as the most powerful ideological state apparatus in mature capitalist societies, and while the emphasis on the development of critical thinking in adult education is to be applauded, most of its concerns have been individualistic, concentrating upon the correctness of the material being taught and learned rather than stepping outside of the process of teaching and learning and examining it as a problem in itself. Teachers have the power to make overt these social processes, but whether they have the authority within the teaching and learning process may well depend upon the content of their teaching sessions.

Teachers, then, are inescapably part of the power processes and they exercise power – especially in the first two dimensions, but they are also part of the processes of power in the third dimension. Clearly the contemporary movement of radical adult education reflects the genuine concerns of many educators about this last dimension of power – and the extent to which it makes adult education a separate social movement is a nice point! This is, significantly, part of the history of adult education, but the extent to which it should pervade every element in the educational process is itself debatable, and a point to which further reference will be made below and discussed further within the framework of the chapter on adult education and social justice.

## Authority

Authority, in the sense that it is being used here, is about the legitimacy to exercise power. Max Weber (1947, pp324–423) postulated three types of authority: rational/legal, traditional and charismatic, and Jarvis (1983a) suggested a subdivision of the last of these.

Rational/legal authority 'rests on the belief in the "legality" of patterns of normative rules and the right of those elevated to authority under such rules to issue commands' (Weber, 1947, p328). Basically this is the type of authority which comes with office, usually in a bureaucratic type of organisation. Teachers exercise this form of authority when they perform the functions of their role as teachers in schools or colleges. They only have the authority because of their relationship to the school, college or university which employs them and only in relation to duties that they carry out in respect of that role. Consequently, they do have the authority to manage the space in the classroom or lecture theatre, *etc.*

Traditional authority rests on the belief that the traditions are respected and that those who exercise authority under them do so in order to comply with their demands. Whilst the tradition of education has been strong, teachers have been able to exercise certain forms of traditional authority because they have been seen as coming from an honourable occupation, *etc,* and this is especially true in more traditional societies. As the traditions lose their status in late modern/post-modern society, this form of authority recedes into insignificance.

Charismatic authority rests with the crowd or group who give the leader the authority as a result of heroism, leadership, *etc.* The demagogue is often accorded this type of authority by the crowd and religious leaders who gain large followings are often regarded as having charisma. Teachers who are superb lecturers or enthralling teachers may also gain such followers who will, where possible, always attend their classes/lectures and confer authority on them. Basically, the authority that charismatic leaders exercise over their followers depends entirely upon what the latter will allow, since the legitimation of that authority rests ultimately with the followers. In a similar manner professional authority lies with those in a profession who accord authority to those whom they view as experts in their subject. Teachers may be granted this form of authority by their students if the students consider that the teachers are experts and know their subject well. In addition, teachers who are experts in their subject might be granted professional authority (recognition) by their peers, but this is not an authority that an expert can assume in the classroom!

The authority of teachers of adults, *qua* teacher, comes from two sources: the employing organisation and the learners. Teachers exercise both to varying degrees, either rational-legal or professional/charismatic and the extent to which they are accorded the latter will determine the amount of the former that has to be employed.

## Relationship between power and authority

It would be possible to explore the inter-relationship of all the elements of power and authority discussed above, but two forms of each appear to be most prevalent: the first two dimensions of power and the rational and professional forms of authority, and their relationship is highlighted in the following figure:

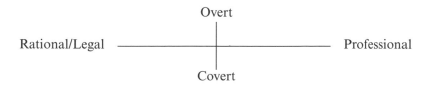

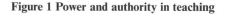

**Figure 1 Power and authority in teaching**

Teachers will clearly not always utilise their power in precisely the same way, or even at all, so that different sessions and different classes may vary; indeed, the degree that power and authority overtly present in any one session may change considerably from one point in time to another. In addition, teachers' own awareness of their power may affect the way that they teach and some teachers of adults may not actually view their relationship with the learners in their group as a power relationship. This is very clear, for instance, from Brookfield's (1990) discussion of teaching. Indeed, Beatty *et al* (1991) assume that the teaching and learning process in the education of adults is egalitarian. This may be the ideal, a point to which further reference will be made below, but it is doubtful whether it can ever be the reality. Teachers do not have to be aware that they exercise power for them to do so since their position is structurally one in which they are automatically accorded it. Conti (1990, p86), for instance, provided an excellent example of this when he wrote that for the teacher:

> . . .To accomplish this (a well disciplined classroom), flexibility is maintained by adjusting the classroom environment and curricular content to meet the changing needs of your students.

In contrast, those teachers who are accorded power by their students may never feel the need to exercise it and may, indeed, see themselves in an egalitarian relationship with them. Consequently, it is now necessary to examine the teaching process – both style and method.

## Teaching style and teaching method

Both teaching methods and teaching styles may contain within them an exercise of power or authority, but the process is more complex than it appears on the surface.

While there is a very wide variety of teaching methods, they can be grouped into three main categories: didactic, socratic and facilitative (Jarvis, 1995a, pp106–139). The didactic method is teacher-centred, in which the teachers or the lecturers provide input into the teaching and learning session as a result of their own limited understanding of the role. It may well be that this is the form of teaching that Rogers attacked in the reference made to him at the outset of this chapter. Some teachers may be experts, and there may be a place for an input from specialists in specific situations, so that it may not always be wrong to have didactic sessions. Indeed, sometimes learners accuse teachers who are experts in their subject of depriving them of the information or the stimulus that input sessions might provide! If learners seek such input from an expert teachers, then the extent to which the teachers are exercising power in responding positively to the request is questionable, although they most certainly have professional authority.

Teachers might also be socratic teachers: they utilise the knowledge, skills and experience of the learners and teach through asking questions, drawing out from them their own understanding and the immediate results of their thought processes. This approach is humorously depicted by Bateman (1990). It is also partly teacher-centred since it is the teachers who lead the students through the teaching and learning process by the questions that they ask. By asking questions, this approach appears to rely less on the teachers' power, but it may still be extremely teacher-centred and there may be little opportunity for the learners to intervene in the process – apart from responding to the questions. In contrast, Bateman does not give the impression of being particularly conscious of the power he exercises.

Facilitative teaching is the form espoused by Rogers, when the teachers prepare the situation within which learning might occur, although they may not be appear to exercise any power in the situation. It may appear to be quite egalitarian but there may have been no opportunity for the learners to discuss with the teachers the fact that they were going to utilise facilitative methods! Additionally, there is always a residue of power and authority located in the teachers' position since they are employed by a bureaucratic organisation.

From the above discussion it is clear that any of these types of methods might be used with or without the conscious awareness of power or even of the process of legitimating the teachers' role. Teachers might never actually be able to escape from the rational-legal position so that there is always a residue of authority – whether they want it or not – but they might perform their roles without conscious reference to it or to the power underlying it. Teachers might be didactic because the students think that they will learn more from teachers who provide information, *etc*. They may be wrong! But it may be that the teachers and learners need to negotiate about this – but this depends upon how teachers use their power and authority in the teaching and learning situation. The methods teachers use do not, therefore, necessarily illustrate anything about the meaning that they place upon their teaching.

Teaching style, however, might actually illustrate the intention of the teachers rather better and while there are a number of different studies of teaching style (see Jarvis, 1995a, pp103–5) two are referred to briefly here. Lippett and White (1958) isolated three styles of leadership: authoritarian, democratic and *laissez faire* and McGregor (1960) discussed Theory X and Theory Y forms of management – both of which are relevant to teaching. By definition the authoritarian utilised overt power to control the group and the *laissez faire* abdicated responsibility for the task. In the same way advocates of Theory X approaches assume that individuals need to be controlled and they will utilise either overt or covert power in order to achieve their ends. Lippett and White found that the democratic approach achieves group cohesion and harmonious working relationships and McGregor claimed that Theory Y advocates are more concerned with the potentiality of growth in others, so that they vary their approach and their method in order to achieve this end. It should be borne in mind that neither of these approaches actually prescribes the manner in which the teachers perform their role – they both point to the intentions of the teachers concerned. The one specifies that the teachers abdicate their power in order to enter negotiation, while the second suggests that the teachers use their power in the best possible way to help their learners achieve.

The point is that the structures reflect the culture of the society and the actual universal moral value lies in the responsible intentions of the actors, whatever their position in society. Morality does not depend upon position. The point at issue here, therefore, is the difference between the performance of the role and the meaning, or intention, that the teachers place upon their actions.

The exercise of power might not be wrong in itself, and it is clearly the intention underlying the act which is more significant than the act itself. Nevertheless, the structural form of power underlies this argument and teachers always possess a residue of power and authority whether it be by virtue of their position in the educational institution or because the learners have accorded it to them. However, it is how they intend to act in the situation which is significant, so that there are forms of pedagogic action which are not symbolic violence, since the teachers have entered into a dialogue with the learners about how the teaching and learning process should be conducted and/or they have no intention of using their power to the detriment of the learners. Significantly, it has been argued in an earlier chapter that the ethics underlying an action is located in its intention rather than in its performance, and it is important to elaborate upon those ideas here.

## The moral paradox of intentionality

Intentionality is a significant concept in the philosophy of Husserl (1962) and the following summary uses Cooper's (1990) analysis of Husserl's understanding of the term. Three main points emerge in his analysis relevant to this argument: firstly, that intentionality is the essential feature of human consciousness since every act intends an object; secondly, no sense can be made of conscious acts unless they relate to a human engagement with the world, which can only occur through mediated meaning; thirdly, that human beings are plunged into a world their understanding of which is revealed through the meanings that their activities project. Basically, Husserl argued that acts are meaningful and intended to achieve some outcome and that intentions actually reveal the meaning placed upon the act by the actors.

Naturally, an objection can be raised about locating value in intention and that rests in the fact that intentions need not result in actions. However, Husserl's position is quite clear on this, since he maintains that it is the acts themselves that project the meanings and not verbally expressed intentions that may be excuses for not acting at all. Hell maybe 'full of good intentions' but they are unacted-upon intentions!

In this brief account there is no moral dimension although there is a potential for a teleological form of argument – that an act is good because it produces a good outcome, eg, the greatest happiness for the greatest number. However, utilitarianism is neither correct nor logical, as it was demonstrated in the second chapter since, among other things, it shifts the locus of morality from the intention to the outcome of the act, and this need not be controlled by the actor. The meaning of the act for the actor, or of the teaching for the teacher, lies in the intention itself.

The moral act is judged by the degree of concern for others demonstrated in the actions themselves irrespective of their outcome, although it is recognised that it is impossible to measure this, and that it may also be almost impossible to ascertain precisely what are the intentions underlying any act. This is exactly the point made in the previous section where it was noted that in one instance teachers could use the power of their position and in another they could abdicate it, so long as the intention of their actions was out of concern for their students.

There is a potential problem here since teachers might act in what they think are the students' best interests but by so doing they might take away the autonomy of the students. This is a problem inherent in the Theory Y approach to leadership which needs now to be resolved. It was argued in an earlier chapter, following Levinas (1991), that ethics begins when the potentiality of relationship between persons exists and that the only value that is always good is Ego's concern for the Other in relationship. Consequently, whenever a person is and there is an intention of concern for another in relationship, however tenuous that relationship, there the universal value of good might be manifest. Herein lies a paradox since if that good intention takes away the autonomy of the other, then it might be construed as an immoral act. Therefore, if this argument is to be sustained, it is necessary to argue that teachers should endeavour to create the types of relationship with students that enables them to decide for themselves on what is in their own best interest in dialogue with the teachers, where this is appropriate. The concern lies in the dialogical relationship between teachers and taught rather than the content of what is taught.

At this juncture, however, it is necessary to recall that there is a third dimension to power and that is the power inherent in the social structures of which teachers are a part – and the question must now be raised as to whether teachers should acquaint learners with the social and political significance of the process of teaching and learning in terms of this structural power. But morality does not lie in what is done, but in the intentions underlying the actions, so that it can be argued that there may be instances when teachers judge it best for the students with whom they relate to discuss the hidden power operating in the teaching and learning processes. There may be others when they consider that it is inappropriate to raise the issues and not in the best interests of the students, but if teachers then raise it they are exercising their own power for their own ends.

However, this might be claimed as dodging the issue because this power is insidious in society and it always affects the students. But this is not denied. What is denied, however, is that it is possible morally to legislate for what is always right in this respect. To legislate is itself an issue of power and this is not the nature of the universal good, so that teachers and lecturers have to decide for themselves what they think to be right in their interaction with their students. As Bauman (1993, p250) claimed:

Moral responsibility is the most personal and inalienable of human possessions, and the most precious of human rights. It cannot be taken away, shared, ceded, pawned, or deposited for safe keeping. Moral responsibility is unconditional and infinite, and it manifests itself in the constant anguish of not manifesting itself enough. Moral responsibility does not look for reassurance for its right to be or for excuses for its right not to be. It is there before any reassurance or proof and after any excuse or absolution.

Teachers and lecturers may use the power inherent in their position to demonstrate concern for their students in the teaching and learning relationship, and for no other reason. If they want to be activists about the power structures of society, in any other situation, then that is also their right and their responsibility. But the manner by which they use their power in the teaching and learning relationship impinges upon the personhood of the learners. This constitutes the final section of this chapter.

## The personhood of the participants

It might be argued that this chapter has concentrated on the relationship between teachers and learners to the exclusion of the content of the actual interaction. But this is not so, for the focus of the chapter is on the relationship in which ideas and information are contained within the process of the interaction of the participants for, as Buber (1959, pp13–14) puts it, 'Ideas are no more enthroned above our heads than resident in them; they wander amongst us and accost us'. In the teaching and learning relationship there is an intellectual purpose and in the academic discourse the personhood of all the participants should be realised. For Buber, being-with-others is fundamental and it is in relationship that personhood develops, so that there is a sense in which it is false to try to discuss the personhood of the learners without recourse to a similar discussion about that of the teachers. Everybody is being and becoming in the world, for to be in the world is to be in relationship.

But there is a paradox about being in relationship: persons freely forego their individual autonomy for the sake of the other and in so doing enrich themselves. In this respect the emphasis of Modernity on individualism is fundamentally flawed since a purely individual existence without relating to others is impossible. 'In the beginning is relationship' (Buber 1959, p18) and only through relationship is the person born and can the self develop. Herein lies the paradox of teaching and learning, since it is in this relationship that persons forego their individual autonomy so that they can be enabled to learn, grow and develop and freely become the unique human beings that they are – individuals! This then is an authentic being-with-others, foregoing and becoming.

But these relationships are always in danger of degenerating into I-It relations, especially those in which power is exercised. Indeed, this also becomes a probability when the academic content of the teaching and learning sessions takes precedence over the people involved, the learners may be turned into objects to be taught (I-It) and the richness of human interaction lost.

When that power and authority is employed to such an extent that the teachers' intention is to mould the person into the type of being that the teachers, or those in power in society, want we are faced with the classical idea of indoctrination. Whether the indoctrination is of an ideological nature of a more practical form, it is always utilitarian and its utilitarian value must be judged by the criteria of the society. Both education and training may, therefore, employ indoctrinational processes because the value of the personhood of the learners is subjugated to the intended end-product of the process.

But teachers cannot escape from the power and authority of their position, but to exercise it without recognising the personhood of the Other through the relationship of teaching and learning may well be an exercise in symbolic violence and, therefore, morally questionable.

## Conclusion

Teaching, then, is about being with others in the learning situation and being available to them, but as MacQuarrie (1973, p111) wrote:

I must be willing to put myself at the disposal of the other. The sad truth, however, is that people are largely unavailable to one another. The unavailable person is preoccupied with himself and thus closed to the other. . .

If the intention of the teacher is to do just this, then there can be no symbolic violence because the intention is to be available for the other in the teaching and learning situation, but the sad fact is that often the relationship is inauthentic and then symbolic violence may well occur in the process because of the power inherent in the teachers' position.

# Chapter Seven

# **Mentoring**

When Odysseus left his home to participate in the siege of Troy, Homer says that he appointed a guardian to take care of his son, Telemachus. For ten years this guardian acted as teacher, friend, advisor and surrogate father to the son: the guardian's name was Mentor. It was not unusual in ancient Greece for young males to be paired with older male citizens so that they could learn from and be guided by them. Similarly, when Dante made his journey through the underworld, he had a mentor – Virgil.

Throughout the history of humankind there have been many instances where older and more experienced individuals have mentored those who were younger and less experienced. The re-discovery of this concept is nothing new. Many an apprentice master was the mentor to his apprentice – guiding, directing, advising and teaching a craft – and the success of the master craftsman was to be discovered when the young apprentice graduated into a master craftsman, able to take charge of the older man's business.

But the world of apprenticeship is one which modern education has abandoned! This 'sitting by Nellie' seems so old fashioned – and so it is, if all that happened was that the young learner (*apprendre* = to learn) sat there and merely tried to copy the master craftsman and learn from him if he had time to explain. Perhaps this image of apprenticeship is a discourse trying to justify it as wrong, rather than an investigation seeking to discover the whole process and what, if anything, was good about it! But this is no defence of a system that had little or no theoretical knowledge to impart, although it is a claim that the practical knowledge might best be learned from master crafts people rather than from teachers of theory in the classroom. It is also to suggest that in some ways the skills of professional practice might best be learned in practice and from those who are experts, even though this might not make them mentors.

Now this latter claim raises a number of questions that are to be explored in this chapter: these relate to learning, practical knowledge and expertise, and reflective practice. In the first part these four elements are discussed and it is suggested here that these lay the foundations for a discussion of mentorship, which occurs in the second part in which it is argued that mentorship is best understood as relationship and function, neither of which is necessarily the same as that of the teacher-practitioner. In the conclusion, it will be argued that this is a successful method of developing human beings, although there are both the risks and the exhilaration of human being and of being human in such relationships.

## Laying the foundations

In this first, brief section it is necessary to explore the underlying concepts that impinge upon the practice of mentoring and, fundamentally, these appear to be the four mentioned above. They are discussed in the following three sub-sections, since expertise and practical knowledge are linked together: learning from experience, practical knowledge and expertise, and reflective practice.

### Learning from experience

The process of learning is central to the whole process of human living and elsewhere this has been very fully developed (Jarvis, 1987, 1992a) so that it is not the intention of revisiting all this old ground again. However, it is important to make the point that all learning stems from experience, whether it be a practical skill or the most abstract theoretical exposition. Indeed, learning may be defined as the process of transforming experience, of one kind or another, into knowledge, skill, attitudes, values, senses, emotions, and so forth.

However, there are fundamentally two forms of experience from which this learning occurs: primary and secondary. In primary experience the individual learns as a result of either sense experience or experimentation, *ie*, an individual sees and feels an object and knows of its existence and can describe it, or an individual tries out a procedure and finds that it works and can be repeated. A great deal of learning from primary experience involves direct interaction with people, talking with them, watching their behaviour and learning from both their strengths and mistakes. This is almost a natural way of learning and occurs frequently in professional practice.

In secondary experience, a person is informed of a discovery or a procedure *etc*, and is told how it works and remembers it. This is learning from a mediated experience, and it may be seen that learning theory in the classroom is learning from a secondary experience. It will be recognised immediately that the mediated experience is much more common, since people are bombarded with information from a variety of media in contemporary society.

Significantly, however, a lot of secondary experiences are mediated through communication from other people, or in dialogue with them, rather than merely receiving a communication via the radio or television. The closer and more trusting the personal relationship, *ie*, the primary experience, the greater the possibility that difficult truths can be mediated through such an interaction and, also, the greater the willingness of individuals to subject their practice to the scrutiny of the other person in the relationship. The interaction is a primary experience, although the message being transmitted might provide a secondary experience from which learning also occurs.

## Practical knowledge and expertise

Through experiencing individuals learn and acquire knowledge, but knowledge is not a unitary phenomenon. Indeed, there are a variety of ways by which it can be analysed and for the purposes of this paper, an extension of the one first proposed by Ryle (1949) is employed here. Ryle made the distinction between 'knowledge how' and 'knowledge that' and this has subsequently become widely used. Benner (1984), for instance, used it in her well-known study *From Novice to Expert*. The distinction is well made that 'knowledge how' is about practice and 'knowledge that' about theory. But this is an over-simple and rather misleading distinction as was demonstrated in the opening chapter of this book, since 'knowledge how' is not the same as having the skill to perform an action, and 'knowledge that' is about knowing that something will most likely occur given specific circumstances in the practical situation – it is still knowledge of practice. In other words, both are forms of practical knowledge. There is at least one other form of knowledge: 'knowledge why', and this is associated with the conceptual framework within which practice can be analysed, and it is based on and driven by the internal logic of the disciplines rather than the practice. 'Knowledge why' is theoretical knowledge and may be less important to basic training for some types of practitioners than the other forms of knowledge, but this level of theory is ignored at practitioners' peril since it is fundamental to any understanding of the context of practice.

Skill plus both 'knowledge how' and 'knowledge that' are vital to improving practice: the skill can only be learned in primary experience (either practice or simulation – and the latter is not precisely the same as practice itself) while 'knowledge how' and 'knowledge that' may in the first instance learned through mediated experience, but later they are also learned as a result of primary experience. (See Jarvis, 1994 for a discussion of learning practical knowledge.)

It is this process of learning, and perhaps teaching, through which the practitioner becomes an expert (Benner, 1984). Following the Dreyfus model, she suggested that practitioners go through five stages to become an expert – novice, advanced beginner, competent, proficient and expert. She acknowledged that not all practitioners reach the stage of expertise and elsewhere Jarvis (1992b) has suggested that for some the process of repetition of performance leads to habitualisation rather than expertise. In that paper it was suggested that there are three forms of practice: thoughtless practice, thoughtful practice and reflective practice.

## Reflective practice

Reflective practice occurs when practice is problematised for the practitioner. This may occur when a taken-for-granted procedure miscarries in some way and the practitioners are forced to ask why a certain event has occurred. But it can also occur when practitioners stop and problematise their own practice for themselves, then ask themselves why their practice was a success or why it was a failure. This is similar to the approach of analysing critical incidents.

The point is that when the question 'why?', is posed, a disjuncture is created between the practitioners' knowledge and the knowledge required to deal adequately with the experience of the current situation. It is this disjuncture, this 'why?', which is the start of the process of learning. When practitioners reflect on their practice, learn from their experience and adapt their practice accordingly, then they are reflective practitioners and they are moving along the part towards expertise. Benner (1984) suggested that many practitioners do not move beyond the competency stage, and this may well be because they do not respond to the challenge of problematising their practice, or because they do not have others who will help them problematise it. Peers may occasionally fulfil this role, managers might also do so – perhaps they should more than they do, but then they are often not trained to act as a teacher-practitioner or a supervisor, nor do they necessarily see themselves in a mentoring role. Practitioners need someone who will problematise their practice for them or help them reflect upon it when they have problematised it for themselves. It is here that the mentor can play an important role.

## Mentorship

Mentorship has suddenly taken on a respectability in professional education and those who use it try to differentiate it from the image of the apprentice master, the teacher-practitioner, *etc*. Indeed, there have been a variety of attempts to define the term. Fish and Purr (1991, p47), for instance, claim that 'nurses who supervise the clinical practice' are called mentors, and they briefly go on to highlight the relationship between the mentor and the student. Sloan and Slevin (1991, p20) suggest that, while there is no real agreement in the literature,

> as new entrants progress through the early experiences, they require considerable personal support *(mentorship)* and directive teaching-learning *(preceptorship)*. Later they require more space, and the clinician's role is more of a *facilitator* – providing tuition at a more advanced level, being available on request, acting as a critic and a "stimulator" of reflection in practice.

The passage then goes on to discuss yet another function, that of the role model. Obviously, these are all different functions in the teaching and learning process in practice and, if they were agreed upon as all being relevant, it would be possible for one or more than one person to perform the various functions stipulated here, and elsewhere. To have a variety of role players, however, as different occupational categories, would perhaps be excessive, so that these may merely reflect the different roles that one person might play. Such a person might be a teacher-practitioner, a manager or a supervisor of professional practice – or even a mentor!

Defining the concept of mentor has run into several of these difficulties in recent years, as Hagerty (1986) demonstrated when she claimed that the literature confuses the person, the process and the activities. But this is no less true of a word like 'teacher' and so the problems surrounding the concept of mentorship are not insurmountable, even though any resolution will not necessarily gain universal support. In this second part, therefore, the concept of mentorship is discussed and this is followed by a discussion on the functions of the mentor.

## The mentor

There seems to be almost universal agreement that mentoring involves a relationship with the learner. Consequently, it is possible to begin to define the mentor relationship as *one in which two people relate to each other with the explicit purpose of the one assisting the other to learn.* The fact is that this relationship is explicitly a personal one-to-one relationship, and this is crucial; in this the relationship comes closer to that of counsellors with those whom they counsel and it is, therefore, a more informal kind of teaching. However, the function of the relationship lies in mentors assisting the learners, or mentees, or protégés, to learn and to perform their role more effectively, and whilst there may be occasions when this involves direct teaching, there are many occasions when the mentor is not the teacher, but may be a facilitator of reflective practice or an opener of doors that provide other learning opportunities. This appears to be a difference between mentoring and teaching. However, it must be pointed out that this is by no means necessarily a relationship which is formed only between teachers and students on educational courses, it is one which exists between adults, and between adults and children, at all levels of society, even between people who are firmly established in their profession, and even well-known within it.

Murray (1991, p5) points out that there are two schools of thought about mentoring: the one suggests that it can be structured or facilitated, while the other maintains that it can only happen when the 'chemistry' between the two people is right. However, these are not automatically exclusive, since a facilitated relationship might actually develop into one where the chemistry appears to be right for the relationship to continue and to deepen. Clearly, in education and training, structured or facilitated mentoring is called for – but this is not something that can just be turned on and off with the passing of every two months' module, *etc*. This has already been discovered in nursing when, as Barlow (1991) reports, short-term mentorship did not seem appropriate for clinical practice with students. Indeed, these mentors were often new staff nurses who would no doubt have benefited from being mentored themselves.

It is the relationship which is important in mentoring – in Buber's (1959) words, it is an I-Thou relationship. But he (1959, pp131–2) takes it even further in his characterisation of the educative relationship:

> . . .I have characterized the relationship of the genuine educator to his (sic) pupil as being a relationship of this kind. In order to help the realisation of the best potentialities in the pupil's life, the teacher must really *mean* him as the definite person he is in his potentiality and his actuality; more precisely, he must not know him as the mere sum of qualities, strivings and inhibitions, he must be aware of him as a whole

being and affirm him in his wholeness. But he can only do this if he meets him again and again as his partner in a bipolar situation.

In the beginning, for Buber, is relationship and it is here in that relationship that mentoring is to be discovered. But, since Buber is describing an educative relationship between a teacher and a child, there is a possibility that it could be interpreted in a non-adult educational manner. This is a fear of some writers about mentoring in general, *eg,* Burnard, (1990), who claim that the mentoring relationship relationship cannot be compatible with the principles of adult education, since the mentor is likely to create dependence and conformity. Such a claim is perfectly understandable, and it is justified if the mentor seeks to be domineering in any way. But in the spirit of the *I-Thou* relationship, this fear has less potency. Elsewhere, Buber (1961, p125) illustrates his concern for humanistic principles that relate closely to those of adult education: 'The relation in education is one of pure dialogue'. He (1961, p125) explains this:

A dialogical relation will show itself also in genuine conversation, but it is not composed of this. Not only is the shared silence of two such persons in dialogue, but also their dialogical life continues, even when they are separated in space, as the continual potential presence of the one to the other, as an unexpressed intercourse.

Such a relationship is at the heart of mentoring. It is in this primary relationship that the mentor can help the mentee reflect on practice and learn. In a relationship of trust and concern it is possible to enable reflection to occur, even about the most difficult and personal concerns, and for practice to improve as a result.

More recently, the original type of mentoring relationship was discovered in the workplace (Jarvis and Dubelaar, 1996) where research into the use of older people at work has shown that certain employers make a conscious effort to ensure that their companies have an age-mix. Some of the elder workers come to see themselves as 'father-figures' and 'mother-figures' in the company. They are there on the shop floor whenever colleagues want them and need advice that can stem from their own depth of experience. They are mentors and they form personal relationships and it is in and through the relationship of trust that they are able to mentor.

Such a close relationship which can be rich and rewarding may also have the potential to become personal and emotionally charged, especially between adults of different genders. Where mentor relationships are facilitated, this possibility has to be recognised and where the relationship emerges because the chemistry just matches, there is also the possibility that emotional relationships might occur. This, then, is one of the other realities of such a relationship which has to be acknowledged – with all its positive and negative possibilities. Murray (1991, p61) cites one way of overcoming the potentiality of emotional involvement between the mentor and mentee when a mentor from AT&T Laboratories claimed that 'having a protégé from a different department helps her to bring an objectivity to the relationship that a supervisor might not have'.

But who is the mentor? On occasions the mentor can be the teacher, but on others the mentor may be an advisor, a senior colleague or an expert. Occasionally, it can be the manager – but it might be difficult to enter such a relationship with an immediately junior colleague, so that where there is a facilitated mentor relationship the mentor is usually at least two rungs higher than the protégé.

## The functions of the mentor

It is clear from this discussion that mentoring is not regarded here in the same light as coaching (Schon, 1987) or supervising in clinical practice, or even personal tutoring (Barlow, 1991). However, there is a sense in which the personal tutor can become a mentor with students, as Daloz (1986) demonstrated in liberal adult education where adults are returning to college to study. But if the mentor is to play a role in education and the professions, especially after the mentee has graduated, then the personal tutor may not be able to perform it and, in some cases, the ex-students may not want it. Hence, it seems that Murray's (1991) distinction between facilitated and unstructured mentoring becomes even more important. During studentship, some form of mentor role might be performed by the personal tutor, especially one who is acknowledged to be concerned about excellence in practice. Mentorship might also be facilitated for junior qualified staff, in the way that Murray indicates. She (1991, p58) records a top level executive as saying:

> I'm always mentoring, both formally and informally. My role is to help my subordinates make decisions. I let them bounce ideas off me and I give my input. But ultimately, I want them to make decisions. If I were making all the decisions for them, I wouldn't need them, would I? So taking on what you call an 'additional protégé is no great hardship for me in terms of time. It's what I do anyway.

Here the distinction between formally and informally is important – perhaps the informal mentoring relationship which just emerges, or which emerges after the formal relationship has been created, is at the heart of mentoring.

In his excellent book on mentoring, Daloz (1986, pp215–35) suggested some of the major things that good mentors do in the situations of mentoring adult students, and he did so under three heads – support, challenge and provide a vision. Each of these are sub-divided into a number of different functions:

- Support – listening, providing structure, expressing positive expectations, sharing ourselves, making it special.
- Challenge – setting tasks, engaging in discussion, heating up dichotomies, constructing hypotheses, setting high standards.
- Vision – modelling, keeping tradition, offering a map, suggesting new language, providing a mirror.

In a sense, in these instances, the role of the mentor is to help the protégés to reflect on their practice, to learn from their experiences and to improve their practice so that they might exercise even more expertise. In mentoring, this is done through an in-depth relationship whether it is structured or informal, a primary experience, Buber's educative relationship. Indeed, it is the relationship that makes mentorship so important – not just to professional practice but to life itself. It is then not only in practice the mentee gains, it is also a life-enriching relationship – but should the mentor also gain from such a relationship?

> But connections achieve . . . only in so far as they make the existence of the connected into *being for each other*, not merely being *with* each other. My continued being 'makes sense' only in as far as there are others who go on needing me. Beckoning to me, making me attentive to their plight, filling me with the feeling of responsibility for them, they make me the unique, irreplaceable, indispensable individual that I am: the entity whose disappearance would make a hole in the universe, create that void. . .Unless I am *for*, I am not.
>
> (Bauman, 1992, p40)

Being open to others is at the heart of human being, but if the mentor smothers the mentee, then the fears expressed by Burnard are justified. Mentorship is about exercising this human characteristic in genuine dialogue, so that ultimately both develop and feel needed through the relationship. With the research reported above about some farsighted employers, the mentors cannot smother the mentees but can only be there, available whenever the mentees need them.

## Conclusions

It might be asked whether mentoring actually works. Murray (1991, p18) reports the following:

> An international management-consulting firm, Heidrick and Struggles, surveyed 1,250 prominent men and women executives in the later 1970s (Roches, 1979, p15) to determine the factors contributing to their success. Nearly two-thirds of those surveyed reported having had a mentor or a sponsor. The positive results were both measurable and had less tangible indicators. 'Executives who have had a mentor earned more money at a younger age, . . . are happier with their progress and derive greater pleasure from their work'.

But if this materialistic assessment is insufficient, then turn to Daloz's (1986) human story of the mentor and see the successful struggles of those adults endeavouring to achieve and doing so, sometimes against great odds, and the way that the mentor is able to be there with support when times are difficult. This is the human side of the story – the I-Thou relationship where people have time for others in order to help them reflect upon their life, to transform their experiences and to learn and grow. For at the heart of all human being is relationship which helps to draw out the human essence from the existant, to create life from existence and to show that human being is always in the process of becoming.

# Chapter Eight

# Self-directed and contract learning

In the previous two chapters it has been argued that teaching and mentorship are about entering concerned relationships and, as it has been claimed elsewhere, that the self emerges in relationship with significant others. It is, therefore, important that this chapter addresses teaching techniques that emphasise the individual and individualism, values emphasised by the Enlightenment, epitomised by self-directed and contract learning. The chapter first examines the idea of individualism within which these two forms of learning have arisen and then it analyses each of these approaches separately. Fundamentally, the chapter suggests that there are some moral questions to be placed over the concept of individualism and that, while both approaches to learning have some advantages, these moral questions need to be recognised.

## The individualism of late modernity

Both self-directed and contract learning imply that the individual is a free agent and able to act independently of the social situation. Heller (1990, p65), for instance, claims that people are thrown into the world and are free to choose their own destiny: they have the possibility of making an existential choice. While this is almost certainly an over-statement of the position, individual freedom is a taken-for-granted concept in Western society and, although it is frequently recognised in the West that some Asian societies do not have such an advanced concept of the individual, many people find it hard to accept the idea that the concept of the individual has not always been so prevalent in Western society either. However, in sociological research, it is not hard to trace studies of the way in which society has changed, so that more emphasis has been placed on the individual. Toennies' (1957) famous Gemeinschaft to Gesellschaft, and Durkheim's (1933) '*Division of Labour*' illustrate the ways that early sociologists were examining the changes in society. It was also the period when Simmel (1908) was suggesting that the mentality of Western people was changing as a result of living in anonymous, urban society and people were becoming more instrumentally rational. Additionally, it is in such urban conglomerations that anonymous people discover a need to develop symbols of their own identity and individuality.

Nevertheless, it should be pointed out that individualism is not a totally new concept and that two early societies stressed individualism: the ancient

Hebrews and the Greeks. In the Old Testament, individual responsibility is discussed by the eighth century prophets seven hundred years before Christ, and self-education was recognised by Socrates two hundred years later. But these were two distinct forms of ancient society, both having writing, conducive in their own way to the development of forms of individualism. Other societies were not so conducive in the first instance, although social changes occurred which enabled individualism to emerge later.

But social changes do not occur in isolation and the birth of modernity and the growth of individualism had many early contributory factors. For instance, the Reformation produced the Protestant churches which were to emphasise salvation of the individual soul, whereas the Church of Rome stressed the communion of saints. Significantly, however, religion has always placed considerable importance on the individual – the holy men/women had to step outside of society in order to be individuals and to achieve the holy life untainted, as it were, by regular human relationship and by the pressures which that placed upon them. The importance of the Reformation was that it was subsequently believed that holiness and salvation could be achieved within the bounds of social living, and Protestantism was to become a major force for social change – yet Protestantism itself was a secularising force. Not only did it emphasise the individual, it also stressed other factors that were to contribute to the birth of Modernity, including the idea of technical rationality and even science itself. As Max Weber (1930) was also to show, it was Calvinism which also played a great part in the development of entrepreneurial capitalism – another individuating factor.

With the birth of modernity, there were both individuating forces that were beginning to fragment society and an ideology of individualism which led to the development of liberalism. Indeed, individualism had achieved a central place in the plethora of new ideas that were about to embrace the Western world. Hamilton (1992, p22) writes of individualism in this period:

> – the concept that the individual is the starting point for all knowledge
> and action, and that individual reason cannot be subjected to a higher
> authority. Society is thus the sum or product of the thought and action
> of a large number of individuals.

By the nineteenth century in England the idea of the individual being an agent was epitomised by Samuel Smiles' self-help philosophy (Smiles, 1996 ed; Thornton, 1983) which permeated a great deal of thought in the nineteenth century. Smiles himself wrote about education in precisely this way:

> Our own active effort is the essential thing; and no facilities, no books,
> no teachers, no amount of lessons learnt by rote will enable us to
> dispense with it. . .The best teachers have . . . sought to make their
> pupils themselves active parties to the work in which they were
> engaged; thus making teaching something far higher than the mere
> passive reception of the scraps and details of knowledge.
>                     (Smiles, 1958 edition, p302 – cited Thornton 1983, p10)

Smiles' philosophy, as may be seen here, was of individuals being active agents who had a duty to better themselves through hard work which, if they pursued it with diligence, would result in them being both happy and successful. Self-education fitted into this ideology. This was the philosophy of the period, an optimistic belief that all will work out well for those who deserve it as a result of their own endeavours, a belief that has now little place in contemporary Western thought. This was also the period when distance education began to emerge, a subject which will be discussed more thoroughly in the following chapter.

By the twentieth century, the idea that society comprised a totality of individuals was assumed and taken for granted, and that the individual was free and able to act independently appeared to be rarely doubted. By this period interesting paradoxes had arisen, however, for the behaviourists were beginning to promulgate the idea that people are conditioned by their environment and experiences, and functionalists in sociology were suggesting that people were the product of the social forces into which they were socialised – but yet most people actually believed that they were free and autonomous. With the demise of functionalism and behaviourism suffering some serious set-backs, the beliefs of individualism and freedom became regarded as even more self-evident and the 1960s demonstrated the strength of this position. However, by the 1980s genetic research and sociobiology were again beginning to question the total freedom of the individual, and it was becoming an age of managerialism which was certainly designed to restrict any freedom that might actually exist!

Nevertheless a number of beliefs surrounding individuals (such as that they are autonomous, that they ought to try to achieve some form of authenticity and self-actualise) have remained prevalent in education, and in society at large. Indeed, Hiemstra and Sisco (1990) have developed this quite thoroughly in a study entitled *Individualizing Instruction*, reflecting the social context within which a great deal of teaching occurs (see also Boud, 1988). However, these are beliefs that require much more careful consideration at this juncture in the argument, although this discussion must be restricted to ethical considerations rather than a full analysis of them – something of which was started elsewhere in relation to learning (Jarvis, 1992). There is considerable confusion in the educational literature between the concepts of authenticity, autonomy and freedom and individuality, but no real attempt is made here to distinguish between them carefully, since they are overlapping and it would not necessarily enhance this study, although they are discussed below.

There are basically three approaches to the idea of authenticity: Cooper (1983, pp8–25) called the two most individualistic ones the Polonian and Dadaist models. Polonius said to his son, 'To thine own self be true', while the Dadaist claims that 'the only requirement for the authenticity of a person's actions and commitments is that these issue from spontaneous choices, unconstrained by convention, opinion, or his own past' (Cooper, 1983, p10). Both of these approaches to behaviour are concerned with the self, they are totally individualistic, and as such they take no account of the Other in any form of action. Consequently, neither of these approaches are considered to be morally acceptable, and yet some leading exponents of education for adults have espoused such positions. Rogers (1969, p295), for instance, has claimed that his theoretical model of the ideal individual is one in which:

> the individual who has experienced optimal psychological growth – the person functioning freely in all the fullness of his organismic potentialities; a person who is dependable in being realistic, self-enhancing, socialized, and appropriate in his behavior; a creative person, whose specific formings of behavior are not easily predictable, ever developing, ever discovering himself and the newness in himself in each succeeding moment in time.

This is the Dadaist position: authenticity lies in changing constantly and acting freely and, perhaps, unpredictably. For Rogers, the authentic person is totally free and not constrained by others. It is also possible to interpret Maslow's self-actualisation need in the same context since for him self-actualisation seems to be the end-product of need fulfilment, even though Maslow himself might have had a more moral approach to understanding human development. Both of these models emphasise individual freedom as the major criterion of authenticity.

In precisely the same way it is necessary to examine Candy's (1991, pp108–9) six traits of personal autonomy which, he claims, underlie self-direction in lifelong learning. Candy suggests that a person may be judged to be autonomous to the extent that he/she

1.   Conceives of goals, policies and plans, and forms purposes and intentions of his or her own, independently of any pressure to do so from others;
2.   Exercises freedom of choice in thought or action, without inward or outward constraints or restrictions on his or her capacities to act or to reason;
3.   Uses the capacity for rational reflection, judging among alternatives
    a.   on the basis of moral defensible, non-arbitrary beliefs as to what is true or right, derived from personal experience and/or reflection
    b.   as objectively as possible
    c.   using relevant and adequate evidence;
4.   Has the will and the capacity fearlessly and resolutely to carry into practice, and through to completion, plans of actions arrived at through (1), (2), and (3) above, without having to depend on others for encouragement and reassurance, and regardless of opposition;
5.   Exercises self-mastery in the face of strong emotional involvements, reversals, challenges, and setbacks, and remains emotionally detached as far as possible;
6.   Has a concept of himself or herself as autonomous.

This is certainly an individualistic charter, although Candy is clear that autonomy is a matter of degree rather than something which is absolute. This list, however, lies at one end of the spectrum: it starts from a Polonian position and moves to to a Dadaist one in the second paragraph, which is almost impossible to sustain, and reverts to a Polonian one in the fourth and fifth! The basis of morality spelt out in the third paragraph is rather intuitive but based upon an idea of rationality which was rejected in the second chapter of this study and is difficult to endorse in late modern society. Candy, himself, feels that the fourth paragraph is the most controversial since he (1991, p109) claims that 'autonomous people are emotionally self-contained and do not need, enjoy, or respond to social interaction'. While he may be correct in this claim, it is certainly one that needs more substantiation and it clearly has psychological implications since it might indicate that introverts are more likely to be self-directed than extroverts. It is here, however, that he indicates his awareness that people actually are not so individualistic as his checklist implies since he emphasises that it is all a matter of degree, although this list certainly revolves around the self.

There is a real sense in which individualism creates situations where the others are strangers and universal strangerhood becomes the norm. But there is a third form of existentialism that finds its expression in the work of Buber and Marcel, among others. Buber (1961, p244) asserts that:

> the fundamental fact of human existence is neither the individual as such nor the aggregate as such. Each, considered by itself, is a mighty abstraction. The individual is a fact of existence in as far as it is built up of living units in relation. The fundamental fact of human existence is man with man.

In precisely the same way Marcel's (1976) analysis of the interpersonal emphasises the availability of one person for another. It is this position which is also espoused by Levinas (1991) and discussed in the third chapter of this book. Commenting on Buber's position, Levinas (1989, p64) wrote:

> The relation is the very essence of the I: whenever the I truly affirms itself, its affirmation is inconceivable without the presence of the Thou.

From a less existentialist position, Taylor (1991, p14) notes that 'individualism involves a centring on the self and a concomitant shutting out, or even unawareness, of the greater issues or concerns that transcend the self, be they religious, political, historical'. Taylor develops the paradox of the authentic individual in contemporary society and he concludes (1991, p91) that perhaps 'the loss of a sense of belonging through a publicly defined order needs to be compensated by a stronger, more inner sense of linkage'. It is in this relationship with the Other that moral value can be made manifest. It is when the Other impinges upon my spontaneity that ethics can begin, which is in opposition to both the Dadaist and the Polonian positions on authenticity, but not necessarily to certain interpretations of personal autonomy. However, the idea of relationship tends to imply that the individuality of the participants is lost but this is a misapprehension since relationships can be inter-subjective in which the individual selfhood of all participants is both acknowledged and respected.

Nevertheless, it has to be acknowledged that there is a fundamental objection to this existentialist position, which was hinted at in the reference to radical adult education in the fifth chapter and which Adorno (1973) attacked quite fundamentally: to what extent is the relationship the end in itself? Should there not be a wider consideration of social justice than just the morality of interpersonal relationships which have been discussed here? This is a position which existentialists themselves recognise, as Macquarrie (1973) points out when he says that power is always a problem for existentialists. It will be argued in later chapters of this book that in a world of strangers, certain people should be treated as if they impinged upon another's individuality, although it is recognised that the *as if* is itself a very problematic concept. This will be more fully discussed in a later chapter on radical education.

At this point in the argument, however, it needs to be highlighted that there are limits on freedom – although individuals freely enter relationship with others and in so doing they curtail their own freedom, so that the contemporary emphasis on individual freedom needs to be tempered by 'an age of responsibilization' (Taylor, 1991, p77). Once individuals consider the Other, then individualism should be tempered by a degree of responsibility, even if not by profound concern. But the responsibility should not only be for the Other so much as for the Other to be free to act and to be him/her self.

Having examined briefly the ideas of individualism and authenticity, it is now possible to begin to assess self-directed and contract learning.

## Self-directed learning

It is clear from the above discussion that people are not absolutely free, although they certainly do have a degree of freedom. Indeed, Candy (1990, pp16–7) recognises that those self-directed learners studying within an educational institution never entirely escape from the control of their teachers. Such an observation might also be true for all self-directed learners, since they rarely, if ever, escape entirely from the influence of others, and even if they do they are still responsible for, and respond to the demands of, their previous decisions. Learning, however, is broader than education so that any discussion of self-directed learning must contextualise it in the wider society as well as within the educational institution.

In the context of this discussion self-directed learning refers to a learning project rather than a single act of learning which goes on throughout life and is as self-directed as is the individual at the time when the learning occurs. However, it is not the intention to seek to define *project* in the way that Tough (1971) did by specifying that it had to be over seven hours in length. A project is more than a single act of learning and takes a period of time to complete, so that self-directed learning is regarded here as a time consuming exercise.

### Self-directed learning outside of the educational institution

This is what Candy (1991, p15) regards as autodidaxy; self-directed learning outside of the classroom. In the wider context, it relates to an understanding of humanity and human maturing since learning occurs in every walk of life; often it is incorrectly related specifically to adulthood, although children are also self-directed in their learning. Perhaps the emphasis on self-directed learning among adult educators reflects the effects of Tough's (1971) work on adult learning projects on adult education. Knowles (1980, p46) also specifically claims that 'the psychological definition of adulthood is the point at which individuals perceive themselves to be essentially self-directing'. While this might be 'a psychological definition' it is certainly not the only one; indeed, Reber's (1985, p365) *Dictionary of Psychology* actually suggests that adulthood covers everyone who has passed their adolescence and makes no reference to self-direction. Deci and Ryan (1981) also indicate that self-directed learning is a fact of life for all age groups and, indeed, many primary schools employ discovery methods in teaching and learning. However, it has to be recognised here that children are more susceptible to adult control in their early years and it may be only during teenage rebellion that they begin to rediscover their own human independence (Eisenman, 1990). Consequently, it is considered unwise to try to draw an artificial boundary around self-direction and relate it to adulthood.

In this wider context the morality of self-directed learning relates broadly to the morality of action in general, rather than to either education or learning in particular. Significantly, the moral issues might relate more closely to adulthood since moral awareness is something which develops with age – as was demonstrated in the fourth chapter. However, learning is a particularly individualistic and individuating act of behaviour, so that it is necessary to recognise that not only is self-directed learning a reaction to the contemporary society, it is also promoting it since society is social, by definition, and so it is within this situation that its morality needs some consideration.

Life is lived in time and space with individual actions occurring at their intersection. Space, however, might be private or social, and in making private space it is important to distance the self from others. By choosing to do something on one's own, individuals put themselves at a distance from the Other, so that people either remain strangers or even are made strangers. In *Sophie's World*, for instance, Sophie was forced to distance herself from her friend, Joanna, when she embarked on her philosophical studies (Gaarder, 1994, p10) and in a sense she put their friendship at risk, and Joanna might have become a little more of a stranger. Strangers are, according to Bauman (1993, p154), irrelevant presences. But strangers are essential to modern society, everything about it is constructed on the assumption of strangerhood – including education! The problem of strangerhood is not eliminating it, but living with it. The extent to which individuals live with it is a part of their moral problem, since they have to decide upon whom they wish to admit to their moral space, their private space.

In a sense, then, it remains the decision of the individual for there are no moral rules to guide it. Bauman (1993, pp167–8) writes:

> In the cognitively mapped social space, the stranger is someone of whom one knows little and desires to know even less. In moral space,

the stranger is someone of whom one cares little and is prompted to care even less. The two sets of strangers may, or may not, overlap. So in all likelihood we will go on committing both irrational and immoral deeds – as well as deeds which are irrational while moral, and such as are rational yet immoral.

There are no moral, or rational, rules about caring for the others. It is the responsibility of the individual to decide relatively freely on how that leisure time and space is to be used and whether the self-directed learning is a moral use of time for the individual actor, or whether some other stranger(s) should be admitted to that space. It is a matter of decision whether to treat others as if they are not strangers, or whether to restrict that activity. This is the responsibility of the individual, as an agent – and it might be argued that the more moral, the more committed, the more time will be devoted to undertaking acts of care on behalf of the Other. (It must be recalled that the morality of concern lies in the intentions as revealed in the actions, rather than in the actions themselves.) At the same time, the ambiguity of contemporary society is such that no rule can be laid down to guide the decision about how to use personal time and space, since it is just as possible to argue that it is necessary to make time for oneself in order not to be entrapped by the demands of society and not free to make moral choices!

There are not just self-directed learning and responding to others in this equation, there are a variety of other activities which individuals might wish to perform in preference to becoming moral agents, and in these they might well become consumers of other commodities supplied by the market and which compete for attention in potential consumers' lives. That choice is based upon want, or desire, but so in part is the decision to admit strangers into that moral space. It may be, therefore, that there is a place for the education of desire in the menu of programmes offered in education for adults – but certainly the education of desire is a significant consideration in contemporary society, and will be returned to in the final chapter of the book.

Consequently, self-directed learning, as a leisure time pursuit, has to take its place within the plethora of potential leisure time activities available to individuals in late modern society and by so locating it here, the choice to pursue it has to be seen within the wider context of individual moral responsibility.

## Self-directed learning as a teaching technique

Self-directed learning is also a teaching technique, used with both children and adults. It is a method which reflects the contemporary society in which all people are different, *eg*, they have different experiences, levels of knowledge, interests, *etc*, and so classroom instruction needs to be individualised (Hiemstra and Sisco, 1990). One approach to individualisation in the classroom is simply to prepare self-directed learning activities, reflecting the facilitator role of the teacher. Knowles (1980) regards this as a form of andragogy, although it is considered here to be misleading to try to locate all forms of self-directed learning occurring within the educational institution, whether they are with children or adults, within the andragogical framework.

As a form of teaching, therefore, the moral issues surrounding self-directed learning revolve around the teachers' understanding of what they are doing. This approach does pose a major problem in the light of the earlier analysis, since it was maintained there that teachers should enter a relationship and be present with the students in order to help them when they are needed. In self-directed learning, however, it is being asserted that teachers should withdraw from the relationship and leave students to fend for themselves in some way, so that the problem posed here is the extent to which these two positions can be reconciled.

However, the distinction between the two is not so clear as it might appear: teaching and learning as a process is not all totally teacher-directed or all learner-directed, and neither does self-directed learning mean that the tutors are not available for their students. In self-directed learning in educational organisations, teachers still have a controlling function. Even in Knowles' (1975, pp31–8) work, teacher interventions are clearly specified since he points out that climate-setting, planning, diagnosing learning needs, setting goals, designing a learning plan, engaging in learning activities and evaluating the learning outcomes are all places in which the teacher has a role. Knowles also correctly points out that many students do not want to work alone and find it a little anxiety-raising. Hence, he (1975, p37) writes:

> ... I have learned to emphasize that we shall be working within a structure, but that it is a different kind of structure from what they have been used to – that it is a process structure; whereas they have been used to a content structure. And I assure them that I am in charge of the process, that I make the decisions about the procedures when they aren't in a position to make them with me, and that I know what I am doing. I assure them that they are being asked to take more responsibility for learning than they used to, and that I shall help them learn to do it.

Knowles is making the point that he, as the teacher, is still in charge of the educational process but that he is allowing students to have responsibility for the manner in which they learn. This is not quite the same as the self-directed learning discussed previously. In this situation, the learning process is one in which many of the parameters are already determined and that there is only a limited degree of freedom within the process. Within Knowles' framework it is clear that the tutors do not leave the students to fend for themselves – indeed, the extent to which it is self-directed becomes rather questionable from the above quotation!

Even when students are given responsibility to work by themselves in what might be called self-directed learning situations, many tutors provide very careful support so that students should not feel too threatened by the new responsibilities that they have in being in charge of some of their own learning. Stanton

(1988, p121), in describing how he ran a self-directed learning psychology class, wrote that he arranged group tutorials when there were sufficient students to justify it and also:

> Individual tutorials were also available. Students could arrange to see either my tutor or myself at a mutually convenient time. Approximately 75 per cent of the students enrolled in the course did make use of this opportunity for personal discussion. Time consuming it was, but it certainly helped me to establish a closer rapport with my students than had been possible under the lecture-dominated method I had previously used.

Giving students responsibility for their own learning is not a means of abrogating teacher responsibility; in some ways it is even more demanding and certainly more time-consuming. This is, no doubt, the experience of every teacher who has tried to give students some responsibility for their own learning but be still be available to support them.

Self-directed learning is not a method whereby teachers stand back and depersonalise learning, what I (Jarvis, 1997) have elsewhere called self-help learning by cutting the teaching costs by timetabling more private study, or library time, into the curriculum. It is a method of recognising the individuality of the students but still being present with and for the Other. The fact that students do still have the opportunity to seek the support of the teachers means that they do still inhibit the teachers' spontaneity and are still, therefore, in a moral relationship with them.

However, self-directed learning becomes an immoral teaching technique when the teachers in an educational institution so distance themselves from the learners that they are not available to them, provide no opportunity for them to impinge on the teachers' spontaneity – that is, when they have created situations of potential strangerhood. Whatever the outcome of this approach, even if it is one in which the learners have achieved an even greater degree of independence than they would otherwise have done, this has become an immoral teaching method. Indeed, independence in itself might not be an aim of education and the fragmentation of society might not be a totally acceptable process.

Having given the students some responsibility for the process of their own learning, there are other actions that teachers might take which remove some of that responsibility from them and have moral overtones. For instance, it is almost natural to assume that teachers, like everyone else, want people to agree with them and they might want the learners to reach similar conclusions to the ones that they themselves hold, or they might see that the learners have taken a direction that will lead them to a false conclusion, *etc*, and, consequently, when asked they guide the students in specific directions. However, it must be pointed out that there are increasingly few totally correct solutions to learning problems in contemporary society and that teachers are much more likely to be interpreters than legislators of knowledge (Bauman, 1987), so that teachers do need to recognise that in any self-directed learning activity, students are very likely to reach solutions that differ from those of their teachers and their peers. Difference is not wrongness in this fragmented society; Baudrillard (1993, pp113–123) suggests that same-ness is hell! While he is more concerned about cloning, he makes the point that 'the abolition of all otherness (entails) the abolition of the entire imaginary sphere' (Baudrillard, 1993, p116). Teachers might, therefore, be more concerned about the process than the outcome of the learning. In both cases, process and outcome, any teacher intervention should be because the teacher is available for the others and that the intervention is intended to assist the others in deciding for themselves what is correct for them, rather than an exercise in teacher authority. Once again, the decision to intervene is the teacher's and there are no rules, other than the principle of concern for the other, to guide those actions.

## Contract learning

One manifestation of self-directed learning that has assumed considerable importance in modern education is contract learning (Knowles, 1986; Thompkins and MacGraw, 1988, pp172–91; Hiemstra and Sisco, 1990, pp104–20, *inter alia*). Unfortunately, the principles underlying learning contracts are not often specified or debated, and the fact that they often work is taken as sufficient justification for their existence (Knowles, 1986, pp46–7). However, it is important that these principles are examined in order to discuss the ethics of the contract in self-directed learning.

The idea of a social contract can be traced back to Lycophron, an elder contemporary of Plato (see Flew 1979, p328), although it was much more thoroughly discussed in the writings of Locke, Rousseau, Hume and Kant. It is no coincidence that the idea of social contract emerged when philosophers were debating the implications of believing in human freedom. Locke, for instance, argued that if all people are free and live in a natural state then some will infringe on the natural rights of others, so that it is necessary that they should join together in a social contract to ensure that every citizen should enjoy his rights (women were not regarded as having citizenship at that time). In more recent political writing, Rawls (1971) has argued that the guiding principles underlying any just government should should be fair. He suggests (1971, p11) that these:

> are the principles that free and rational persons concerned to further their own interests would accept in an initial position of equality as defining the fundamental terms of their association. These principles are to regulate all further agreements; they specify the kinds of social co-operation that can be entered into and the forms of government that can be established. This was of regarding the principles of justice I shall call justice as fairness.

On the surface they appear to be a reasonable ground for the principles of government but it should be noted that underlying them is the idea that everybody should be concerned to further their own interests. But this is not the principle of moral goodness upon which the argument of this study is based. Neither, however, are the utilitarian principles that writers on contract learning produce, since they are based on outcomes rather than intentions, to justify its use. This does not deny that learning outcomes are not important, only that they can be used to justify the morality of the method.

Knowles does argue very strongly for a contract based upon an agreement between teacher and learners, with the first draft of the contract being prepared by the learners. In this way the learners have to specify what they perceive to be their own learning needs, objectives and resources. Knowles (1986, pp30–1) even mentions that they should designate their own criteria of evidence of accomplishment and the method of its validation. It is only at this stage that the teacher, consultant, mentor, *etc*, should be consulted. Thompkins and MacGraw also argue for a negotiated contract, and this is often the basis of much educational practice. However, it still has to be recognised that the educational institution and the teacher control the educational process, so that while there is a democratisation of the educational process the control of the process remains ultimately where it has always done.

There are differing practices about whether such a contractual relationship, if embarked upon, should be written or oral and taken in trust. For some individuals, the written contract appears to be more legalistic and less likely to foster the type of teaching and learning relationship which will enable concern to be expressed. For some learners, however, it provides the type of stable framework within which they feel more confidence to embark upon a different form of teaching and learning. It is not possible to argue that either is more, or less, moral than the other – it is a matter of making a decision and abiding by it and often the educational institution or the teachers will exercise their judgment and decide upon the form of practice that they wish to utilise – it is in the intention behind this decision that the morality lies. For whose betterment has the decision been made? Is the contract framed in such a manner as to enable to tutor to be available whenever the learners might need that support, *etc*? Is the envisaged practice aimed at depersonalising the teaching and learning process or is it aimed at facilitating human relationships within which there might be a mutual enriching? It is only in the actual practice of contract learning that the teachers' intentions become evident in their actions, so that the morality underlying the actual practice is only evident at this point.

Contract learning, therefore, offers the opportunity for teaching and learning to be a moral interaction, although it is clear that there are many contractual situations when such an interaction might not be possible and teaching and learning degenerate into an impersonal facilitation of knowledge acquisition which fall short of the high moral principles of education for life.

## Conclusion

This is an individualistic age in which society is fragmented and it is easy to see that those forms of self-directed education which reflect this type of society can easily lose some of the high moral principles of human interaction. At the same time, it is clear that many educators are endeavouring to remain available to work with learners who need them whilst still respecting their autonomy and individuality. This inter-subjective relationship is one in which the value of human concern can flourish is still to be found within these practices. At the same time, it has to be acknowledged that there are many learning situations in which the learners do not seek a human relationship; they seek to acquire knowledge independently, the morality of which was discussed in the first part of this chapter. However, learning and the market is a topic to which further reference will be made below.

Chapter Nine

# Distance education

Distance education is rapidly becoming a common form of education, reflecting characteristics of late modern society. It is, in a real sense, a child of its time and any analysis, ethical or otherwise, of distance education necessarily involves a reflection on contemporary society as a whole. This chapter has three main sections: the first examines the characteristics of distance education; the second examines the ethical implications for teaching in distance education; the third examines the distance education organisation as an expert system selling its commodity in the market place of learning. Finally, there is a conclusion in which the relationship between distance education and the risk society is briefly explored.

## The characteristics of distance education

In examining the history of distance education it is possible to see that it has always utilised the contemporary technology for the transmission of information. It is difficult to determine precisely when distance education began – but it was certainly about a century before the foundation of the Open University in the United Kingdom. The Chautauqua Movement (started in 1874) commenced the first integrated core programme in adult education throughout America in 1878 which led to correspondence courses being started in 1879. Even prior to that an organisation called The Society to Encourage Studies at Home was founded in 1873 and in 1883 a Correspondence University was also founded in America (Knowles, 1977). In Britain, there were a variety of similar types of educational initiative at about the same time. It might be claimed that the self-help ethos of this period is reflected in this approach to education. However, distance education has changed quite fundamentally from those early days of correspondence, and now educational institutions are able to transmit their courses by satellite, cable, internet and interactive video compact disc – to name but a few. One of the significant things about this variety of courses is that the choice of course is firmly the responsibility of the individual learner. Two main characteristics common to all these forms of distance education are the re-alignment of space and time and the mode of production of the learning materials.

## Space-time re-alignment

The re-alignment of space and time in late modern, post-modern, society has occupied the minds of a number of contemporary thinkers, including Giddens (1990) and Harvey (1990). Giddens utilises the idea of space-time distanciation, while Harvey depicts the process as space-time compression. At first sight these two ideas appear contradictory but they are, in fact, quite complementary.

Space-time distanciation is clearly relevant to distance education since it has always involved a separation between teachers and learners. Prior to the development of distance education, teaching and learning always took place in the same space and at the same time, space-time instantiation. But now distanciation has occurred. Teaching materials prepared in one place are learned in another and at another time. It is regarded as advantageous to the students because they can study at their convenience but, obviously, it has also been seized upon by employers because it means that employees can study subjects relevant to their work situation out of work time – an illustration of the potentially exploitative nature of the capitalist system!

This in itself reflects another feature of late modern society – it depends to a great extent on the individuation of society. While there are clearly advantages in emphasising the individual, there are disadvantages both for learning and for aspects of life itself; the former will be discussed later in this chapter, but while there is a sense in which the latter lies outside of the scope of this book there is another in which it has already been discussed since it has been argued here that it is only in relationship that the universal moral good can be manifest. It is when the Other impinges upon Ego's spontaneity that there is the possibility of a positive ethical manifestation, therefore it might be claimed that the individuation of society is a denial of the ethical.

Giddens makes a number of other points relevant to distance education, since he argues that there are two other mechanisms in the process of space-time distanciation: symbolic tokens may be passed between people and institutions, such as money and credit; expert systems emerge, systems of technical expertise, which organise large areas of the material and social environment. The second of these points is discussed later in this chapter and the former elsewhere in the book.

Space-time compression is also very relevant to distance education. Harvey points to the fact that the speed of production of commodities has changed and accelerated production results in accelerated consumption. People become used to consuming a commodity rapidly and changing to another according to fashion or whim. The issue of consuming in education has been discussed fully elsewhere (Jarvis, 1992, pp143–54). Obsolescence is built in to some of the commodities; the market cannot function without it. As individuals consume material commodities, so they also consume cultural ones, and in education the module has become the means by which this is undertaken. People can consume (learn) a module and, without seeking to plumb the depths of the whole subject, they move on to another. But consumption is no longer local – it costs the same to transmit a programme on satellite television 500 miles as it does 5,000. Now people can and do consume information from all over the world and educational institutions are becoming global in their orientation and so time and space are compressed into the global village. Individuals can now consume information and increase their cultural capital in short bursts by careful selecting of what programmes they watch and what modules they select to study, *etc.*

Soon people will be able to plug their home computer into the same system as they do their cable television and telephone and access information directly through the computer system from any part of the world, so that printed distance education courses may soon be outdated.

It can thus be seen that distance education is responding to the ethos of late modernity: already courses are shorter and modular catering for accelerated consumption in a flexible market. People can now study alone for a degree by combining modules from different educational institutions and, soon, it will be possible to take them from different institutions in different parts of the globe. But the fact that they can study alone emphasises the individuality of the learners so that distance education actually capitalises on the individuating tendencies of modern society. At the same time it must be acknowledged that once relationships are established it is easy to maintain them at a distance through electronic mail, *etc*, so that these new developments in communication can also facilitate community. Nevertheless, in order to produce these courses, distance education has to have a system of production.

## The mode of production

Distance education has been regarded as a form of mass education and the production of the teaching material has been by mass production. It was the German scholar Otto Peters (1984) who really analysed the production and distribution of distance education materials in this manner, and he rightly recognised that education was beginning to employ industrial production techniques, which might now be called Fordist. His analysis might be summarised as follows – in the production of distance education materials there is:

- rational organisation from the outset;
- a carefully planned programme of production and marketing;
- a principle of rationalisation – the craftsman's trade is
- changed into production based on the division of labour *eg,* the teacher's role has changed;
- mechanised and automated production – there is an assembly line mentality in production;
- standardisation of product;
- depersonalisation throughout the whole process;

- only a place for large organisations, since small concerns are no longer able to raise the initial capital to invest in the developmental work;

- a need for the whole enterprise to be centrally controlled and rationally organised – a centralised bureaucracy – if it is to be economical.

There has recently been some debate about the extent to which all of these points are valid (Rumble, 1995), but it is clear that for large distance learning institutions, like the British Open University, certain mass production (Fordist) techniques have been utilised. However, Peters' analysis is flawed when it comes to small institutions, since many of them are undertaking distance education courses and are, perhaps, using post-Fordist approaches in production of course materials.

The Open University, then, takes the form of the age in which it was born – rational, industrial, mass market. Walton Hall might be described as a knowledge factory! The factory is not necessarily a producer, in the research sense, of knowledge but a producer of marketable knowledge. However, there is one major issue here that has to be recognised – the production of knowledge that is going to be disseminated to a mass market is controlled by relatively few people; the selection, packaging and marketing of cultural knowledge contained in the teaching and learning packages is tightly and centrally controlled. In this sense, centralisation does not only include the production process; it determines the content of the course and since many purchasers of the commodity might not automatically refer to other materials about the same topic, this centralised system might be producing the only information that the students endeavour to learn about a topic.

But the Open University is more than Walton Hall: there are regional offices and part-time staff. How does that fit into this Fordist model? This is the same process. Many large industrial companies need to personalise their image and so it has to have a 'face' – and the staff at the Regional Office are the face of the large bureaucratic production organisation in the regions able to offer a personal and local service. Then the part-time staff – both tutors and counsellors – are rather like the after-sales service! Without the part-time staff the product is not very useful for some students because they are unsure about how to use it or get the best from it. The part-time academic and counselling staff are there to help them, but they are actually servicing a cultural product which has already been sold. Perhaps a course is only a course when it is taught – but the actual point is that not all people need the 'after sales' service, although the commodity purchased (the educational course) is clearly enriched if students utilise it – after all they have bought that too in their initial purchase price. However, the amount of tutorial and counselling support provided must depend upon the size of the market: it gets less as the courses become more specialised and cater for fewer students and when the cost of the product has to be kept low in order to enter market competition.

The smaller educational organisations providing distance education might not be in a position to provide much of the educational support because they do not have the income from the course to build up structures like that of the Open University. This is a significant point since the educational support, which is very important to some learners, is lessened unless there are sufficient finances to provide it. As competition grows to market courses, so there will be a need to cut the fees to make the courses more marketable and, while production costs can be curtailed, the educational support-type services would also suffer.

Distance education has, therefore, transformed the nature of teaching and learning and the marketing of learning materials has made the more traditional welfare-oriented education appear to be redundant. This lack of support might prevent weaker students from benefiting fully from the learning materials that they purchase. It may be seen from this discussion that there are a number of profound ethical issues that need to be examined in a little more depth.

## Teaching in distance education

From the above description of distance education there are three issues that require further analysis here: the role of the teacher, the educational support staff and the control of the knowledge within each course. Each is discussed now.

### The role of the teacher

In most traditional education teachers prepare their lessons and deliver them to the class face-to-face, but in distance education there is some difficulty in determining exactly who is the teacher. The whole process of production, as Peters points out, is a rational assembly line-type of production. There is a course team which decides what topics will go into the course and there are writers, graphic artists, designers, *etc*, who then prepare the material which is then produced and marketed. In a large organisation there might be a part-time tutor who 'teaches' the material and marks the assignments. The teacher's role has grown and changed and is apparently played by a variety of different people. Even in smaller organisations the persons who write the course might also assess the assignments but they probably do not perform all the other roles.

Now this not only changes the role of the teacher, it also changes the ethical responsibility of teaching. It has been consistently argued that ethics begins when the Other impinges upon Ego's spontaneity and it was argued in an earlier chapter that teachers should put themselves at the disposal of the Other. Teaching is a matter of entering a relationship with the Other solely for the benefit of the Other. By its very nature, however, distance education separates whoever plays the role of the teacher from the taught. Writers of course material, *etc*, are no longer in relationship with those who are going to learn from their writing, so that it might be argued that they now have no responsibility for the Other, only to the employing organisations by producing a high standard course which will gain student approval. Only in large distance organisations where local tutors/counsellors are employed is there any possibility of relationship and concern. That is between someone who is at the periphery of the organisation and the learners and whose presence depends on the success of the organisation in marketing the product.

For the course team there are potential students and they might think about them as they are preparing the course, but there is no I-Thou relationship with the learners; there is no putting oneself at the disposal of the Other. The distance education university, for instance, tends to remove this potentially ethical relationship with the learners and leaves only the relationships within the course teams themselves. It is part of the inevitability of bureaucratic organisation and, as such, part of the neutralising of the distance educational process.

The course team, however, are employed by the larger organisation and are responsible to the organisation for the production of the learning package/module that they are producing. They have their roles and responsibilities within the organisation and in the production process and they are be expected to perform those – they have no responsibility for the learners. This is the process which Bauman calls adiaphorization, which is the process of stripping human relationships of their moral significance. He suggests (1995, p149) that this is an accomplishment of bureaucracy, aided and abetted by technology. Since none of the course team are in relationship with the Other during the preparation of the course, then the ethical component of teaching has been removed and since the team members' relationship with each other is functional within the work situation, they have their professional ethic – but this is profoundly different to the ethic of human relationship, for it specifies how the professional should behave in specific situations, rather than emphasising that the professional enters a relationship with the Other out of concern for the Other.

## The educational support

The amount of support offered to students varies with the size of the distance education institution and the financial means available to organise that support. Support is a type of welfare, it is also providing a service at a cost, but as the competition to provide distance education courses increases the cost of production and after sales services have to be re-considered and the expensive educational support is threatened. Like the welfare state, funding for those who need the additional support appears an expensive luxury and one which the institutions might be able to forego.

Where the support exists, however, the ethic of being available for the Other's benefit still obtains. No fee can repay that willingness to put oneself at the disposal of the Other, but it is a willingness that can save the drop-out and strengthen the struggling. Most distance education organisations are aware of the way that this support can help some of those who are struggling to overcome their problems and be successful and so they try to provide it. However, it is impossible to measure the cost benefit of educational welfare, a willingness to respond to another's need for no other reason than that they are there is the moral imperative and one that is threatened by the competitive market of education and the government's concern that education should be reasonably self-supporting.

**The control of the selection and presentation of the content of each module**

It might be claimed that this is always the responsibility of the academic, or academics, teaching a course and so why should it be different in distance education? There are number of reasons why it is different, namely: the nature of the way the material which is presented is treated and the situation within which many distance education students study.

Distance education material is prepared and transmitted to the students through the types of process that have been discussed above. At some stage a course team, or an individual, assumes responsibility for the content of the module and or for a unit within it. There might have been much discussion between members of the course team before the final decision is made, but once the decision has been made the course can be prepared. The content of the course is, in some way, fixed at this moment in time. The content is written down, printed, *etc*, and presented. It is less personal than in the traditional teaching and learning situation – and it represents the distance education organisation's course. The material assumes the mantle of the distance education institution, rather than being seen as the course of an individual teacher. The content of a distance education module seems to have some specific authority by some of the students just because it is included in the course – it is as if the material is almost holy writ – and this impels the students to learn it rather than read more widely. While the course team might not regard the selection of material as any different from any other course which they might teach through other means, the fact that it is distance and encapsulated in a fixed and unchanging, but not quite unchangeable, syllabus gives it a different aura.

Because distance education materials are public, the selection of course content is also a much more public phenomenon than it is for traditional education but, paradoxically, the learning process is much more private. Distance education institutions reflect the privatisation of the individual in late modern society. In traditional educational institutions, students can participate in a teaching and learning situation and then debate amongst themselves about what has been presented. In addition, they usually have access to a library where they can go and read around the course, checking for accuracy and studying other interpretations of the same phenomenon, *etc*. Neither of these is normally possible with distance education – it is designed for students to work at their own pace, in their own time, wherever they wish to study. By virtue of the nature of the distance learners, they are individuals in private situations and as learners they have fewer opportunities to assess the validity of the content.

Consequently, it is easy for distance education course teams to produce situations where the learners place greater authority on the content of a course than it might actually demand and yet have fewer opportunities to assess its accuracy. This places the learners in a rather disabling situation in respect to the course content. Course team members, therefore, have considerable potential power over the personhood of those who might wish to study their course. The power of the teacher was discussed in an earlier chapter and so there is no need to rehearse those arguments here, but it is important to recognise that there are additional factors to be taken into account in distance education.

But distance educators cannot enter relationships with all the Others (strangers) who might follow the course, although that does not rule out the basis of the original argument. The existence of the Other still impinges upon the spontaneity of those who select and present material but in a different manner since they will study it in a different time and space. The morality of the act lies in the intention of the actors to be concerned about the potential students in their own particular situation, especially since there is an even greater danger of generating inauthenticity in learners who might regard the learning materials in different manner. Consequently, they should make their selection and presentation as if the Other were present and taking into consideration the Other's special circumstances. The idea of 'as if' becomes most significant when it is realised that contemporary society has re-aligned spece and time and so there is a sense in which distance education may be seen as a re-alignment of the teaching and learning process in space and time.

## Trusting the expert system

The distance education institution becomes a much more impersonal phenomenon to the students who might live only a short distance from it but who could live at the other side of the world. They do no necessarily know the names of anybody, unless the institution has deliberately tried to provide itself with a 'face' through either having a local office or giving a name to the role player whom students, or potential students need to contact. The phenomenon of naming, or giving a face to, can be seen in nearly every supermarket where the employees all wear a name badge with some logo about their being of service to the client. The need to give a face to the institution is obvious – it does appear to be an impersonal system with which it is harder to interact and trust.

Giddens sees this as one of the two dilemmas to be experienced in late modernity, which are: security versus danger and trust versus risk. He writes (1990, p7):

> Modernity, as everyone living in the closing years of the twentieth century can see, is a double-edged phenomenon. The development of modern social institutions has created vastly greater opportunities for human beings to enjoy a secure and rewarding existence than any type of pre-modern system. But modernity also has a sombre side, which has become very apparent in this present century.

It is the two faces of modernity which pose many problems for people of this age. In the case of the distance education institution it may not be as problematic as it is for other institutions, but individuals might well be anxious about embarking on a distance education course. Learning, for instance, is itself a risk-taking activity because it means leaving the security of what is known for the insecurity of the unknown. While it is not necessary to rehearse all of the arguments that have been discussed elsewhere (Jarvis, 1992) it is necessary to recognise that from the earliest days philosophers and tellers of myths recognised that it was possible to live in harmony with the sociocultural and physical environment without learning, but to 'eat of the tree of knowledge' resulted in the harmony being broken and the recipients of the knowledge having to create a new world for themselves. Learning is just this, a breaking away from what is known and finding out new things – it is a risk-taking activity.

But there is not only the personal risk, there is an investment of both time and resources into the learning activity. Potential students might ask themselves whether the investment is worthwhile for them as persons as well as for them in their social situation. Can they take the risk, trust the distance education organisation with themselves, as well as their time and money?

These questions are similar to those which could be asked about other expert systems which are going to process people to a definite outcome. Can the airline be trusted? Can the double glazing company be trusted? *etc.* In an impersonal society, people are forced to deal with expert system – can the distance education institution be trusted?

In this impersonal society, one which Bauman (1990, p68) epitomises as universal strangerhood, the students may remain strangers all the way through the process of studying for whatever qualification they might be seeking – but the organisation should not be organised in such a way as to treat them as strangers. In some way they impinge upon the spontaneity of the institution and in so doing they have to be treated as human beings who become persons. This does not specify which procedures distance educational institutions put into place: there is no deontological rule that specifies what things have to be done – but there is a universal ethical principle that if the stranger impinges upon Ego's spontaneity, then that is the beginning of ethics. The organisation should be run in precisely this way, as if the stranger is impinging upon the spontaneity of the role players and the role players should act for the benefit of the Other. This is as much an attitude of the role players as it is a set of procedures for the organisation.

In a sense, then, the distance education institution has to earn the trust of the stranger who is confronted with the dilemma of trust versus risk. There is risk in learning, but the learners need to be able to trust the organisation which is providing the opportunity to learn at a distance.

## Conclusion

The discussion on risk in the previous section related to individual risk, but there are two social risks that have to be recognised at this juncture: the risk of control of educational information in an individuated society and the risks of large distance education institutions taking ownership of smaller institutions and even putting them out of business.

It has been pointed out already that distance educational institutions capitalise on the individuated nature of contemporary society and on the fact that many of their students do not have the opportunity either to discuss with other students or have access to an academic library. This means that small groups of academics are assuming control of the dissemination of academic information to potential large numbers of students – tens of thousands. This is changing the nature of education in a variety of ways but it also poses a risk both to education and to society as a whole. Such control could change the nature of the educational enterprise so that it becomes even more of a legislative agency for 'correct' knowledge than were the ancient universities in pre-modern times. This also means that if these institutions are controlled by either governments or, even more problematically, multi-national companies, then the legislation of 'academically correct knowledge' lies in the hands of the few, and education has lost whatever little independence it has had to be an independent critic of society.

In addition, some distance educational institutions are growing at a rapid rate and exercising educational influence in many countries. With the develop-ment of new technologies, resulting in both time-space distanciation and time-space compression, it is possible that these larger institutions not only become rivals of smaller institutions in other countries, but actually put them out of business. The market has little place for the weak or the small, and this could easily become a new form of colonisation of small state education and indigenous cultural knowledge.

Distance education is itself a manifestation of the risk society (Beck, 1992) and one of which educators need to take cognisance. As was pointed out at the outset of this chapter, distance education inevitably epitomises much of contemporary society and it is exposed to the same problems. These include the problems of the market, but it has to be recognised that unless educational institu-tions are financially supported by government, or other foundations, their social costs might be higher than managers of some other forms of business organisa-tion would anticipate. But these final reflections on the nature of distance educa-tion pose other ethical problems of the educational market and these are discussed in the following chapter.

# Chapter Ten

# Learning and the market place of knowledge

> Much adult education will never know itself as such, and will be recognized only by leaders and teachers of real insight. It will go on in clubs, churches, cinemas, theatres, concert rooms, trades unions, political societies, and in the homes of people where there are books, newspapers, music, wireless sets, workshops, gardens – and groups of friends. But it will have its impetus in our more definitively organized agencies of education – Schools, Colleges, and Universities, WEA branches, Adult Schools, Women's Institutes, YMCAs and YWCAs and Settle-ments. The need is that these should realize the possibilities of it, and set themselves to foster it and minister to it.
>
> (Yeaxlee, 1929, p155)

This rather long opening quotation is taken from one of the very first books to have been written specifically about lifelong education – for that is its title and it was published in 1929. In these words are both the insights and aspirations of the early scholar of adult education: insights which have come to fruition in ways that his aspirations would neither have foreseen nor wanted. Indeed, the adjuncts of education, as he saw them, have become part of something much more complex and have now to be seen as independent providers of learning themselves rather than as appendages of the educational system. But then Yeaxlee was writing in a different age and reflecting a different culture than the one about which this book is written.

The thesis of this chapter is that learning has become a lifelong process and learning materials have become commodities which are sold in the market place, which raise profound questions of an ethical nature for educators since the market knows no compassion and caters only for those who are able to function financially within it. In order to lay the foundation for this argument it is necessary first to explore the changing nature of knowledge and, thereafter, to examine the ethical implications of this position.

## The changing nature of knowledge

While the history of the university can be traced back at least to the medieval period (Boyd and King, 1964), there is another sense in which education is a peculiarly modern phenomenon and, certainly, the growth of education as we know it today is a product, or an epiphenomenon, of the modernity project. Modernity, as we have already suggested, is typified by an emphasis on scientific knowledge, empiricism, rationality, universality, individualism, secularism and progress. Thus it was that as a result of the Enlightenment, Western society reflected many of these values at a time when its power was dominant and its culture regarded as having reached the apex of civilisation. These were also the values embraced by the intellectuals who were, to some extent, the guardians of a culture that supported the power of the modern state. However, there was a gradual dissolution of the bond between the intellectuals and the modern state for, as Bauman (1992, p14) argues, the political technology 'developed by the modern state was soon to render the legitimizing services of the intellectuals increasingly redundant; or reduce them to a subordinate role. . .', although it will be argued later that this legitimising force may be finding a new expression in late modern society. Bauman goes on the qualify his claim since intellectuals have not suffered too much material inconvenience, nor have they lost their freedom of thought, although it might be argued that even this has been under attack in the United Kingdom during the 1980s.

However, the decline in the status of the intellectual is reflected in the declining status of universities, with the movement towards a system of mass higher education in UK and lifelong learning. This form of education reflects a later form of society which, for the sake of convenience, is referred to here as late modern. Late modern society has lost some of its emphasis on some of those values which marked modernity, such as scientific knowledge, empiricism, rationality and progress, and the power of the state has itself declined with the dominance of global technological capitalism. Indeed, the nature of knowledge itself has undergone change and four major changes are suggested in the remainder of this section. Knowledge is now regarded as: relative (almost narrative); its rational basis has changed; its modes of transmission have altered; it has become a marketable commodity.

### The relativity of knowledge

When Lyotard (1984) wrote *The Post-Modern Condition* he claimed that all knowledge had become narrative, but later (1992, p31) he recognised that he had over-emphasised his position and he now thinks that different forms of knowledge have to be recognised, even though he still considers some forms of scientific knowledge to be narrative. The point about a great deal of narrative is that it reflects the dominant theories of the day and, as is now widely recognised, the prevailing received knowledge does appear to change with great rapidity.

The question might well be posed about the extent to which there is unchanging scientific knowledge, and clearly nobody is going to reject the idea that there are some universal and unchanging laws of nature, although it has been recognised that these are much less frequent than was previously claimed. Advances in scientific research do tend to modify prevailing theories and this has also come to be rather taken for granted; new discoveries reveal more about phenomena than was previously known; new technological advances mean that what was impossible a year or two ago now becomes possible and tomorrow becomes the everyday. Scientific knowledge, therefore, has become recognised as relative and its validity can always be questioned, and other evidence produced to refute or recast a current theory. Academics who previously legislated on what was correct knowledge have now become interpreters in a world of new knowledge (Bauman, 1992) and, perhaps, legitimators of learning.

Other disciplines, such as the social sciences, have tried to be scientific in their approach and as they have approximated to the scientific, they have discovered that there are myths about the claims about the nature of scientific knowledge. Indeed, it is perhaps significant that the term 'learning' is sometimes preferred to 'knowledge' since the latter term implies a finitude, or an end-product, while the former suggests that what is known is only partial and that the progress of discovery is incomplete.

In the light of all these recent changes, it might be argued that there is surely a sense of optimism about the progress that is being achieved, but this is also far from the truth, for, as Fukuyama (1992, p4) suggests, the 'pessimism of the twentieth century stands in sharp contrast to the optimism of the previous one'; perhaps humankind has lost its way and its confidence – where is history going, and why should new knowledge be produced if it is only relative? This is a world in which old questions are being asked anew.

## The rational basis of knowledge

The birth of modernity brought with it an increasing emphasis on empiricism at the time of the Enlightenment. The traditional narratives about the world were being destroyed by the scientific discoveries and rational arguments of the age. The then new universities grew up in this age of modernity, often with the express intention of disseminating this new scientific knowledge to an eager population – the history of adult education is littered with mechanics' and scientific institutes, literary institutes and stories of many hundreds of people coming to lectures about recent scientific discoveries. Knowledge was regarded as empirically true and, therefore, valid. Empiricism was regarded as the basis on a great deal of this new knowledge and those who discovered it were the legislators of what was correct. The universities were in a position to pronounce on what was correct and true knowledge.

But now the basis of knowledge is changing. Increasingly it is becoming apparent that many statements about society are ideological rather than empirical, and claims about it seen to be discourse rather than factual. These may still be firmly based in reason although they are less possible to substantiate. Indeed, there has also been an increase in narratives about what society should be like, rather than what it is – more ethical studies and even a return to utopian studies (eg, Kumar, 1987; Levitas, 1990). In a sense, this is a response to the pessimism that Fukuyama described. Yet young people increasingly opt to study the humanities and social sciences – a symbol about life that the universities can hear only partially because of the strident demands of the complex commercial system, reinforced by the state, which has become their master.

But there is another basis to knowledge that is now being accepted and this is clearly described by Lyotard (1984, p48), who argues that the knowledge that is taught by universities is now only socially legitimated by the criterion of the performability in the social system. This argument can be made for education and knowledge generally, so that although educators no longer have to produce an elite the production of skilled experts must be the outcome of learning, since:

> The transmission of knowledge is no longer destined to train an elite capable of guiding the nation towards its emancipation, but to supply the system with players capable of acceptably fulfilling their roles at the pragmatic posts required by the institution.

> (Lyotard 1984, p48)

He goes on to argue that once knowledge ceases to be an end in itself its transmission is no longer the exclusive responsibility of scholars and students – a point to which further reference will be made below. Knowledge is now based on pragmatism. This is not the place to explore the philosophy of pragmatism, but it might be claimed now that knowledge is legitimated by its utility. If something works, then it can be transmitted to others. However, the issue is perhaps deeper than this since universities are being urged to seek research funding from industry and commerce – the knowledge being produced is based on its perceived utility. Once produced, it has to be transmitted to those who need it, so that another new concept has become quite central to universities and colleges in recent years – continuing education. Continuing education used to be called 'adult education' and then there was a combination of terms such as 'adult and continuing education' and now the adult has been dropped from much common usage and 'continuing education' has become the accepted term. People need continuing education so that they can continue with their work, *etc.* Universities are also being increasingly asked to conduct an impact evaluation on what they are teaching – that is, the performance outcome in the organisation from which the students come. To a great extent, the validity of continuing education is pragmatic since its value depends on its impact on society.

## Transmission of knowledge

At the birth of modernity, there were basically two modes of knowledge transmission, spoken and written, and the universities were undertaking both. The lecture theatre was the locus for the transmission of learning and the publishing houses, with such illustrious names as Oxford and Cambridge, were the other major mode of knowledge transmission. When wireless became the third major mode, the universities were notably absent, as they were with the birth of television. Eventually, with the birth of the Open University in the United Kingdom, the universities tried to reclaim a place in the modern mode of knowledge transmission. Clearly, the Open University was a great success and its knowledge production is of a Fordist nature – mass production for a mass market, with some courses prepared for 100,000 students – and we have discussed this topic in the previous chapter. Significantly, questions are now being raised about post-Fordist methods of production, and perhaps there is a place here for the more traditional educational system in this late modern world of learning.

### Knowledge has become a marketable commodity

Knowledge, then, can now be packaged and marketed. It might not now be called teaching but learning packages, or learning materials, *etc*, are now familiar names. This is a knowledge-led society and knowledge has become a commodity that can be sold, like any other. However, it is even more important than many of the products on the market. Lyotard (1984, p5) wrote:

> Knowledge in the form of an informational commodity indispensable to productive power is already, and will continue to be, a major – perhaps *the* major – stake in the worldwide competition for power. It is conceivable that nation-states will one day fight for control of information, just as they battled in the past for control over territory. . .

The educational system now purveys knowledge but it is now part of a large complex scene in which it is rarely the largest player. Indeed, the transnational companies that are able to invest millions of dollars in the research and production of these means of transmitting knowledge are also able to invest the same amount in the research and development of knowledge itself. They are, therefore, able to produce their own learning materials and market them to whosoever will purchase.

The educational system still to a large extent relies on local and instantaneous transmission of knowledge, *ie*, the learners have to be present when the lecture is delivered although they are slowly moving to other forms of open and distance learning, but the new market has both space-time distanciation (Giddens, 1990) and space-time compression (Harvey, 1989): knowledge can be transmitted and learned not at the teachers' convenience but at the learners'. This can be done worldwide and instantaneously since the market is now global, *etc*.

Knowledge, then, is an important, relative commodity that is being marketed by many different organisations. Its basis has changed and become more pragmatic, and the culture of late/post modernity is one where there are ample opportunities to acquire such learning packages and opportunities. Having laid the foundations, it is now important to examine the place of higher education in lifelong learning.

## Lifelong learning

The status of knowledge has been changed in the culture of late modernity. Indeed, the concept of knowledge has itself been challenged to a considerable extent, and now 'learning' is perhaps a more correct term. However, neither the concept of learning nor its relation to education have been fully explored, so that this part consists of three sub-sections – the first examines the concept of learning, the second relates it to the institution of education and the final one draws together the threads of the argument and suggests that one relationship between learning and education is that of legitimation of learning, but not its legislation, although these institutions can easily award their own sign of success. A return is also made to this topic in the final chapter of the book.

## Learning

Educationalists have tended to have had a restricted understanding of learning, one which probably stemmed from the earliest experiments into learning – those of Pavlov and, later, of the behaviourists and the Gestalt theorists. In a sense, all of them highlighted the fact that the lower animals needed some form of teaching in order to learn. Hence, limited definitions of learning, such as learning being 'any more or less permanent change in behaviour which is the result of experience' (Borger and Seaborne, 1966, p14) have become prevalent in the literature, and in everyday thinking about it. Such definitions also reflected the scientific approach to knowledge that was discussed above. However, it has been more widely recognised in recent years, especially since Dewey (1916), that learning is more than a change in behaviour and that it is perhaps more basic than that suggested by the behaviourists. Interactionists, for instance, regard learning as the process of transforming all experiences of the human being throughout the whole of life.

I (Jarvis, 1992), for instance, suggested that learning is the process of transforming experience into knowledge, skills, attitudes, values, emotions and the senses, and I would now want to extend this slightly to suggest that beliefs need to be included as well and that experience is created or recreated rather than just apprehended. The human being is, therefore, essentially a learned phenomenon. Learning is possible whenever human beings do not take their experiences for granted, and when people seek to respond to any disjuncture that occurs between their experiences and biographies. Obviously, in times of rapid social change it is less possible to presume on experiences than ever before – everything about society seems to be undergoing change and so the conditions for continuous learning are present – indeed, the conditions for a learning society have been created by the rapidity of social change and the ensuing relativity of knowledge. The type of learning society which has emerged, however, is a far cry from the idealistic type of society envisaged by Yeaxlee (1929) and Hutchins (1970) and other humanistic thinkers. For them, the learning society would be a humanised, democratic society offering part-time education to all adults during their leisure. For them, it was effectively a benign educative society.

While the late modern age has created a situation where learning is the norm, it is also clear that there is a reaction against this. People like stability and there is a sense in which they like conformity. Indeed, the market has already recognised this, so that there is a conformity in sales – shopping centres have the same shops and the same designs, every McDonald's burger is the same, *etc.* (Ritzer, 1993). Individuals learn to conform and then merely to repeat what they have learned and from which actions they learn nothing new. Non-learning is something that people apparently want, so that it should not be assumed that the learning society has no stability within it – indeed, learning is a paradoxical phenomenon (Jarvis, 1992).

Thus far, learning and non-learning have been viewed as individual processes in which experiences are transformed or repeated. The word 'learning' is treated here as a verb – but it was suggested above that the word has other connotations, one of which is that, as a noun, it means the sum total of what has been learned – by either society as a whole or by individuals. Society's learning is cultural and transmitable. However, the term 'learning' carries no inference about what has been learned being correct or legitimate in any manner and, merely that it has been acquired in some way, so that it carries none of the connotations of 'knowledge'. Moreover, it does not imply that there has been a teacher or an educational system.

Significantly, however, the learner may be regarded as the consumer of cultural knowledge, who is also at the end of the value chain, as economists would call it (Kyrö,1995). However, such a value chain might be said to reflect the marketable value of the learning rather than any ethical value. To have the knowledge is perhaps more important in this society than being the appropriate person, since the end is often more important than the means.

## Learning and education

In a great deal of literature these two terms are treated as synonymous, reflecting the restricted ideas about learning – such phrases as 'adult learning' frequently mean 'adult education'; and 'lifelong education' and 'lifelong learning' are used in precisely the same way. However, it can be seen that there is a major distinction between them, and for the purposes of this book 'education' is regarded as 'an institutionalised process of teaching and learning' and it is suggested that an institutionalised system of lifelong education is hardly possible and certainly not desirable in society.

Education may be viewed as a social system within society providing learning opportunities for those who enrol within it. The state demands that young children be educated to a certain age and beyond that there is a degree of freedom since it is abdicating its responsibility beyond a specified age. Education is an expensive provision in this contemporary world and the point at which its responsibility is being relinquished is insufficient to equip many young people for their occupation, especially throughout the whole of their working life. They need to continue in education not only to the level of a first degree but increasingly to that of a taught Master's qualification, which is becoming the norm for many of the high-status professions. But even this is not sufficient to last for the whole of working life since knowledge is changing and growing at such a rapid rate; and so continuing education has become a major concern of all institutions of higher and further education. Yet many industrial companies, especially the smaller ones, are finding it difficult to release their staff for continuing education courses in campus-based universities, so that universities are having to find other ways of purveying their products and a variety of distance education courses are beginning to emerge. Now the emphasis is upon the learner and learning.

Education is an institutionalised process of learning, but educational institutions have not had the capital to research into all the ways through which culturally accepted knowledge can be transmitted, and neither do they have a monopoly in offering knowledge for people to learn. As Yeaxlee pointed out there are other adjuncts to education, but now they are no longer adjuncts. They are partners or competitive providers in the same market. It is now possible to purchase face-to-face courses from a variety of providers and it is also increasingly easy to buy videos, computer-based learning, interactive compact video discs, *etc*, all providing opportunities to learn. Soon, with the Internet, it will be possible to access information stored on computers throughout the world and cable will enable everybody who has the basic equipment to gain access to a vast number of learning opportunities. Lifelong learning is an ever-increasing reality and opportunities for learning far exceed those that the educational institutions can provide – there are many purveyors of learning materials in the market of late modernity but higher education is only one of them. Universities may seek to provide opportunities for lifelong education, but the conditions exist whereby individuals may purchase opportunities for learning throughout their lives.

## Legitimation of learning

Thus far it has been argued that learning has become a marketable commodity and that education is but one purveyor of learning materials, often by one of the least cost efficient ways of selling it, although that does not imply that it is one of the least popular. Certainly, the desire for personal contact with a teacher, or teacher assistant, is something that many learners appear to desire. Even the Open University, with its excellent publications and use of the media, still finds a great demand for the tutorial. Personal contact remains an important element in teaching and learning, at least with this generation who have not been brought up in such an impersonal society. Whether interactive technological media will take its place with future generations remains an unknown at the present time. Certainly the nature of teaching will have to change as the emphasis is placed on the marketing of learning materials.

However, the market is a complex phenomenon – it is not just a matter of supply and demand, which is the rationality of modernity and one which does not reflect the realities of a late modern society. Marketing is about selling brand names and signs. Indeed, Baudrillard (cited from 1988, p22) highlights this in his discussion of consumption in *The System of Objects*:

> Consumption is *the virtual totality of all objects and message presently constituted in a more or less coherent discourse.* Consumption, in so far as it is meaningful, is *a systematic act of the manipulation of signs.*
>
> (Italics in the original)

Baudrillard has argued that for phenomena to become objects of consumption, they must become signs. It is at this point that the educational system currently has a great advantage over other purveyors of learning – it has an established and widely recognised system of signs, which are the educational qualifications. It is these that educational institutions can advertise in the market place. An advertisement appeared in a national UK daily paper (*Guardian*, 19 October, 1993) which had these words: 'If you have paid for your training – make sure you get your receipt'. Underneath the caption was a picture of a National Vocational Qualification certificate – Level 3!

Educational qualifications demonstrate that the learning which has been undertaken is legitimate and that it is recognised as such. The qualification has become a currency in the market for occupation and possession of such a qualification demonstrates that the individual has the necessary learning to undertake the work. But jobs are changing and becoming more complex. Knowledge, since it is relative, is rapidly dated by new discoveries. Additional signs are required by the market: potential candidates for work must have the recent knowledge necessary to undertake the work. Qualifications become outdated and new ones are required. A new phenomenon is emerging – qualification inflation – for the Bachelor's degree and then the Master's degree becomes devalued and the taught doctorate will become the new sign of a well-qualified professional.

Higher education, therefore, can legitimate learning throughout the whole of life. At the present moment, educational institutions hold a monopoly in the United Kingdom when it comes to legitimating learning, but the question has to be asked for how long this will continue. Already there are commercial organisations which award their own qualifications. As Eurich (1985, p85) notes:

> A new development on the scene of business and education is the growing number of corporate colleges, institutes, or universities that grant their own degrees. It is the Rand PhD, the Wang or Arthur D. Little Master of Science degree. No longer the purview of established educational institutions alone, accredited academic degrees are being awarded increasingly by companies and industries that have created their own separate institutions and successfully passed the same educational hurdles used to accredit traditional higher education.

If this development, which has already started in UK in a co-operative manner, continues it might not be long before corporate educational institutions are marketing cultural knowledge for educational qualifications in the same manner as they are in the United States. Higher education must recognise that lifelong learning opportunities are being provided by other institutions, and that the commodification of knowledge means that higher education may well be competing to provide learning opportunities with institutions whose record in commodity production is much better attuned to the market. Perhaps they will have to discover that there are niche markets and that the relativity of modern knowledge is not conducive to Fordist modes of production, so that in a post-Fordist age of production they have a significant role to play, albeit in co-operation with other providers.

In contrast, a grey market is emerging in which the transmission of cultural knowledge is undertaken in voluntary organisations, like the University of the Third Age, for learning's sake and without any form of accreditation. Its emphases are different and reflect many of the aspirations of those early thinkers about the learning society – but they will stand as a symbol of what learning without the capitalist market might have been. It is now necessary to explore the nature of the market and its morality.

## The nature of the market

There are at least two ways of looking at the market: that proposed by Schumpeter (1976) and the neo-classical model. Schumpeter (1976), writing in 1943, regarded competition as a force for change; competitors in the market have to be efficient, changing both production processes and products in order to sell commodities in the face of their rivals' efforts. Schumpeter argued that producers would go out of business if they were not efficient and, consequently, we have witnessed governments arguing that 'lame duck' companies should 'go to the wall'.

We have witnessed the validity of his claims in education since it has changed its methods of providing courses eg, distance education, flexi-study, etc, and in the wide variety of new courses being produced at every level. Schumpeter argues that this process is conducive to efficiency and quality. With the production of many commodities we have seen the truth of these claims, although the concept of quality is more problematic, since it is not possible to reduce labour costs where the quality of a product depends upon the amount of time put into its production. A work of art, for example, will not achieve the same quality if an artist fails either to put time into technique or to ensure that the finishing touches are made to the painting. Neither can a nursing process be performed adequately without the nurse spending time with the patient – although some present policies towards the health service seem to assume otherwise! But neither can a really good educational course be produced without the scholarship of its author(s) or teacher(s) and this takes time.

The second model of the market is the neo-classical one, which suggests that in perfect competition the commodity demand for goods will equal supply, and that in these cases the price of the commodity will stabilise (Arrow, 1974). If, however, there is greater demand for a commodity than its supply, then the price will rise, and the price will fall if there is an over-supply. This means that suppliers have to judge their price by the demand factor in the market. If suppliers have to bring their prices down in order either to meet the competition or to survive, then the production costs have to fall. This is also increasingly happening in education, especially in a wider market where educational providers are competing for students, in both local and global markets.

Educational providers are clearly functioning in a learning market, competing not only with each other but increasingly with other providers of learning materials and qualifications. At least three things emerge from this that need discussion here: the nature of the commodity being sold and the cost of the production process and, therefore, its quality; the competitive nature of the market and the educational needs of the learners.

## Nature of the commodity and the cost of the production process

It is clear from the above discussion that the nature of the commodity being sold is no longer self-evident: it might be the qualification or the learning process. What is clear, however, is that recognition of this is important, since if it is the qualification being sold, then it matters less if the production techniques have not been quite so thorough or the quality has fallen a little, in order to make the price more competitive. This is clearly seen with MBA courses, which have tradition-ally taken two years but which are now being reduced to as little as 10 months. Bickerstaffe (1997, p14) records how fast-track, or crash, courses have been introduced and he notes that students 'tend to be less concerned with self-development and the pursuit of academic interests, and more with getting back to work'. They are also appreciative of 'the lower cost of studying'. He goes on to suggest that 'there is probably little to choose between the two lengths of courses' and he claims, with little evidence and no specified criteria, that both 'provide an excellent education'. Finally, he says that 'what they are willing, or able, to pay are likely to be the determining factors'. In other words, the MBA is the com-modity and the price is a determining factor.

On the other hand, if the learning process is what is being sold, then the amount of tutor availability, time taken to study/reseach the materials being taught, the number of students being taught at the same time, the type of educational provision (face-to-face or distance) are all factors in the process, and part of the commodity itself. These, however, are often extremely expensive and have relatively fixed costs so that if the quality of the teaching/ teaching materials provided for the learners is to be high then the commodity cost will be fixed and high.

Consequently, it is necessary to reduce tutor-time on face-to-face courses and this is being undertaken in many ways, some of which educators of adults applaud, but the reasons for their introduction may be less laudable. I have already referred to the fact that self-directed learning is becoming more prevalent – in itself it helps retain the autonomy of the learner and is, therefore, commendable. But it might be being introduced introduced as a form of self-help learning (see Ritzer, 1993), when it is seen as reducing the production costs and making the process more efficient! In the same way, the great majority of educators welcome the introduction of Accreditiation of Prior Learning and the Accreditation of Prior Experiential Learning. These are both processes for which adult educators fought to get into the educational system for many years because we wanted to have adults' learning and experience recognised. But remission of time from a course both reduces the amount of tutor contact and makes the course financially more attractive to, but by no means all, potential students. In other words APL and APEL sometimes become synonymous with SALE – commodities on sale here cheaply and so come and purchase! In this case we see, once again, the significance of the markets for the processes that are occurring in education.

High quality educational materials are not necessarily cheap and if they are exposed to the competition of the market, the quality might fall in some instances. In this case, it is a matter of seeing two cultural values juxtaposed, efficiency and quality, and recognising that the dominant value – efficiency – reflects the ideology of advanced capitalism, and that it is fundamentally an ideology rather than a value! It does appear that this is actually happening in education, despite vehement denials from many interested parties.

## Nature of the market

The market might engender efficiency but, it must be asked, is economic efficiency synonymous with good education? The answer must be in the negative. I am not, therefore, encouraging the inefficient production of educational materials, but I am arguing here that adoption of economic market principles does not automatically result in high quality education. This is tacitly recognised by the educational institutions by the introduction of quality assurance and quality control mechanisms. But there are two other features of the market that need to be touched upon here: if a producer is unable to compete in one market, then new markets have to be found and, secondly, only those who can afford to purchase the commodities actually buy them. Consequently, there has been a growth in distance education abroad and the search for new markets at home, *eg*, expanding the age range for each educational offering – older adults on the university campus, *etc*. But it also means that many people who do not have the financial means necessary to purchase them will be denied them, but this is something that the welfare state was more able to do – offer educational opportunity to those who could not otherwise afford it! Indeed, there is no room for any kind of moral concern in the market whatsoever. This is a point well made about the Third World in an excellent chapter by Hall (1996) in a book that looks at adult education from a Third World perspective.

## Educational needs of the learners

Education is now no longer about learning needs but learning demands – but what of those learning needs? Clearly governments have recognised this and have begun to introduce schemes which enable potential students to borrow money, *etc*, in order to pay for their education, on the assumption that having gained the educational qualification the students will get a better job and be able to pay back the loan. But not all education, especially for adults, is vocationally orientated. Neither should it be – but the cost of the commodity is too great for some who might wish to participate. Some Educational Authorities have introduced voucher schemes in order to help individuals join adult education (see Jarvis, *et al*, 1997), while other voucher schemes actually tend to 'ration' the amount of education that can be received, *etc*. But underlying this debate is another issue – the extent to which education is a human right or entitlement and, if so, how much education in the lifetime should be provided freely?

Article 26 of the *Declaration of Human Rights* specified that everybody has the right to education, but having provided some free schooling, governments might claim that they had fulfilled their obligations under this Article, and that it does not apply to lifelong education. This type of response gave rise to the discussions in the 1970s about recurrent education, in which it was claimed that people had a right to a specified amount of education beyond compulsory schooling. The concept of recurrent education disappeared into obscurity with the advent of continuing education and with it went the idea of an educational entitlement.

Nevertheless, not all people achieve their full potential as a result of their initial education and a part of the tradition of adult education has been that it reaches out to those whose potential might be developed through education and offers another route by which this may be done. There is, however, no place in the marketplace of education for this form of outreach. Indeed, there is no place in the market for welfare! The market caters for those who have rather than those who have not – and the educational market is doing likewise.

Education, as we know it, embodied many of the cultural values of the Enlightenement, but today even some of these cultural values are taking second place to the ideology of advanced capitalism. In addition, the universal value reflected in teachers being available to students and relating to them because they are faces who have impinged upon their spontaneity can only occur within the context of already overloaded teaching timetables as educational institutions seek to lower the production costs of education. The universal value is manifest in those dedicated teachers who give much time over and above that for which the educational institution pays them and, ironically enough, often recues the reputation of the educational institution and encourages the policy makers to continue to exploit the moral teachers for the ends of the market.

## Conclusion

This chapter has argued that education has become a marketable commodity and that the market has no place for welfare or the common good. But this concern to respond to the educational needs of the underprivileged is part of the tradition of adult education which might be beginning to disappear at the present time. Indeed, the cultural values of education are being swallowed up within the advanced capitalist system. However, the universal value of concern within human relationships is still being manifested between teachers and students. Paradoxically, those who put their concerns into practice, and go the extra mile, enable their institutions to retain their good reputations without paying for it. The dedication of these teachers actually reinforces the market system.

It is now necessary to explore this relationship between the process and the product a little further. This is undertaken in the following chapter.

# Chapter Eleven

# Being and having

In the previous chapter, the distinction between the educational process and the educational qualification was deliberately drawn; it was argued that the educational market is forcing a situation where the product being sold, the qualification, is taking precedence over the learning process. Indeed, the learning market brings to the fore the distinction between being and having – something that I have explored previously (Jarvis, 1992, pp143–54) and what follows is a revision of that argument. In the first part of the chapter this distinction is explored, in the second it is related to learning and in the third part to education. Finally, there is a concluding discussion.

## The distinction between being and having

The human body is born into this world as a physical phenomenon, a biological mechanism, and as such has its own needs. As infants begin to develop they reach out for things, and these attempts to possess actually occur before the formation of their self. Maslow (1968) places these needs at the lower end of his hierarchy. Once the distinction between body and mind is drawn in this way, though, it is difficult to sustain the idea that a hierarchy exists at all, since his five levels fall into two distinct categories. The lower ones are *having* needs, whereas the higher two are *being* needs. In a similar manner, Fromm (1976, p12) differentiated between them:

> In the having mode of existence my relationship with the world is one of possessing and owning, one in which I want to make everybody and everything, including myself, my property. . .
> In the being mode of existence, we must identify two forms of being. One is in contrast to *having*. . .and means aliveness and authentic relatedness to the world. The other form of being is in contrast to *appearing* and refers to the true nature, the true reality of a person or a thing in contrast to deceptive appearances.

Not surprisingly, the being mode has been regarded as a higher order than having. Human beings, then, are situated in a body that has physical needs, the satisfaction of which are necessary in order to exist, though the being and having modes are not totally opposed to each other. There is a complex interdependency between them. But during most of the following discussion, we will treat the two modes as antithetical to illustrate their differences without presupposing that one of more significant than the other.

The having mode is self-explanatory in many ways, but a number of important points needs to be made about it. We consider five briefly.

First, for the mind and the self to begin to emerge from the body, communicative relationships must exist between the young baby and other human beings. These relationships are of crucial importance to the growth of the human essence. Indeed, the significance of this human relationship has already been discussed earlier in this book in respect of the non-cognitive learning of the universal value through relationship, since young children experience the care of their significant others. The relationship through which the universal value is learned occurs as much through the caring of the body as it does through the moulding of the mind.

Second, the having mode attaches significance to things that have existence but not being, or if the phenomena actually have being, they are treated as if they are objects (Buber, 1961). Hence to treat persons as objects to be taught (I-It relationship) is to dehumanise them and to treat them as if they merely have existence, which destroys the potential for a dynamic relationship between persons.

Third, as Marcel (1976) points out, having always implies some act that is already over when the thing came into the possession of the one who possesses it, but being is an ever-present, a living, phenomenon. Having the qualification, then, indicates that the process of learning has been completed!

Fourth, possession lies at the heart of contemporary Western civilisation and is a fundamental assumption of capitalist economies. A person who possesses many things is often given high status – including those who possess many educational qualifications! Advertising encourages people to purchase commodities that they do not need, and conspicuous consumption is a major feature of the system. This way of life has become deeply ingrained. Any other set of values has come to be regarded as deviant, if not wrong. There is a certain irony in the fact that capitalism will not function unless there is a flow of money and a continual purchasing of new commodities, because its own philosophy is grounded in the having mode.

Fifthly, possession invariably affects the possessor in some ways. Macquarrie (1973, pp87–8), summarising Marcel's work, writes:

> To have something is not just to stand in an external relationship to is. The very having of something affects the person who has it. He becomes anxious about it and instead of having it, it begins, so to speak, to have him. There is a real danger to our humanity as the world becomes increasingly industrialised, computerised, automated . . . Rising affluence brings new dangers. It leads to the acquisitive society, the rat race, the infinite desire to possess. In its relation to the world, as in so many other aspects, human existence finds itself at the centre of a tension and must survive in the face of opposing pressures.

The body does have needs and these must be satisfied. The having mode is important for human existence, but contemporary Western society has over-emphasised its importance, which enables the capitalist system to function effectively. The tension indicated in the preceding quotation between the human being and the cultural values of the contemporary world perhaps indicates that there should be a critical relationship between the two, and that the taken-for-granted, presumptive response to the world as we know it may not always be in the best interests of humanity. The culture into which people are socialised and the cultural values which dominate society are biased in favour of those who exercise power and consequently towards those who support the current system. Hence, reflective, critical learning is necessary in people's relationship with the world, though the paradox is that people seek to exist in harmony with their world.

Having, or possessing, can therefore be detrimental in some respects. But, by contrast, being refers to experience – something that cannot be possessed and retained since it occurs at a particular time and then survives as a memory. Though people sometimes try to capture, or recapture, an experience they invariably fail since they are attempting to ensnare being within having. All experiences of being offer the opportunity of learning and growing, and all shared experiences offer the opportunity for the manifestation of universal value. Being then is about active involvement in experience, through which I might engage with the Other. Being is about being alive, and in that sense always about becoming. There is always more human potential to be realised and more relationships with others into which individuals might enter through which they might both express and experience the universal value of concern for the Other in mutual relationship.

Being and having are, in sum, two very different approaches to life, and their emphases diverge in many ways. Because of the nature of contemporary society, having often seems to predominate, as we demonstrated in the previous chapter. This is true even in the use of language, as will become apparent in the next part of this chapter. However, it will be recalled from the fifth chapter that learning is at the heart of human being itself and so it will be useful to examine it within a society which emphasises having.

## Being, having and learning

Mind and self are learned phenomena (Jarvis, 1987, 1992, 1995) and so learning is at the centre of the process of growth. As was pointed out above, the learning that is involved in being is active, participative, and reflective. Gadamer (1976, p50) suggests that 'understanding . . . cannot be grasped as a simple activity of the consciousness that understands, but is itself a mode of the event of being'. Learners engage in a relationship with the world, with their teachers, in both primary and secondary experiences and in informal, non-formal and formal situations. They bring their own biographies to the teaching and learning situation and enter a participative dialogue and a moral relationship; in the learning relationship the learners' knowledge, skills, attitudes, senses, emotions, *etc*, become fused with those of the teachers, and of other learners. The same considerations apply outside the formal classroom situations and as individuals learn, so they grow and develop. In discussion with others, they try to establish an active, constructive relationship from which everyone benefits. As people learn, so their knowledge becomes part of their being and their experience, and they have no need to display their expertise. Others, in dialogue, will acknowledge that expertise and give credit where it is due. Authorities do not need to demonstrate that they have the knowledge, for it is part of their being and others recognise it. They do not have to display that they have it!

There is a profound difference between knowing and having knowledge in the learning situation. It is the difference between active participation in the process of creating knowledge, on the one hand, and digesting what others transmit, on the other. Having knowledge can imply having a certificate in such and such a field. We see this in other ways in the educational process – students take notes during sessions rather than engaging in the active discussion through which knowledge is generated. Students have books and seek confirmation from authorities that they possess the correct knowledge. Indeed, they seek handouts during sessions, so that they know that they have to learn. When business people attend a seminar, they have to be given the knowledge in expensively produced folders, so that they can see that they have value for money. Having got the lecture notes or the handout, the learners might seek to memorise them, inwardly digesting – or consuming them! For the educational commodity is now being marketed in a consumer society.

Knowing, then, can be used in the sense of 'having knowledge' – as if it is a commodity. It is this which Marcel (1976, p83) condemns when he suggests that having is always about assimilation. He writes (1976, p145) that:

> knowing is a mode of having. The possession of a secret. Keeping it, disposing of it – and here we get back to. . . the 'shewable.' The absolute possession of a secret or a mystery – mystery being by its very essence I cannot dispose of. Knowledge, as a mode of having, is essentially communicable.

Students expect to take possession of what the teacher expounds, or the author has written, and communicate it back at the examination. Teachers sometimes encourage this approach; they see themselves as the fount of wisdom and demand that the students learn and regurgitate what they have. But in exercising the authority of their position, they *have* authority rather than *are* the authority.

Educators of adults are frequently confronted with the results of this process, and sometimes facilitate it. Learners appear to be only happy when they have something tangible from their learning experience – something that they can digest. I am not suggesting here that teachers should not produce handouts, *etc*. Far from it – it is an essential element in a great deal of teaching – but we have to beware of the students' need to consume and sometimes we have to move into the being mode!

## Education as having or being

Throughout this book, I have claimed that education is a social institution which reflects the cultural values of late modern society. But education involves the institutionalisation of learning; from this standpoint we might expect it to encourage the being mode. It is, in short, trapped in a dilemma: will it emphasise the having or the being mode? It is argued here that it tends to adopt the rhetoric of being but the practices of having, and that this is inevitable because of its institutional status.

Some writers clearly distinguish between the two types of education – one orientated toward being and the other toward having (Jarvis, 1985). With respect to the latter approach, Freire (1972, pp45–46) offers these disparaging remarks:

> Narration (with the teacher as narrator) leads the students to memorize mechanically the narrated content. Worse still, it turns them into 'containers', into receptacles to be filled by the teacher. The more completely he fills the receptacles, the better the teacher he is. The more meekly the receptacles permit themselves to be filled, the better students they are.

> Education thus becomes an act of depositing, in which students are the depositories and the teacher the depositor. Instead of communicating, the teacher issues communiqués and 'makes deposits' which the students patiently receive, memorize and repeat.

As 'depositories' they are then assessed to discover if they have actually retained the material. If they can repeat it non-reflectively, but correctly, they are judged successful – see the following chapter for further discussion on this.

The final step is the awarding of credits and certificates. Modern society demands that courses culminate in credentials that demonstrate to the world that the learners have acquired specific knowledge and skills. Without the proper certificates, students cannot continue to the next level of education – becoming imprisoned in a global classroom (Illich and Verne, 1976) – or cannot obtain work. Because of the educational market, certification has developed enormous importance, and education sells its wares (certificated courses) in the market place. Fake certificates are also cashing in; there is a market for bogus qualifications and fake certificates, often purchased at exorbitant prices from pseudo-educational institutions. Even the most respectable of universities have to award certificates for the shortest of courses so that, through the mechanism of credit transfer, students can construct portfolios of awards to demonstrate to a sceptical world the amount of knowledge and skill that they have. Even if they have forgotten it or have rarely used it, it does not matter – all that counts is that they have the certificate. The certificate is the currency of this market!

This is not a diatribe against certification; it is a criticism of the abuse of what might be a necessary system in education. Learning occurs in a private sphere, and society is to some extent anonymous and depersonalised. People move between locations and occupations. How can applicants for a place on a course or a job be assessed when they are not known? References can be written about the person, but they cannot tell the whole story. How can potential students determine the value of courses that they want to take, unless there is a reputable certificate at the end? Public certification is a guarantee of something – even if it is only that the learners attended a reputable educational institution, or that they once possessed the knowledge and skill, or that they were given the opportunity to gain them by taking specific courses. Certification, then, might be important for education in the being mode as well, because the privatisation of learning and the anonymity of the public world provide almost no other way of recording and communicating learning experiences.

However, we have witnessed government policy in the United Kingdom which has endeavoured to impose certificated outcomes to all educational courses. It is as if the government now sees the labour market as a market of certificated persons competing for jobs, and that education is merely the process of providing fodder for this market. Education, then, is being interpreted in the having mode, although there is often the rhetoric of the being one. Since the government in the United Kingdom will fund only certificated education, learning for learning's sake – a manifestation of the being mode assumes a less significant place in government policy.

Freire (1972, pp56–7) has this to say about education in the being mode:

> Problem-posing education affirms men as beings in the process of becoming – as unfinished, uncompleted beings in and with a likewise unfinished reality. Indeed, in contrast to other animals who are unfinished but not historical, men know themselves to be unfinished; they are aware of their incompleteness. In this incompleteness and this awareness lie the very roots of education as an exclusively human manifestation. The unfinished character of men and the tranformational character of reality necessitate that education be an on-going reality.

RS Peters (1965, p110) offers a similar view of education but with less emphasis on the relationship between the participants in the process:

> Education . . .can have no ends beyond itself. Its value derives from principles and standards implicit within it. To be educated is not to have arrived at a destination; it is to travel with a different view. What is required is not the feverish preparation for something that lies ahead, but to work with precision, passion, and taste at worthwhile things that lie ahead.

Peters certainly related his understanding of education to the quality of life for he continues, on the same page, about education providing 'that touch of eternity under which endurance can pass into dignified, wry acceptance, and animal enjoyment into a quality of living.'

The educational process must, therefore, involve the opportunity to enter dialogical relationship in which human beings communicate and share experiences. Herein lies the potentiality for the manifestation of universal moral value – which Levinas (1969) points to by using the term 'infinity'. Significantly, vocational training courses may also be viewed in precisely the same way, since they do not all rule out dialogical relationship, even if their objectives are more limited in scope. What mitigates against the dialogical relationship between students and students as well as between students and teachers and against the recognition that the process is about human becoming in relationship, is the desire of either the students, the teachers or their employers to view the process as a means to an end to be achieved in a specified time period. Let it be said immediately that the end-products are frequently far from wrong in themselves, and that specific educational and training courses should have ends which have relationship to the cultural values of society. But, as was pointed out earlier, having and being have a complex inter-relationship. The elevation of the end-product is teleological and utilitarian, reflecting the contemporary cultural values, but it is something which has logical weaknesses. Indeed, to lose sight of the learning process in education by looking only at an end-product is to downplay the being mode in human life. It is only when I am, when I have time to be, that I can relate to others and through dialogue create new knowledge.

## Concluding discussion

One of the most significant words in that last sentence is 'time' – if I have the 'time'. Yet many adult students on continuing professional education courses do not have the time; and employers cannot give their staff time from work because they cannot afford it in a global market which, in turn, exacerbates the competitive educational market in which providers offer shortened courses in order to compete with their rivals, *etc.* It is the shortest time to gain the qualification legitimately that becomes the order of the day. It is necessary to be realistic in this age: the market is not just internal to a single country; every company and industry is competing in a global market. So it seems to many managers that employees need to have the specific knowledge and skills for the benefit of their company, and they cannot waste time developing themselves at the expense of their employers through longer courses. This reflects the cultural value of efficiency but loses the universal value of people being with people, ready to enter a relationship – in this case an educative one – with others. To have the product is more important than to be enriched by the process!

Jacques Delors (1996) recently chaired a UNESCO commission into education which suggested that there are four learning pillars to education: learning to do, to know, to live with others and to be. For many, the educational process is about the first two; but learning to be and to be with others allows for the potentiality of the universal value to emerge, when I have time for the Other because the Other has impinged upon my spontaneity.

# Chapter Twelve

# Assessing students' work and evaluating curricula

Thus far we have examined the teaching and learning process without making reference to the assessment procedures, but this is a significant part of the process, one in which teachers exercise expertise and authority; it is, therefore, a moral process and one which we will examine here. In order to do so, it is first necessary to understand assessing and evaluating and this will comprise the main part of the chapter. It will be argued that assessors have to distinguish between the students' work and the students themselves in this process because students might identify themselves with the work being assessed. The chapter itself has four parts: the first discusses the relationship between measurement and assessment and evaluation; the following two relate this to the processes of assessing students' achievements and evaluation of courses or curricula; the fourth examines this discussion from a moral perspective.

## Is it a matter of degree?

Nearly everybody knows that there are 360 degrees in a circle and that it is possible to measure with great accuracy the number of degrees in a fraction of a circle, or an angle. By contrast, not everybody has associated this process with that of awarding degrees for academic work, but the degree refers to degrees of knowledge, *etc*. A degree is usually awarded at the end of a course and reflects an academic assessment of the students' achievements (rather than knowledge), and often at the end of the course the students are asked to evaluate the course on which they have studied. The distinction between assessment of students' work and the evaluation of courses is maintained in this paper but it is on the similarities of these processes that this chapter focuses. Both assessment and evaluation have some similarities to the process of measuring, although what they are endeavouring to measure is much more problematic and profoundly different. Indeed, one definition of 'to assess' is 'to estimate' and one of 'to evaluate' is 'to assess the worth of', and this paper discusses the underlying problems of trying to equate measurement with assessment and evaluation.

Most children learn how to use a protractor at school in order to measure or draw angles. They know that when they measure an angle for a second time, they should get the same result as they did the first, since the same angle is fixed and unchanging. If they want to be more accurate in their measurement they use a more sophisticated instrument. In the same manner if they want to measure distances accurately and precisely they can take a micrometer, and do so. A variety of micrometers, gauges and callipers, and even more accurate instruments exist, to allow the scientist to measure an external object with degrees of utmost precision. The phenomena that they measure, in these cases, are empirical and the measurements that they take can be replicated to ensure that they are correct. The measurement is of an objective phenomenon and is apparently objective knowledge, but more precisely, it is subjective knowledge about an objective phenomenon. In exactly the same way chemists can take any substance and analyse its contents and specify precisely its constitution. Once again, providing that the analysis is correct, the outcome will always be the same, since the substance is objective and unchanging – but the knowledge is still subjective.

There has been a significant confusion in measurement and its relation to knowledge that is evidenced in the above paragraph – because the phenomenon being measured is an empirical and objective thing, it has been assumed that knowledge about it is objective and external to the knower. But this is untrue, since it is the object which is external and nothing else. The fact that it is empirical and unchanging means that when it is measured, the measurement is always the same and this can be read from an instrument, learned, or memorised, without being altered by the differences of perception, perception itself being a human characteristic. It is as if the knowledge were external, although it is subjective knowledge about the same external unchanging phenomena.

Ever since the Enlightenment, at least, knowledge has been treated as apparently objective, and anything other has been regarded as less than scientific and, therefore, less valid. Having this high status has resulted in other academic disciplines seeking to produce similar forms of knowledge with the same degree of precision as the scientific measurement of external and objective phenomena. But this is not possible since the phenomena being measured are not objective, empirical and unchanging!

If an educator seeks to assess a student's academic work, such as an essay, it would look rather strange if the assessment read rather like this: the essay is 5,231 words long, has been printed in courier type face on 17 pages and 8 lines. But it is accurate, it is replicable and it is unchanging. It is an accurate measurement of an objective phenomenon. But it tells us little about the content or the standard – whatever that is!

However, when the scientists seek to account for their measurement, then there is some likelihood of disagreement between them, especially if the fundamental principles underlying the way that the phenomena function are not agreed upon. If there is agreement that certain physical laws apply to the phenomena then disagreement about explanations for the measurement might begin to disappear, since physical phenomena apparently tend to follow set laws. When the laws are unknown, however, the scientists' explanations are more likely to contain degrees of difference, but the significant point now is that they are not trying to measure the phenomenon but to explain it or account for its functioning.

When teachers mark essays, they are not trying to measure them; neither are they are looking at the constitution of the content of the phenomenon, such as 'this essay is constructed of 453 verbs, 657 nouns', *etc*. But they are examining the level of knowledge, the accuracy of its use, the power of the argument, *etc*. It matters not how accurate the marking scheme is, the assessment of the essay is now a matter of judgment – for there is nothing empirical in the essay to measure along these more traditional dimensions. It is now no longer a measurement of an objective phenomenon. The words are objective but their meaning is not – there is no way by which meaning and argument can be treated as objective. If different people view the words, then they will probably see the same thing and read the same words but when asked to provide a meaning to what they see they will probably begin to diverge. Indeed, research on reading itself by Marton and Saljö (1984) shows that different styles of reading result in different meanings being given to that which is read. The more sophisticated the interpretation, or meaning, given to the work, the more subjective is the assessment because the assessors are endeavouring to understand a problematic phenomenon from their own perception, understanding and knowledge. Indeed, reading an essay is an exercise in hermeneutics! It is no longer measurement! It has become something different but akin to it. However, the problem is exacerbated because the results of the assessment are recorded symbolically, *eg*, in the form of a percentage – 64%, or a grade – this is a 'B' essay, *etc*, because the symbols look like measurements.

The point about the grade is that it is a the symbol of a subjective assessment but once that complex assessment has been lost in the symbolic recording of the grade, it is treated as if it were an objective assessment of the essay, which it is patently not! Because many assessment processes seek to get agreement between at least two markers, it is as if the agreement constitutes an objective measurement rather than a general agreement of two or more subjective assessments. The grade objectifies the assessment process. People treat it as if it were objective, and that the knowledge is objective knowledge, so that an essay which has been assessed and graded a 'B', becomes a 'B' essay, *etc*. In fact this process is one of confusing a label with a measure!

Thus it appears that the assessment process has been a process of measurement, often with a statistical outcome, and that it is scientific. But the conclusions to this brief discussion must be that measurement can only occur when the phenomenon being measured is in some manner empirical; that this is usually external to the person undertaking the measurement; and that this need not be the case with assessment. Trying to emulate the apparently scientific has been an aim of all the social sciences – sociology, psychology and economics especially – but even the scientists are themselves beginning to recognise the limitations of their approach (see Miller 1995 for a scientist's critique of the scientific approaches). For education to copy the other social sciences is not only to do a disservice to education, it is to embark upon an outmoded process, since postmodern thinkers (*eg*, Lyotard, 1984) are beginning to question the validity of the Enlightenment perspectives, of which positivism is one. In addition, it constitutes a misunderstanding of the phenomena being assessed since meaning and argument are not objective and measurable. Additionally, it may be seen that the equation of measurement and assessment is a logical nonsense. If assessment is not measurement, it is necessary to ask precisely what it is.

## The nature of assessment and evaluation

Assessment is a normal part of any social interaction. Whenever a person is introduced to another person and thereafter spends some time in social intercourse with that person, the first individual is quite likely to comment afterwards: 'he's a nice guy' or 'she's really quite delightful', *etc*. These comments contain the essence of assessment – they are not measuring the person at all, not suggesting that the other is 5'8" tall and weighs 12 stone, *etc*, but they are evaluating various aspects about either the person or the interaction they had with the person. They are placing a value upon a phenomenon, something which cannot be measured because it is not objective, and in a rather problematic manner it is not actually factual. (This process was discussed earlier in the book since it reflects the emotivist position in moral philosophy.) The phenomena being assessed are ephemeral, they have neither substance nor presence. Consequently, the assessment may be illustrating that the first person enjoyed meeting the second, or was impressed by the other, *etc*, but this cannot be proved empirically. In any interaction, the Other makes an impression on the Ego and Ego's reaction is evaluative. However, the Other will meet other egos – will make other impressions and so people might agree or disagree about people, but their assessment of the Other might well be affected by what they already know about the Other from different sources. Assessment is quite subjective – but should there not be more objectivity in a professional's assessment of a student than this? It really does make the process pretty precarious if it relies solely on this form of appraisal! Clearly there are other factors to be taken into consideration, such as the professionalism of the assessor – but at its core, this is precisely what the process is about, and this is true for both assessment and evaluation. Consequently, it is now necessary to turn to the processes of assessing students and evaluating curricula.

In the first part of this chapter the idea of measurement was quite fully discussed and clearly there have been a number of attempts in education to create tools that enable this measurement to take place. For instance, certain forms of test instrument, such as intelligence tests and sets of questions, have been designed to enable the assessor to measure a score and it is true that they do allow a score to be measured – but what are they measuring? Herein lies the problem, they may only be measuring the ability of the individual to respond to that test on that particular day. Two people getting the same score will not necessarily have answered the same questions in the same way, so that the same score hides the individuality of the respondents. The same person doing the same test on different days may not always answer it in the same way; for instance, students responding to Kolb's Learning Style Inventory responded to it differently on different days and came out with different learning styles as a result! Instruments are always going to be questioned for their reliability, since they assume that the respondents will always be consistent and this denies the individuality and autonomy of the human being.

Nevertheless, some educators endeavoured to discover more accurate tests, such as multiple choice questions. Like the intelligence test, the multiple-choice question is an instrument to measure something and the score gained on the test can be accurately measured and recorded. Once again, the scientific ethos has come to the fore – but the question has to be asked as to whether the multiple choice question measures what it claims to measure. It is significant, and rather surprising, that Mehrens and Lehmann (1991) almost assume that objective tests actually measure what they claim to measure and that most of their discussion thereafter is based upon this assumption. For instance, in the weaknesses that they (1991, p133) suggest for multiple choice questions, there is no questioning of whether they actually measure what they claim to measure. Perhaps this indicates the strength of the scientific assumptions in psychology – assumptions that need to be questioned, claim Usher and Edwards (1994). Later in Mehrens' and Lehmann's (1991, p249) study, they define reliability as 'consistency between two measures of the same thing' but they do not suggest that a reliable score might be one which reflects perfectly the phenomenon being measured.

Instruments do not necessarily measure what they claim to measure and they fall short of the large claims that are sometimes made for them, although the best of instruments do provide some approximations and indications about the types of persons and their abilities. But because they are tools that enable measurement to take place, they are often treated as if they are providing the same precise information as the micrometer furnishes – but they do not. What they do provide is an indication of the people and their abilities and as such they are useful – but they have not the reliability of the scientific instrument since they are not dealing with inanimate phenomena but human beings – and no human being can be measured!

But human beings and their work are being assessed – indeed, they assess each other all the time. They are always placing their value on another or on another's performance – but it is their value! How individuals perceive a complex phenomenon will vary between people and between situations – it is almost as if there is no objective phenomenon to be assessed. Herein lie the dangers of the subjective approach – that assessment may change according the perception of the assessor, according to the time of the day, the day of the week, the mood of the assessor, *etc.* It is relative to the perceptions of the assessor, *etc.* But this is what occurs all the time in everyday life – but everyday life is not necessarily fair and the perceptions of those with power dominate so that excellence, whatever this is, does not always rise to the top – but can be smothered and lost.

But it might be asked why there is so much agreement within a profession? Does this not reflect some objectivity about people? People are different and their performances do differ – so that there are some objective differences upon which agreement can be reached. In closed professional groups there can be a consider- able amount of agreement but that reflects the similarity of approaches of people with the same training and background – they may perceive things similarly, so that their assessments may converge. This is a form of inter-subjectivity rather than objectivity. It is their similarity that sometimes enables them to do this – but give thirty examiners the same essay to mark at the same time and it is most unlikely that they will all give it the same grade! They are placing their values on the essay and they do perceive things differently – that is what life is about! They may be the examiners and it is their decision whether to pass or fail a candidate, *etc.* It might be fair, but if there is a great deal of difference between them, as there frequently is when this exercise is carried out, then they are clearly reflecting their own perceptions rather than measuring an objective phenomenon. Hence, this approach is not sufficient.

Education, then, should not go down the road of trying to emulate the apparently scientific, neither should it accept that the natural, everyday approach to assessment is the best – for there are no perfect ways of assessing, so that it may be that it is necessary to triangulate a number of approaches in order to come closer to whatever is the reality of the phenomenon which is being assessed.

It is, therefore, argued here that there are no objective phenomena in the educational process that can be measured, even though some of the instruments that are used tend to imply that there are. If there are no objective values, then the question might be posed as to what is a standard, or a value – and this is an important point to which further consideration must now be given. What actually makes something good? What is a standard?

If a student in a class says that she got 85% for her essay, there might be a feeling amongst her listeners that she did well – until she says that everybody else got 100% and she was bottom! She might have done well because she included most of the knowledge and ideas in her answer that the assessors required – and so according to those criteria she got a high grade. But by the norms of the class, she did badly. Consequently, it is difficult to say precisely what a standard is, since it depends on how it is assessed. In this case, there is a profound difference between criterion- and norm-rating.

This is rather like the processes that a moral philosopher goes through in seeking to determine whether an action is good, as we have seen earlier in this study. The judgment reached depends on which approach is subscribed to and the type of argument utilised.

While assessors may consider a piece of work as something which is good, this really means that it has reached a high standard in their opinion. 'Good' is used in a non-moral sense, meaning that the work is of a high standard – usually it is judged according to predetermined criteria in order to ensure a degree of objectiveness. Assessors endeavour to make a judgment according to the specified criteria – but it is still their judgment and not a precise measurement, in the assessment of students' work and the evaluation of curricula.

## Assessing students' performances and evaluating curricula

This section is divided into two sub-sections, but not quite by the sub-sections that might appear to be the most obvious. The two sub-sections relate to what is being assessed or evaluated: firstly, objective phenomena such as essays and curriculum documents and, secondly, practical phenomena that once performed remain only as a memory.

## Assessing the contents of an empirical phenomenon

Students' work is frequently assessed as a result of a written assignment, or a test, *etc*, and a grade awarded. In a similar manner when a new course is being accredited a large written document is often prepared and a validation committee take hold of the document and evaluate it. In both cases it is an objective, empirical entity which is being examined.

Many written assignments are in an essay, or project, form and it has been clearly demonstrated that there are major difficulties in seeking to assess the actual meaning and the strength of argument contained in an essay. The very many differences obtained from different approaches to reading the material and the attempts to devise instruments to measure intelligence, *etc*, have already been alluded to.

Consequently, in some instances, self-assessment is practised but, crudely, this might be no more than the blind assessing how blind they are! Yet, there is also a self-assessment when the self-assessor is able to say 'once I was blind and now I see' – or, 'I know that I have improved and that I have learned', and so this approach should not be ruled out completely

This problem is a profound one, in fact it is a hermeneutical problem – Gadamer (Warnke, 1987) has argued that the only way of understanding other people's meaning is to reach an agreement with them about their subject matter and, if he is correct, then the written assignment should constitute the basis for a discussion with the writer. Clearly this does not happen in normal undergraduate teaching because of time constraints and so the problems remain. At the higher levels of education, for instance in the *viva voce* examination for a doctoral degree, there is an attempt to enter a dialogue in order to tease out the candidate's meanings and intentions and to try to reach agreement. However, time does not permit this type of dialogue for most written assignments and so the assessment techniques used are rarely ones in which a dialogue has occurred and so the grade may reflect the judgment of the assessor, rather than the agreement between the assessor and the assessed.

In a similar manner when a curriculum proposal is being evaluated, the course team prepare a written document and they submit it to a validation committee. After having considered the document, the validation committee usually meet the course team to tease out their intentions and discuss their ideas. After having had a dialogue, the validation committee makes its evaluation about the proposed curriculum but it does so from a much more informed position because it has entered dialogue. There is no attempt to measure anything – only that the experts invited to evaluate the proposal do so after having entered a dialogue with the proposers and having understood their intentions.

In all of these instances, both assignments and proposed curricula, the writers have endeavoured to encapsulate their ideas and knowledge, *etc*, in a written document. While the physical attributes of the document might affect the manner in which the assessors or evaluators approach it, what they are fundamentally trying to do is to understand the level of knowledge, the arguments, the intentions of the writers and, clearly, the best way of doing this is for the interpretations of the assessors and evaluators to be tested in a dialogue with the writers. Having more accurately understood the writers' intentions, the assessment or evaluation made might more closely reflect the knowledge, understanding, argument, intention, *etc*, of the writers. This is not a measurement of an objective, empirical thing – it is an assessment or an evaluation of a subjective, ephemeral phenomenon that might actually have no substance and no form.

## Reflections on a practical process

Teaching is a practical occupation and students have to be assessed in practice. Similarly, tutors ask students to evaluate the curriculum: often at least twice – once during the course and once at the end. Increasingly, in continuing education there is a third evaluation – after the student has returned to work – in order to evaluate what impact (Robinson and Robinson, 1989) the course has had upon the work performance. On occasions these evaluation instruments are actually sent to the managers rather than the students and this raises significant questions which distinguish the student (learner) from the client (manager) who might pay the course fee or release the learner from the workplace in order to study the continuing education course. In these instances, the practical performance cannot be replicated – it is a one-off – and neither can the curriculum. Both the practice and the curriculum implementation occurred in time, they were experienced at a specific time, and cannot be replicated although additional practice or another course can occur at a later date. This is obvious – but the same water cannot flow under the same bridge twice!

What is being assessed in practice? Practice has many dimensions, *eg*, knowledge, its application, the ability to think/analyse, the ability to empathise, to communicate, perform, process and manage case load and to learn from practice. When Bloom (1956) produced his famous taxonomy of educational objectives, it was those in the cognitive domain which gained prominence. In 1964, he, with others, produced a less well-known volume about the affective domain, but the third volume on the psycho-motor domain never materialised. This is perhaps of no surprise since skills were considered to be the lower status aspect of education at that time and in many ways it is even harder to delineate. However, a number of scholars did produce a taxonomy of the psycho-motor domain following his approach, notably Simpson (1966) and Harrow (1972).

Harrow suggested that there are six levels of skill: reflex movements; basic fundamental movements (like crawling); perceptual abilities (such as co-ordinating the eye and the hand in catching a ball; physical abilities (such as precise control of the movements); skills (such as typing); non-discursive communication (such as the use of skilled movements to express emotions). This taxonomy may reflect the maturation process of the individual, but it does not provide a great deal of help when it comes to preparing individuals to enter professional practice. However, Simpson's (1966) earlier taxonomy does offer a some help in considering this process. Once again there are six levels: perceptual ability – awareness through the senses; readiness – knowing what to do and how to do it; learning parts of a skill – by imitation and practising; habitualisation – internalising the skill performance; performing complex acts automatically; adapting and devising individual ways of undertaking the skills performance.

But practice is more than skills and so the taxonomy of Krathwohl *et al* (1964) about the affective domain is also significant: receiving; responding; valuing; organising; characterising. When these two approaches are combined, assessing is seen to be a rather complex process – and it is not one which has led to the design of performance criteria to measure it, *etc*. It is recognised as being something very subjective. It is hardly scientific. In more recent times there has been a movement away from the affective and back to breaking down an occupation into a number of skills, or competencies, that can be assessed which has also resulted in a movement to competency-based education. In this each competency is assessed individually in order to decide whether someone is fit to practise. In a sense, this reverts to the old list-of-skills approach that a number of professions, like community nursing in Britain, used some twenty years ago. One of the major weaknesses of the approach is that there are no definitive lists of skills for any one occupation and, even if there were, the assessment of every single skill is still a subjective process, so that it is ultimately compounding subjective assessments! Even if this approach were to be possible, the question remains as to whether the ability to pass the majority, or all, of competencies creates a competent practitioner.

If it is impossible to encapsulate the total practice in competencies then another problem arises: the whole of practice is not being assessed, whereas experienced practitioners might be in a much better position to evaluate another's practice because they understand the totality of practice, even though they might not always easily be able to articulate their tacit knowledge. This is extremely clear from both Ryle's (1963) and Nyiri's (1988) discussion about the expert, in which they point out that the expert might not be able to articulate practical skills but recognises them in practice.

A few years after the attempts to create a taxonomy of skills for assessment, Dreyfus and Dreyfus (1980) produced a five-stage model of skill acquisition which contained a number of similarities to Simpson's work. Benner (1984) utilised this model in her work on clinical nursing practice:

**novice** – someone who is taught the rules of performance, which is similar to Simpson's second stage of readiness;

**advanced beginner** – 'one who can demonstrate marginally acceptable performance' (Benner, 1984, p22);

**competence** – this stage is achieved when a practitioner has been doing the job for two or three years and begins to feel mastery and ability to cope with the contingencies and complexities of clinical practice;

**proficiency** – where the clinical nurse knows that plans have to be modified in certain situations and she has the confidence to undertake this, which is very similar to Simpson's final stage.

The **expert** has a great deal of experience and appears to rely on intuition to respond to situations in clinical practice, although this intuition is tacit knowledge rather than intuitive in the way that the word is often used.

It will be seen that Benner's approach is not really an advance on Simpson's, although it is one which has become extremely well-known, and still the problems of the affect remain. It is still a subjective process and if the skill is only being assessed on a single occasion, it may not be performed the same way on another one. It is ephemeral in this sense and so continuous assessment in practice is necessary and very time-consuming – if every aspect of practice is to be assessed!

Should the competencies approach be rejected? Perhaps it is a good *aide memoire* for teaching, mentoring, formative assessment – but it is no more objective than the holistic approach in deciding whether a student has passed or not!

In a similar manner when asked to evaluate a course that students have undertaken, what are they evaluating – their learning, the excellence (whatever that is) of the teachers, the organisation of the course, their enjoyment, *etc*? If they evaluate their learning as 'good', that they now have confidence to practise as 'high', but the University Department as 'bad' and 'uncaring' and the standard of the teaching 'low' – has it been a good course? What then is a good course? Rarely do all the students agree about any single element of the course, for they are imposing their own values upon the experience that they have had.

Impact evaluation presents different problems – the employer evaluates the course as cheap, quick and the effect on practice as achieving the desired outcomes – then it might appear to be a good course. However, this could occur even though the teaching was indoctrinational, the learning experiences unchallenging and the department uncaring. Has the student had a good course? Naturally impact evaluation is problematic, and subjective – but it appears to be another way of evaluating the curriculum. It is logically false but beguilingly attractive! The students might actually not have enjoyed the course and considered it to be poor, but the employers might have considered it to be good value for money and so they send more students on it – but not for educational reasons.

## The persons or the work

The implication in the first part of this chapter was that assessment and measurement are similar and so we might ask now: what is being measured? In one sense, the answer must be that nothing is being measured – for the positivist tradition is itself under threat and the modernity project is itself being re-evaluated. But that something is being assessed or evaluated, even if it is not an empirical and objective phenomenon. This is a hermeneutic process which Gadamer (1976, p28) asserts as a fusion of the the assessors' perception of a phenomenon and the assessors' reflections upon it – it takes into consideration both the differences in the phenomenon and differences in the assessors' reflections upon it, for assessors cannot escape their own ontological condition or their own subjectivity. In this fusion, the assessors create a new meaning situation in every assessment. But in this fusion of the perception of the performance and the assessors' own understanding, the assessment or evaluation reflects not only the thing being assessed or evaluated – it also reflects the assessors and evaluators themselves so that this demands that the professionalism of the assessors or evaluators be self-evident.

By its nature, however, assessment and evaluation give the assessor access to the Other through their work. Any form of access to the Other, especially that in the role of assessor, gives the assessor power and authority over the assessed. There is both authority and power in the role, but there is also a residue of power that resides in expertise. Many examination systems try to remove this personal power relationship in the process by ensuring that the assessment system is anonymous and that there is professional agreement between assessors. In short, they try to ensure as much fairness as possible, although they sometimes make claims for the objectivity of the final grade that are harder to sustain. It is clear that all the procedures that have been put in place by these Examination Boards are valiant attempts to remove the subjectivity in assessment, as far as possible, in order to be fair to all the candidates. The intention to be fair is not questioned here and I have no intention of assessing these systems here; my concern is much more with the normal processes of marking assignments and assessing professional practice, *etc*, in which the assessors do have access to the Other.

Except where the assessment being made is about an unquestionable phenomenon, such as 2+2=4, is correct, the majority of assessments and evaluations are of a subjective nature. In all of these cases the assessors are trying to understand what the students or candidates have written or how they have actually performed in practice. The assessment is of the students' work or performance and not of the students themselves. Nevertheless, for many students their work or performance is part of themselves; they have put themselves into it. It becomes, therefore, an inter-subjective and a moral process. Assessors might see themselves as assessing the students' work or performance but the students see the process as one of being assessed.

However, the assessor can rarely get access to the students to discuss their work or performance with them, although only through dialogue is it possible to understand fully their work or performance. Consequently, three things are clear about this common everyday educational process: the assessment is subjective; the assessor is not always clear what precisely the student intended to write or do; the students might well regard the outcome of the process as a judgment about themselves rather than about their work. Hence, this is a much more delicate moral relationship than it appears on the surface. Through the work or performance, the assessor has access to the Other, although the Other may not have access to the assessor! Consequently, the assessor has to treat the process as if it is inter-subjective; must empathise with the Other and seek to ensure that that concern is communicated in the process. For example, the assessor might point out that she thinks the work is of average quality, that the assessment is only reflecting her assessment of this piece of work and it does not necessarily reflect the student's abilities, *etc*. She might make comments on an essay – that she does not quite understand the logic of the argument, or ask how was this conclusion reached – rather than marking something as wrong, *etc*. To mark something as wrong, when it is a subjective and hermeneutic assessment, is an exercise of power rather than an inter-subjective process in which the human relationship is expressed.

As was pointed out earlier, it needs the communicative relationship where Ego is accessible by the Other in order for the assessor to tease out the intentions behind the work or the performance. This would enable the assessment to be more exact although, realistically, this is too time-consuming for most teaching and learning processes. It is not efficient and may not be regarded as an efficient use of the tutors' time. At the same time, tutors might invite students who wish to discuss the grade, comments, *etc*, to enter a dialogue with them but if every student responded to this invitation, it would soon be regarded as inefficient, however rich the teaching and learning relationships that emerged might be.

It is for these reasons, among others, that such processes as self-assessment, peer-assessment and even contracting the grade before the work is undertaken and agreeing the criteria by which it should be assessed have become more popular. There are, naturally, strengths and weakness about these processes, and none of them actually answer all the problems of assessment. It remains a human process in which people relate, even if they do not interact, with each other and one in which the assessor might have access to an unknown Other and in any process of assessment the human criteria must apply as well as the professional ones on which the judgment is made.

# Chapter Thirteen

# The education of adults as a social movement

Thus far in this book we have examined the educational process in the light of both universal and cultural values. Traditionally, however, adult education has embraced those cultural values and adult educators have regarded it as a radical social movement – it has always had amongst it ranks activists who have espoused good causes and protest movements. But as the era of modernity appears to be reaching something of a crisis point in the United Kingdom and Western Europe, at least, and adult education has been incorporated into mainstream education as continuing or lifelong education, the possibility that adult education is still a radical social movement, or even a social movement, or even a separate part of education, has to be recognised.

In order to do this, it is necessary to understand social movements and locate adult education within their context. And this constitutes the first part of this chapter; the second part explores the way in which society is changing and demonstrates how it is now impossible to regard adult education as a social movement or even as a separate and distinct educational phenomenon; the third part points to the disillusionment that is apparent in this age and to the fact that as a risk society there is still need for social concern; lastly, there is a discussion about the role that education can play in future social movements. This points to the universal ethic of responsible concern.

## Adult education and social movements as phenomena of the Enlightenment

The Enlightenment occurred over a period of history in Western Europe, mainly in countries that had been profoundly influenced by the Protestant Reformation. While it emerged in an historical time, it was a series of intellectual innovations that occurred over a century which called into question many of the central ideas of the previous centuries. It will be recalled that Hamilton (1992, pp21–22) summarised the Enlightenment's main characteristics as: reason and rationality; empiricism; science; universalism; progress; individualism; toleration; freedom; uniformity of human nature; secularism. An examination of this list reveals that this system is a logical outcome of the Protestant Reformation; these are also the beliefs and values that undergirded the development of Western Europe as it achieved economic and political dominance in the world. It contains the optimism of the age, the belief that the world is becoming a better place and that utopia is just around the corner. Consequently, it is easy to see how social movements could emerge which embraced this optimism and which endeavoured to bring about the new age. The most well-known of all of these is contained in the writings of Karl Marx, who thought that the working people would recognise that the wealth which was being created at this period was being generated by their efforts although they were not receiving all the benefits of their labours. Since they were being exploited by the capitalists who were accumulating the wealth, he anticipated that they would rebel and create the new classless society.

There were many other movements during this period, some reformist and others more radical, all reflecting this optimism – people believed in progress and felt that history was going somewhere. They also thought that they could plan rationally to make this a better world, and so education also emerged amongst all the other social movements. Indeed, for Tilly (cited in Scott 1992, p130) social movements 'are a product of modernity'. Tilly (cited Scott, 1992, p129) suggested that:

> People have, to be sure, banded together more or less self-consciously for the pursuit of common ends since the beginning of history. The nineteenth century, however, saw the rise of the social movement in the sense of a set of people who voluntarily and deliberately committed themselves to a shared identity, a unifying belief, a common programme, and a collective struggle to realize that programme.

The concept of social movement is not well-defined although according to Scott (1992, p132) most social movements had some of the following features:

1. at least occasional mass mobilisation;
2. tendency towards a loose organisational structure;
3. spasmodic activity;
4. working at least in part outside established institutional frameworks;
5. bringing about social change (or perhaps preserving aspects of the social order) as a central aim.

There are two fundamentally different types of movement: there are structural ones and social action ones. The structural ones reflect changes in the structures of society whereas the action ones reflect changes that exclude groups of people from playing a full part in society.

In the immediate post-Enlightenment period many social movements were action-orientated and had most of these features, as they endeavoured to create a better world for the working classes. Their members usually directed their activities towards those in authority in the State.

Adult educators certainly had a vision of a better world and what they endeavoured to do clearly reflects the hopes and aspirations of the period. Kelly (1970) documents many educational movements among adults during this period which fit into this category; all were committed to providing education to the working classes, such as the adult school movement, the mechanics institute movement, the co-operative movement, *etc*. These movements all appeared after the beginning of the Enlightenment. Other writers have also demonstrated how a variety of adult education enterprises since that period, in different parts of the world, have acted as social movements and have been active in endeavouring to create a better world for the working classes and peasants – amongst the most well-known of these have been all the activities in Canada (Welton, 1987; Selman, 1991 *inter alia*); the work of Highlander in the USA (Adams, 1975; Horton, 1990 *inter alia*) and, in a different cultural context to which further reference will be made below, the work and writings of Freire (1972, 1972a).

Fundamentally, adult educators have been involved with movements which have petitioned the State:

- to make more educational opportunities available and open to more people – from literacy to vocational education;

- to provide education as a right to all in the same way as other welfare provisions;

- to allow greater democratic participation by citizens in policy decisions as the people became more educated, *etc*.

Significantly, in late modern society in Western Europe, many of these aspirations have been achieved: there is now a greater access to educational provision than ever before: it can occur at any time during life: there appears to be more opportunity to learn about the complexities of the world and to voice an opinion about them through the media, *etc*; the welfare state has been introduced and now become a matter of history and its dismantling is beginning to locate morality where it belongs – with people. Although in the process of dismantling, there is a danger that the State's protective functions towards all its citizens will disappear.

Having achieved many of these educational objectives, however, there is a certain irony which has caused adult educators considerable concern – adult education as a separate educational entity appears to be under threat, and in order to understand why this is, it is necessary to understand something about the changing world in which this is occurring. It is also significant that the nature of social movements is also changing and this is a point to which further reference will also be made below.

## The changing world

It is generally accepted that late or post-modernity is a feature of Western European culture in which the consequences of the Enlightenment are being questioned. The fact that it is by and large a Western phenomenon is important to this debate, since it is suggested that its emergence in the West is a product of the classical market forces which were enabled to operate from the time when the free movement of capital between countries was allowed which generated conditions closer to a universal free market. Before that time, it could be claimed that the world was developing along regional lines, and the following paragraphs outline a simple theory of this change.

Basically, the theory of regional development means that a regions's employ-ment structure will be enhanced through the investment of capital in the area and, as a result of the multiplier effect, this will generate even more wealth throughout the region. Consequently, regions where capital exists get richer in contrast to those regions where there is less capital to invest. For as long, therefore, as there is not a free flow of capital between countries, those countries with wealth have more capital to invest and generate more employment opportunities and get richer, so that the West got richer at the expense of the remainder of the world. The fact that each state had boundaries within which capital could be invested meant that there was only a limited workforce for companies to employ and nowhere else for companies to invest their wealth. This had a number of outcomes, amongst which was that it gave the trades unions considerable power enabling them to wrest privileges from the elite for the working classes. This also meant that these countries were able to tax the large and successful companies and so generate sufficient wealth to create and sustain a welfare state, which also enabled the further growth in the provision of educational opportunities for all people, including the emergence of adult education as a leisure time occupation.

However, as the barriers between countries were lowered in respect to the transfer of capital, the conditions of the classical market began to emerge on a worldwide scale. Large companies seeking profit were no longer constrained by the restrictive practices of the trades unions or the high taxation of the welfare state. They were able to seek more profitable places in which to invest their capital, which they did. Some less developed countries with cheaper and more malleable labour forces became the focus of capital investment, although there were still many countries that were a bad risk or in which capitalist companies were unable to invest capital, *eg*, the Eastern bloc and China. Classical economists would argue that until such time as an equilibrium is reached in the cost of siting produc-tion in different locations, companies will always tend to invest in the most profit-able ones and so there will be a gradual enrichment of poorer countries at the expense of the more wealthy ones. The poorer countries have, consequently, embarked on the process of modernisation while the more wealthy, and less competitive ones, faced a period when they could no longer take their wealth or income for granted and they appeared to stagnate or, in other words, they entered a new phase of modernity – late modernity. Some first world countries, like Germany, with reformed labour relations and new industrial investment, have until comparatively recently still been able to compete successfully in the market while other countries with practices embedded in the past and outmoded produc-tion techniques have faced a more difficult period. As a result, there has been a gradual change and the taken-for-granted world view of the modern society is rapidly disappearing and many of the values that were espoused during the peak of economic prosperity in West Europe including the development of the welfare state and educational provision are now open to question.

Naturally, the above paragraphs contain an over-simplification of the globalisation process which had been going on long before the free movement of capital through colonial imperialism. Since some transnational companies now undertake their production processes across a variety of countries, introducing an international division of labour, they have also lessened the significance of national economies and the state, and have emphasised the globalisation process even more.

Among the theorists who have endeavoured to explain globalisation in economic terms is Wallerstein (1990), whose theory contains six elements: capitalism is worldwide; it has always sought wider markets which has created the contradiction between modernisation and Westernisation; the problem of getting workers to work harder for lower pay is an inherently difficult one; modernisation as a central universalising theme gives priority to newness and change; the capitalist world-economy does not merely reward unequally, it is the locus of increasing polarity over historical time; the strongest and wealthiest states have risen and declined. Most of his points are apparent in the above argument, although they are not all accepted here uncritically; for instance, his final point implies that history always repeats itself, which is not logically correct. It is also significant that Robertson (1992, p13) criticises him for being too one-sided and concentrating too much on the forces of economics. Even while it is recognised that information technology and the traditions of culture have also played significant parts in these changes, the control of capital is central to the processes of change and to the way that lifelong learning and continuing education have developed. It is hardly possible to understand what has happened to adult education in the contemporary world without reference to the globalisation process.

During the period in which the West was modernising and achieving dominance (the West and the rest) those cultural values which it had adopted during the Enlightenment were assumed to be the apex of civilisation, and they were not only taken for granted but were often exported around the world by the mechanisms of both capitalism and colonialism, including education – even university extension (Steele, 1994, *inter alia*). However, as other parts of the world modernised and the dominance of the West appeared more fragile – even though many of the transnational companies are still controlled from the West – it began to question its own values. As Bauman (1992, p167) has also pointed out, communism 'was modernity in its most determined mood' seeking to create that better world by the fastest possible methods, but when the Berlin Wall fell, the ideals of modernity crumbled with it. Late, or post, modernity had apparently arrived! A number of scholars then began to write about this new era (Lyotard, 1984; Harvey, 1989; Jameson, 1991; *inter alia*). Whether it actually is a new era has certainly been a major feature in the debate – with many scholars, notably Habermas (1985), denying that modernity is over. It is because of this debate, which is not really discussed here, that 'late modernity' rather than 'postmodernity' has been adopted. Clearly the values of advanced capitalism dominate Western society, some having become more prevalent and others having taken new form, while some of the cultural values which were expounded during the dominance of the West are now being questioned by postmodern scholars.

It is in these conditions that other parts of the world are now apparently modernising and it is not surprising, therefore, that social movements are emerging in these countries that embrace some of the similar values and expectations as did people in Britain and Western Europe in its period of modernisation. Consequently, writers like Freire can be contextualised in a modernising culture and he mirrors the concerns that existed amongst adult educators in the West during that period, so that his approach has been seized upon in the West as reflecting the values of adult education, and he is lionised by many who seek actively to espouse the radicalism of adult education's history. However, his activities in the modernising world might actually be providing us with another symbol:

> one message comes through loud and clear: contrary to a widely shared view of modernity as the first universal civilisation, this is a civilisation singularly unfit for universalization.

> (Bauman, 1993, p215)

Even so, this process is occurring and other parts of the world are modernising. With this, the economic dominance of the West has become more questionable and society itself has changed into an Information Society – the speed of dissemination of new knowledge has increased, the nature of work has been transformed and with it the nature of education and educational priorities altered.

It was as early as 1926 that Scheler (1980, p76) suggested that scientific knowledge was changing hour by hour and he regarded this as artificial knowledge since it never becomes embedded within the cultural system. Now knowledge is changing much more rapidly and it has assumed a relative nature. The very nature of relativity had led to constant change, experimentation and the emergence of the reflexive society, which Beck (1992) regards as 'risk society'. Knowledge itself can be disseminated through modern technological means which is bound to affect the nature of education itself in the coming years, since technology can by-pass education and transmit information directly to the learners.

These rapid developments have also led to a changing structure of work in Western societies. Reich (1991, pp171–84) suggests that there will be three main types of work in the future: routine production services, in-person services and symbolic analysts. In addition, he notes that there will remain a few who work in the primary industries, like farming and mining, and others who are government employees sheltered from global competition – although many of these are actually less sheltered from global competition than he implies. Finally, there are the unemployed and the retired. Each of these categories is now very briefly examined.

The routine production workers are both the blue and white collar workers who perform simple sequential steps in production – whether manual or supervisory or data processing – and they need literacy, core skills, and the ability to perform simple computations but they must be reliable, loyal, hard working and malleable. In 1990, about 25% of the American workforce fell into this category and while these statistics will not be the same for other societies they do provide an indication of the structures of the workforce in late modern societies.

These occupations can be performed anywhere within the global company so that they are frequently undertaken in countries where the costs to the company are cheapest.

In-person services are those undertaken on a person-to-person basis, so that they cannot be sold worldwide. They require the same qualities as the routine production workers but they also demand a pleasant demeanour so that they make those whom they serve feel good. Some 30% of the American workforce were employed in this manner in 1990.

Symbolic analysts comprised 20% of the workforce in 1990, but this percentage has been rising rapidly over the past quarter century. They identify, solve and broker problems, they often work in small teams and their work is knowledge-based and worldwide. Much of the initial preparation for this category of occupation comes through high calibre university education, mostly provided by Western universities and it is in Western societies where this type of occupation finds its place, although many of symbolic analysts have global missions and work for the transnational companies.

The primary occupations are also undergoing changes with the introduction of new technologies and there are substantially more people unemployed for a variety of reasons which include structural, frictional and demographic ones. There are also many more unemployed because of the short-term nature of many jobs. Additionally, more people are retired since many people are stopping work earlier and living longer.

It is within this context that adult education has been transformed into continuing education which, significantly, responds to the educational demands of all groups in the workforce whether it be routine production workers, in-person service workers or symbolic analysts. Indeed, industry and commerce are, themselves, beginning to provide education for the workers. Now, there is access for the greater majority of people and a chance to gain educational qualifications at most stages of their lives, so that lifelong education has become a realistic possibility – for at least as long as the working life! It could be claimed that every successful social movement will be incorporated into the mainstream and, consequently, what has happened to adult education is a sign that it has been a successful movement. Indeed, more recently, lifelong learning is being adopted as a slogan by governments, so that we have the European Year of Lifelong Learning, *etc.*

Continuing education has become incorporated into the mainstream provision of education and as a major section of institutionalised education it can no longer be regarded as a social movement. The idea of adult education itself appears to be an almost outdated concept – after all, it was a product of the Enlightenment. There is almost certainly no future for it as a separate form of educational provision. Many of its ideals have been achieved and others introduced by right-wing governments – so that rather ironically the radical ideas of the left have been introduced by the right – indeed, the new right has been the truly radical political force in UK, and probably Western European, politics over the past two decades. At the same time, the welfare state has been tried and shown to be impracticable in a global capitalist society, even though its intentions are clearly ones that most educators still espouse. The radicalism of the Enlightenment, therefore, seems either to have been impracticable or practicable within the conditions generated by the very forces of capitalism which radicalism sought to destroy. It is not possible to regard adult education as a social movement any longer. One element of the education of adults still lies outside of mainstream provision – education for the elderly – and this might still be regarded as a social movement, albeit not a very radical one, and this is a point to which we shall return later.

## The risk society and social movements

Many of the tenets of the Enlightenment have been questioned and history no longer seems to be going anywhere. Academic discussion has re-emerged about both utopia (Kumar 1987) and, even, the apocalypse (Bull, 1995). Fukuyama (1992, p3) opens his book on the end of history with a statement that is the antithesis of the Enlightenment hopes:

> The twentieth century, it is safe to say, has made all of us into deep historical pessimists.

No longer do we have a view of history going somewhere. Indeed, for many the pessimism of the period has created a situation where people are beginning to ask profound existential questions about the meaning of life, *etc*. Others, perhaps not wanting to face the situation but reflecting the reality of the contemporary world, have tended to sloganise their response: Leave it to the market! Clearly the market reigns supreme since it is now global and, as we have seen, it has been one of the main generating forces of the contemporary condition. If the optimism of the immediate post-Enlightenment period was a reason for the growth of new social movements, this current pessimism must affect the way that current social movements manifest themselves.

But the capitalist world, which constantly needs to innovate and expand, is having constantly to manufacture new commodities and discover new resources. It is having to produce new products, often without the resources, or the time, to test them fully. Even if it were possible, the long-term effects of this drive to produce and, apparently, to improve the living conditions of the people has generated a new world – one which Beck (1992) calls 'risk society'. More recently, Giddens (1994, p4) has claimed that contemporary global capitalism has generated the condition of 'manufactured risk', by which he means that the risks are now 'a result *of* human intervention into the conditions of social life and into nature'. The uncertainties that have been created are new and the world is now more concerned with damage control world-wide, and the peoples of the world are finding it increasingly difficult to co-operate. Giddens (1994, p207) suggests that:

> Modern civilization proceeds through the attempted imposition of human control on environments of action, including the natural

environment, which were once largely external to such action. This orientation to control, strongly bound up with the stress of continuous economic development but not reducible to it, comes up against its limits as it is generalised and globalised. One such limit concerns the prevalence of manufactured uncertainty, which compromises the very control orientation itself; another concerns the effects that such a control orientation has on basic moral questions and dilemmas of our existence.

Perhaps it will take an apocalyptic event to produce the type of co-operation necessary to respond to the world thus created. Clearly, the world is not perfect but because of better standards of education and communication, people are more able to join in the political debate about the future directions that this world will take. Herein lies the rationale for the growth of ethical debate in contemporary society.

The people are also more aware of the fallibility of politicians and political decisions as a result both of their own learning and the more significant place the mass media have in society. But often, however, they feel that they are denied the opportunity of participating in the decision-making process – there is still, therefore, a place for radical politics and social movements. Giddens (1994, pp12–20), himself, proposes a six-point plan: concern to repair damaged solidarities; centralise life politics – a politics of life style; create a situation of generative politics (in which people can make things happen); generate dialogic democracy; rethink the welfare state; confront the role of violence in human affairs. In order to create a society in which these things happen, Giddens discusses the possibilities of what he calls 'universal values', although these are actually cultural values that have emerged as a result of globalisation and are transcultural, rather than universal in quite the sense that the concept is being used throughout this study.

However, the nature of social movements has changed and new social movements are arising. Unlike the movements of the post-Enlightenment period which were predominantly economic, workplace, concerned with citizenship and rights; the new social movements are knowledge-based, issue-orientated rather than class-focused, more involved in civil society, act in defence of the public realm and are basically concerned with the autonomy of the people (Scott, 1992). Frequently, these movements arise in response to the conditions, created by global capitalism, which are apparent in the risk society but, significantly, they are often 'beyond left and right' (Giddens, 1994) and 'too heterogeneous in their aims and modes of activity to play the role of substitute for the workers' movement' (Scott, 1992, p145 citing Melucci, 1989). Indeed, as Giddens (1994, p21) points out there is now no single group – such as the proletariat in Marx's thinking – that can carry the hopes of humanity. This does not rule out the need for some form of political engagement, although it is beyond the politics of left and right.

Adult education, then, is rapidly ceasing to be a separate educational entity and, even if this were not the case, the nature of social movements in contemporary society has changed so that it would not be able to play such a radical role in the future. And so, it might be asked, does the education of adults – or education itself for that matter – have any reformist or radical role in this new late modern world? This, it seems, is the major question and one which is not easy to answer, but one which needs to be tackled.

## The education of adults and social movements

Now we recognise that we cannot plan and build a better world through rational thought and things are being increasingly left to the market, or at least to those who control the market, and this will not produce a utopian society – of that we are aware. The market may produce more commodities and it may produce a land overflowing with 'milk and honey' but it cannot produce a human utopia. Since all the goods in the world cannot produce a perfect world, there will always be a place for the people to influence those who have power and, as Giddens (1994) points out, there is always an agenda for radical politics. However, there is certainly no agreement about where society should be going or even if it is going anywhere – for there is certainly no agreed philosophy of history. Social movements do not all necessarily espouse the same thing, nor the same approaches to disseminating their ideologies. There is a diversity of concerns and no agreement about what would be a desirable outcome.

New social movements have arisen, *eg*, the green movement, feminism and the elderly, some of which are structural and others action-orientated. For instance, education for the elderly might at present be viewed as a structural social movement, but feminism and the green movement are action-orientated and these latter require a knowledge base. Their foci are autonomy and the public realm. Others, like the peace movement and animal rights, might also be viewed within this category. They reflect a changed world, but they are the movements which will help shape the next stage of global policy development since they advocate a better society from within the imperfections of the present one. These are not revolutionary movements, they all have to educate people about the justness of their cause. Indeed, both Beck and Giddens are clear that the nature of contemporary risk society is one of reflexivity, and reflexivity by its very nature is a learning process. These movements, therefore, need people who have the necessary knowledge and skill to operate in this type of society – an information society, a learning society – some of their tools must be educational in nature if they are to be successful. People need to be presented with the information but this is only one phase in the process – for, as I shall suggest below, the information is not sufficient to produce action although it may be an important factor in the process.

Education, therefore, is not a separate movement but there is a sense in which the education of adults has become a part of every social action movement; each one needs self-directed learners, humanistic teachers and leaders. In an ironic sense educators of adults, having this reformist persuasion, may have to discover a pre-modern approach. Adult education itself was not then a social institution or a social movement, so that people like Winstanley viewed the educational process as something that could be used by a variety of other organisations, such as the church. Those who practised it were not seen by others as educators but, in this case, they were clergy and, similarly, the past may also be the future (Kelly, 1970). Those who see education as having a role in social responsibility and action-orientated social movements may have to be educators within those other movements, and education will have to be seen as a process rather than a movement or an institution.

## Conclusion

However, in this late modern, or postmodern world – we are pessimistic and know that policy and planning will not produce the utopia, so that we are still faced with a major problem and perhaps it remains a problem because we still think in a cognitivist – modern – manner. We are still seeking a place for education in the creation of the utopian society – a society which is essentially a moral society, about which there would probably be little universal agreement since most moral values are cultural and relative. But, as Bauman (1993, pp247–8) argues:

> . . .moral issues cannot be 'resolved', nor the moral life of humanity guaranteed by the calculating and legislative efforts of reason. Morality is not safe in the hands of reason, though this is exactly what the spokesmen of reason promise. Reason cannot help the moral self without depriving the self of what makes the self moral: that unfounded, non-rational, un-arguable, no-excuses-given and non-calculable urge to stretch towards the other, to caress, to be for, to live for, happen what may. Reason may be about making correct decisions, while moral responsibility precedes all thinking about decisions as it does not, and cannot care about any logic which would allow the approval of an action as correct. Thus, morality can be 'rationalized' only at the cost of self-denial and self-attrition.

Morality, which is universalisable, is pre-knowledge and lies beyond the cognitive sphere of reason. It is about desire and, paradoxically, we are faced with an almost unresolvable problem – the education of desire – since desire as we understand it lies beyond the realm of education. Indeed, universal moral value also lies beyond the realm of education, and so we have to learn one of the lessons of the end of modernity – planning, rationality and education are insufficient to produce a better world. People have to want to work for that even when it means subsuming their own interests for the benefit of the whole. They have to desire it – and that is something that they alone can do and all that education for adults can do is to act as teachers within the different social movements helping them to present their own arguments, but then leaving it to the people, as autonomous and authentic members of the learning society, to reflect upon their experiences and – perhaps – re-orientate their desires and then their acts. In this, the education of adults is being true to the philosophy of liberal adult education.

The final chapter of this book considers these ideas further: the learning society and the education of desire.

# Chapter Fourteen

# The learning society and the education of desire

Running through this book has been a constant theme that there are two sets of values; the first are universal and the second are cultural and relative. It has been suggested that the universal value is pre-knowledge and learned through experience in early childhood, whereas the cultural values are relative, cognitive and experiential and learned as we grow and develop as members of both the family of origin and the wider society. We have shown how these two values interrelate in every educational setting, but that the cultural values of modernity predominate in the way people think and in the way education functions in society. In some cases, the cultural values are corruptions of manifestations of universal value. Indeed, that is perhaps to be expected for it enables them to be presented slightly differently from the practice or intention and yet so closely to the universal value that it makes it very difficult for holders of the latter principles to protest – but it is still a corruption of them. Their interrelationship will be traced through this final chapter in three parts: the cultivation of desire, the learning society and the education of desire.

## The cultivation of desire

Educators of adults used to start their programme planning by trying to determine the educational needs of potential students. Griffin (1987), however, indicated a view of needs analysis as a social control model of education, although he recognised that adult education was traditionally understood in terms of welfare. Education would be provided to meet the needs of potential learners. But 'needs' comes very close to 'wants' and 'demands' and so with the development of the market of education it was easy to understand how 'needs' are transformed into demands, which the educational providers would supply, rather than meet. Now education is a marketable commodity and its signs are widely advertised in order to attract potential learners.

Education and learning have become commodities to be marketed to potential consumers – something to be enjoyed. Usher and Edwards (1994) have argued that at the heart of this movement is 'experience' and 'experiential learning' since its adoption signifies the move from modern to postmodern. Campbell (1987), however, argues that experiencing the pleasure of consuming is a late Protestant phenomenon which emerged after the Industrial Revolution and which has helped to mould the consumer society ever since. Fukuyama (1992, p333), on the other hand, allies reason with desire, but his argument is always in the realm of the cognitive. Usher and Edwards, however, develop their argument by suggesting that experience is the site in which desire is cultivated – people want to experience new things, novel techniques and so 'experience collapses into consumption' (Usher and Edwards 1994, p188) and so, through advertising, providers of learning materials can create a demand for its new products. People can keep on experiencing the new in an ever-changing world and enjoying the process; individuals become self-disciplined consumers. It must be pointed out here, however, that Usher and Edwards might be over-emphasising 'experience' itself and underplaying the pleasure of experiencing which then, as Bauman (1992) points out, enables seduction to replace repression as a form of control.

Now people can keep on learning throughout their lives and the providers can keep on cultivating the learning desires of the consumers so that learners can continue to have new and pleasurable experiences. Indeed, at least one adult education institution has used the slogan 'learning is fun' to encourage people to enrol on their courses. As the learning market emerges, so a variety of providers of learning materials grow, not all of them being from the educational sectors of society in the first instance – but in this late modern society boundaries are being blurred in any case. Now there are providers of learning materials from a variety of sectors which are causing education to change and compete. And governments, and even educational institutions, can publish their own learners' charters!

Usher and Edwards also suggest that the cultivation of the desire to learn underlies the postmodern and, at the same time, the learning society is born! But there are many more factors in the learning society than this, although there would be no learning society if there was not a demand to learn.

Naturally this is not the way that many educators interpret their provision, but this is because they have always sought to meet the needs of potential learners and have planned their programmes from this philosophical viewpoint. In a sense, adult education providers have always given the power to the learner, because the learners' needs have been paramount to the providers' own philosophy. Hence, the consumer-market-driven education comes close to the educational-needs-driven rationale of the welfare state; but 'close' is sufficiently different to turn the whole philosophy on its head! Both the desire to market the educational products and the desire to consume them contribute to the movement towards the learning society. In this sense, desire is cultivated and more educational products are purchased – even if they are not always consumed and learned thereafter! It is a learning, or learners', utopia!

## The learning society

When the early theorists of the learning society, Yeaxlee (1929), Hutchins (1970) and Lengrand (1975), postulated the future, they had rather idealistic interpretations of the type of society that would emerge. They thought that the provision of liberal education throughout the whole lifetime would constitute the type of 'civilised' society that a learning society should be like. In a sense, some of the more recent writers have also regarded the learning society in a similar manner. Ranson (1994, p105) suggests that:

> The challenge for the time is to create a new moral and political order that responds to the needs of a society undergoing a historic transition.

He actually regards (1994, p106) 'the creation of a learning society as the constitutive condition of a new moral and political order'. He goes on to suggest things that should occur when in the new order. Few would question that the establishment of the type of society that he envisages would be more democratic and excellent to live in, but it is visionary. It presupposes that children's education can lead to the creation of a new moral community and, unfortunately, he rarely looks at the literature of adult and lifelong education. Yet the values of the community he advocates are cultural, they reflect the values of the age and rely on the idea that teachers and educational managers 'can . . . play a leading role in *enabling* such a vision to unfold not only among young people but across the public domain' (Ranson, 1994, p129). But learning is amoral, what people intend to do as a result of their learning is where the morality lies. Additionally, if teachers try to produce children of a certain type, seeking to live according to a certain manner, they might be accused of reducing education to a form of indoctrination. In addition, even if I learn that this vision is of a better type of society for everybody, there is nothing in this cognitive approach to suggest that I should seek to put its ideals into practice and seek to bring it to fruition. He does, however, point to the significance of mutual responsibility and friendship within society. His study presents a vision of a civilised society in which people are free to learn.

However, the learning society is not necessarily a civilised society, nor is it *The Land of Cockagyne* where learning materials flow in abundance to be consumed at the whim of the learners, nor any other form of utopia, for that matter. Yet the language of utopia is being used about it. Longworth and Davies (1996, p145), for instance, write:

> What we have tried to describe . . . is the end of the age of education and training and the beginning of the era of lifelong learning. As a necessary companion to the age of information it will allow us to understand better its implications for the lives of everyone of us and allow the human race to develop its potential in more positive ways than hitherto. Already commentators are looking at the world as it is and predicting descent into a new dark age of the human spirit – mean-minded, aggressive, parochial, utilitarian and without the ideals which allow us to reach for a more civilised way of co-existing on this small planet.

> We believe that lifelong learning offers an alternative to that bleak scenario . . . Lifelong learning is not just desirable, it is a survival issue for us all.

Unfortunately, they do not offer us a way to overcome the issues that we have highlighted in this study. They look to prosperity and efficiency and the values of modernity – cultural values – but not beyond them. While few would dispute that there is a better world to be created than the one that we currently experience and that even some of the cultural values point to the possibility of a better world, it will not emerge merely as a result of lifelong learning – for, as we argued earlier, learning *per se* is amoral, and what learners do with their learning is where values become pertinent. EP Thompson (1977, pp790–1) also recognised this in a completely different form, when he wrote:

> And in such an adventure two things happen: our habitual values (the 'commonsense' of bourgeois society) are thrown into disarray. And we enter Utopia's proper and new-found space: *the education of desire*. This is not the same as a 'moral education' towards a given end: it is rather, to open a way of aspiration, to teach desire to desire, to desire better, to desire more, and above all to desire in a different way.

It is not the cultural values of moral education that are required for a better world but is something more: it is the education of desire. Here then lies the paradox – it is not in the cultivation of the desire to consume (learn) that the way to a better world might be found, but in the education, or cultivation(?), of desire to produce a better world – a desire to practise the universal value.

## The education of desire

Of course we all want to produce a better world! Few people would argue with that. Indeed, educationalists have long regarded education as a necessary component in creating that world as is clearly indicated in Ranson's (1994) study, but this is perhaps because this conception of the better world emerged with modernity, in parallel with our modern educational system. Education cannot produce the good society. People can, and do, pass through the educational process very successfully without doing anything to produce a better world, although they may try to produce a good life for themselves!

Significantly, this book has not argued that the good life is a product of education, or of anything else for that matter. It has argued that the only universal value is when I am open to the Other because the Other is and has impinged upon my space, and I am prepared to respond to the Other out of concern. At least two things emerge from this: firstly, I must be willing to respond to the Other and desire the Other's good without impinging upon the other's autonomy and, secondly, the structures of society within which I function must at least enable this to occur, even if they do not facilitate it. It is, therefore, necessary to discuss the education of desire, once again, and then to juxtapose the cultural values – especially that of efficiency – with the universal value of concern expressed in relationships, which will mean that we examine briefly the concept of time in the educational process.

## Education of desire

From the outset of this study, it has been argued that universal value is precognitive and learned through experience in early childhood. Consequently, placing too much emphasis upon experience in the emergence of a post-modern society might mean underplaying the significance of experience itself in every age. As was pointed out above, it is the pleasurable experience that ensnares the consumer, so that learning has to be fun if this form of learning society is going to emerge. But this is not the education of desire that will produce a better world.

In that early childhood experience which was discussed in the fourth chapter of this book, the young child learned through experience what it means to have another care for it. I learn preconsciously the universal value. As strangers become faces many people still desire their good, and most of us have experienced being helped, sometimes by people whom we do not know but frequently by our friends. Many people desire the other's good – for that early preconscious learning experience is stored as a memory. As EP Thompson wrote, it is not a form of moral education which is called for, since that teaches the cultural values of our society, but the education of this desire to do good. What is called for, is an approach to learning that enables people to recall their own experiences of being cared for, and their experiences of caring for others, and realising that the world would be a better place – irrespective of either social structures or structural change – if individuals living within whatever structures that exist do so out of concern for the Other. Indeed, the very presence of the Other actually questions the authenticity of the I. How do I respond to the Other? How authentic are my intentions? Do I allow for a relationship to emerge? Do I desire to be concerned for the Other?

As Levinas (1991, p39) wrote:

> A relation whose terms do not form a totality can hence be produced within the general economy of being only as proceeding from the I to the other, as a *face to face*, as delineating distance in depth – that of conversation, of goodness, of Desire . . .

For him, desire is something personal, unless it stems from a lack or a need in the I – it is subjective and, as importantly, he claims (1991, p298) that we 'have thus the conviction of having broken with the philosophy of the Neuter'. To be impersonal and objective is be beyond the relationship, almost beyond the expression of care and concern and beyond the universal value. Desire is something embedded deeply in the human person – it is embedded in being itself, learned in that early experience.

How then can there be an education of desire? If teachers try to teach someone to want to respond to the Other because the Other is, and that it is universally good to respond to the Other out of concern, then we run into the danger of advocating indoctrination. Indeed, we might be said to be cultivating desire, in precisely the same way as the market does through its advertising. Advertising might be viewed as a form of indoctrination even though, in this latter instance, the outcome might be claimed to be good. We have already argued that the ends do not justify the means (the teleological argument), and so we are faced with a moral dilemma – how can this desire for the good be taught? Or even, can it be taught at all or only caught?

Perhaps the idea of being caught is significant in this context: we can learn from the everyday practical example. Indeed, we have discussed in this book how practical knowledge is coming to the forefront once again. Perhaps we can learn to desire to do good rather than be taught it in a traditional manner. Learning, it will be recalled, involves the transformation of experience into knowledge, skills, attitudes, values, emotions, senses and beliefs, *etc.* The first two are the ones most frequently emphasised in education, but if we begin to emphasise the 'attitudes, values, emotions, senses and beliefs' a little more, we might begin to see these other outcomes of learning coming to the fore. Perhaps they might be more emphasised in teacher training – teaching styles as much as teaching methods, *etc.* Perhaps the education of desire can only be taught by example – people who experience another doing good and wishing to emulate the other – since this universal value has already been experienced by nearly everybody and if the conditions are conducive to its practice, then we might see it begin to emerge. But utopian thought is rather like a mirage, it always lies in front and beyond the thinker, as Levitas (1990, p191) suggests:

> Utopia expresses and explores what is desired; under certain conditions it also contains the hope that these desires might be met in reality, rather than merely in fantasy. The essential element in utopia is not hope, but desire – the desire for a better way of being. It involves the imagining of a state of being in which the problems which actually confront us are removed or resolved. . .

This then is the fundamental problem – the conditions are not always conducive to its practice! Indeed, the universal value may act as a norm by which we assess the transience of the cultural values of this modern age. It allows us to look at the current system, to recognise its shortcomings and to seek to change it into something better.

## Time

The cultural value of efficiency is beginning to take precedence in education at this present time, indeed we have been introduced to the idea of efficiency savings in education so frequently that they have now become inefficient: courses have to be produced and marketed at the lowest possible cost, so that course producers have to lower production costs or expand the market, or both, This means that class sizes get larger, small classes are uneconomic and are closed, that more time is given to library and private study, that there are fewer tutorials, that production costs for distance education courses are cut, that markets are expanded, *etc, etc.* But more significantly, the time taken in marking assignments, checking the quality of the work, attending course team and institutional meetings are often not included in the production costs – they are the hidden times which educators are expected to give, often, over and above their work time. Basically, it means that educators are expected to do more in the same amount of time. They become stressed because of all the pressures placed upon them.

But, as Adams (1995, p68) argues correctly, research 'in education . . . has barely begun to focus on the most explicit aspects of time in education', although everything that we do is timed! The whole of children's educational experience is located against the clock, and adult educators cost, market and evaluate education by the number of learning hours. Even though we produce our courses in time which are expected to take a specified amount of time to study, we have not yet researched into the efficiency of learning; for instance, learning may be more effective if it occurs in small blocks of time over a longer period, or it may actually be more effective if there are longer blocks of time over a short period. We know little about the relationship of learning and time, although we know considerably more about time and the preparation and marketing of course materials!

Efficiency is a cultural value that predominates the educational world – as it does many other worlds of work – so that we get time-management courses! It is also a non-moral good. Clearly, the market demands this in order to be more competitive, and so these cultural values become explicit. Teachers have less time to spend with students – they have to go to a meeting, *etc.* Teaching becomes less important to the educational process. Of course, we emphasise, correctly, that we want people to be independent learners, *etc*, and students are kept a little at a distance! But what begins to disappear are the conditions under which the universal value might be made manifest – of people being there for the sake of the Other. Being present takes time! Time costs money – it is an economic variable in education! Being present may seem like a waste of time and wasting time is irrational, instrumental rationality being another of the cultural values of modernity. The universal value is lost as cultural values dominate the educational process, and yet this universal value still enables us to assess the validity of the cultural values – and they are found to be less than perfect.

Increasingly, it is being suggested that children are suffering because parents do not have the time for them; health care is rushed because doctors and nurses do not have the time to be with their patients, *etc.* Even in midwifery ('mid' meaning with – German *mitt – with*) practitioners are claiming that they do not have time to be with the mothers-to-be. In the Delors Report (1996), four learning pillars of education are specified – learning to do, to know, to live together and to be. Perhaps the third one needs a little reformulation, or we need to add a fifth – *learning to be together*. Significantly, the Delors Report does not place all its emphasis on the cognition, nor upon the doing, and so it is necessary to recognise the significance of the other factors in learning. In these conditions, education itself needs reconceptualisation so that it might still be seen as a site in which people meet to help one another even though the conditions under which this can occur might make education a little more costly! This is in no way condemning the current moves towards the learning society – it is pointing to the fact that in these new learning conditions call for new ways for people to make themselves available for people and new forms of teaching and learning must be found. In addition to all its obvious strengths and advantages, which we can all applaud, the values placed upon it remain cultural and relative and learning *per se* remains an amoral and natural process.

## Conclusions

The argument running through this book is that there is one universal value – being concerned for the Other – and that ethics begins when the Other impinges on my spontaneity. By contrast, there are a number of cultural values – some are non-moral goods whilst others are moral goods. We are beginning to see the dominance of cultural values – both moral and non-moral – over the universal moral good. Indeed, there are now forms of education where the universal value has almost been totally eradicated from the learning process – the amorality of learning within an advanced capitalist system is becoming the order of the day.

The universal value is not cognitive, neither is it instrumentally rational. Indeed, it is learned preconsciously and so it does not fit the modern paradigm. It is a universal value but its practice actually questions the excessive practice of some of the cultural values – values which have strong ideological overtones – and so attempts are being made to bury it quietly. But its universality means that it will not go away – for unlike the cultural values it is not relative!

This book is by no means a Luddite analysis of contemporary education for adults but it does ask questions about the processes that are currently occurring. Indeed, we might note that we do not know if people actually learn more efficiently without teachers, we do not know if people would not be even more creative and adventurous in their learning if they had mentors, we do not know if the use of teachers might make education and learning more enjoyable, we do not know what are the best use of the structures of time for efficient learning to occur.

What we are claiming here, however, is that the processes of teaching and learning are processes where putting the universal value of people caring for people into practice costs money and so it is becoming less dominant in the educational system. When people have no time for people the face becomes a stranger, the Other no longer impinges upon my spontaneity and the universal ethic is subsumed into relative, cultural values and education has become depersonalised. If this were to occur the learning society, hailed by many, would be impoverished. Educators should strive to avoid this – for, paradoxically, it might be that individuals being available for learners might also produce a better and more efficient teaching and learning system where each individual's potentiality stands a greater chance of being achieved and, perhaps, it might be a step towards the good society to which many of us who advocate the learning society look forward.

# Bibliography

Aboulafia M (1986) *The Mediating Self: Mead, Sartre and Self-Determination* New Haven: Yale University Press

Adam B (1997) *Timewatch: The Social Analysis of Time* Cambridge: Polity

Adams F (1975) *Unearthing Seeds of Fire* Winston-Salem: John F Blair

Adorno T (1973) *The Jargon of Authenticity* Evanston: Northwestern University Press.

*Adults Learning* (1991) Bill of rights for the adult learner. Vol 3 No.4

Althusser L (1971) Ideology and Ideological State

Apparatuses. In B Cosin (ed) (1972) *Education: Structure and Society* Harmondsworth: Penguin

Anderson J and Ricci M (1990) *Society and Societal Science* Milton Keynes: Open University

Apps J (1989) Providers of Adult and Continuing Education: A Framework. In *Handbook of Adult and Continuing Education* eds S Merriam and P Cunningham. San Francisco: Jossey Bass

Argyris C and Schon D (1974) *Theory in Practice: Increasing Professional Effectiveness* San Francisco: Jossey Bass.

Aristotle (1925 ed) *Nichomachean Ethics* Oxford: Oxford University Press

Arrow K J (1974) General Economic Equilibrium: purpose, analytic technique, collective choice. In American Economic Review Vol 64.

Atkinson, RF (1969) *Conduct: an Introduction to Moral Philosophy* London: Macmillan

Ayer A J (1971) *Language, Truth and Logic* Harmondsworth: Pelican Books

Bacon R and Eltis W (1976) *Britain's Economic Problem: Too Few Producers* London: Macmillan

Barlow S (1987) Impossible Dream: why doesn't mentorship work in UK nurse education. In *Nursing Times*

Bateman W (1990) *Open to Question* San Francisco: Jossey Bass.

Baudrillard J (1988) A System of Objects. In *Jean Baudrillard; A Selection of Writings* edited by M Poster. Cambridge: Polity Press

Baudrillard J (1993) *The Transparency of Evil* London: Verso (Trans: James Benedict)

Bauman Z (1987) *Legislators and Interpreters* Cambridge: Polity Press

Bauman Z (1991) *Modernity and Ambivalence* Cambridge: Polity Press

Bauman Z (1992) *Mortality, Immortality and Other Life Strategies* Cambridge: Polity Press.

Bauman Z (1992a) *Intimations of Postmodernity* London: Routledge

Bauman Z (1993) *Postmodern Ethics* Oxford: Blackwell.

Bauman Z (1995) *Life in Fragments* Oxford: Blackwell

Beatty P, Benefield L and Linhart L (1991) Evaluating the Teaching and Learning Process. In Galbraith M (ed) *op cit.*

Beck U (1992) *Risk Society* (Trans: Mark Ritter) London: Sage.

Benhabib S (1986) *Critique, Norm and Utopia* New York: Columbia University Press.

Benner P (1984) *From Novice to Expert* California: Addison Wesley.

Berger, P L (1977) *Pyramids of Secrifice* Harmondsworth: Pelican Books.

Berger P, Berger B and Kellner H (1974) *The Homeless Mind* Harmondsworth: Penguin

Bickerstaffe G (1997) The Long and the Short of Choosing an MBA in *The Observer Business* p. 14. Sunday 25 January

Bloom B 1956 *Taxonomy of Educational Objectives Book 1 Cognitive Domain* London: Longman

Bocock R (1976) *Freud and Modern Society* Walton-on-Thames: Nelson

Bohm D (1987) *Unfolding Meaning* London: ARK

Borger R and Seaborne A (1966) *The Psychology of Learning* Harmondsworth: Penguin

Boud D (ed) (1988) *Developing Student Autonomy in Learning* London: Kogan Page (Second Edition).

Bourdieu P and Passeron J-C (1977) *Reproduction* (Trans: R Nice) London: Sage

Boyd W and King E (1964) *The History of Western Education* London: Adam and Charles Black (Revised Edition)

Brockett R (ed) (1988) *Ethical Issues in Adult Education* New York: Teachers College, Columbia University.

Brookfield S D (1990) *The Skillful Teacher* San Francisco: Jossey Bass.

Brown V (1992) The Emergence of the Economy. In *Formations of Modernity* (eds) S Hall and B Gieben. Cambridge: Polity Press

Bruner J (1968) *Toward a Theory of Instruction* New York: W W Norton and Co

Buber M (1947) *Between Man and Man* (Trans: RG Smith) London: Collins (Fontana Edition – 1961)

Buber M (1959) *I and Thou* (Trans: R G Smith) Edinburgh: T & T Clark. (Second Edition)

Buber M (1961) *Between Man and Man* Glasgow: Fontana Library

Bull M (1995) *Apocalypse Theory* Oxford: Blackwell (ed)

Burnard P (1986) The student experience: adult learning and mentorship revisited. In *Nurse Education Today* Vol. 6 No 5

Campbell C (1987) *The Romantic Ethic and the Spirit of Modern Consumerism* Oxford: Blackwell.

Candy P (1990) More than Meets the Eye. In Long H and Associates *(op cit)*

Candy P (1991) *Self-Direction for Lifelong Learning* San Francisco: Jossey Bass

Caplow T (1954) *The Sociology of Work* Minneapolis: University of Minnesota Press. Cited in Vollmer H and Mills D (eds) *op cit*

Carr-Saunders A and Wilson P (1933) *The Professions* Oxford: Clarenden Press in Vollmer H and Mills D (eds) *op cit*

Conti G (1990) Identifying Your Teaching Style. In Galbraith M (ed) (1990) *op cit*

Cooper D (1983) *Authenticity and learning: Nietzsche's Educational Philosophy* London: Routledge

Cooper D (1990) *Existentialism* Oxford: Blackwell.

Daloz L (1986) *Effective Teaching and Mentoring* San Francisco: Jossey Bass.

Dearden R F, Hirst P H and Peters R S (eds) (1972) *Education and Reason* London: Routledge and Kegan Paul

Deci E and Ryan R (1981) Curiosity and Self-Directed Learning. The Role of Motivation in Education. ERIC Clearinghouse: document number ED206307 cited in Eisenman, 1990 *op cit*

Delors J (chair) (1996) *Learning – the Treasure Within* Paris: UNESCO

Dewey J (1916) *Democracy and Education* New York: Free Press

Dews P (ed) (1986) *Autonomy and Solidarity: interviews with Jürgen Habermas* London: Verso

Dreyfus S and Dreyfus H (1980) *A Five Stage Model of the Mental Activities involved in Directed Skill Acquisition* University of California: Unpublished cited Benner *op cit*

Durkheim E (1933) *The Division of Labour in Society* New York: Free Press

Eisenman G (1990) Self-Directed Learning – a Growth Process? in Long H and associates *op cit*

Elliot P (1972) *The Sociology of the Professions* London: Macmillan

Eurich N (1985) *Corporate Classrooms* Princeton: The Carnegie Foundation for the Advancement of Teaching

Faure E (chair) (1972) *Learning to Be* Paris: UNESCO

Fish D and Purr B (1991) *An Evaluation of Practice-Based Learning in Continuing Professional Education in Nursing, Midwifery and Health Visiting* London: English National Board, 1991.

Fletcher C (1975) *The Person in the Sight of Sociology* London: Routledge and Kegan Paul

Flew A (Editorial Consultant) (1979) *A Dictionary of Philosophy* London: Pan Books

Frankena W K (1963) *Ethics* Englewood Cliffs, New Jersey: Prentice Hall

Freire P (1972) *Pedagogy of the Oppressed* Harmondsworth: Penguin

Freire P (1972a) *Cultural Action for Freedom* Harmondsworth: Penguin

Fromm E (1976) *To Have or to Be ?* New York: HarperCollins

Fukuyama F (1992 *The End of History and the Last Man* London: Hamish Hamilton

Gaarter J (1994) *Sophie's World* London: Phoenix House

Gadamer H-G (1976) *Philosophical Hermeneutics* Berkeley: University of California Press (Trans: D E Linge)

Galbraith M (ed) (1990) *Adult Learning Methods* Malabar: Krieger.

Galbraith M (ed) (1991) *Facilitating Adult Learning* Malabar: Krieger.

Giddens A (1990) *The Consequences of Modernity* Cambridge: Polity Press.

Giddens A (1991) *Modernity and Self-Identity* Cambridge: Polity Press

Giddens A (1994) *Beyond Left and Right* Cambridge: Polity

Greenwood E (1957) Attributes of a Profession. In *Social Work* Vol 2 No 3 pp.44–55

Griffin C (1987) *Adult Education as Social Policy* London: Croom Helm.

*The Guardian* (1993) 19th October – an advertisement

Habermas J (1987) *The Philosophical Discourse of Modernity* Cambridge: Polity Press

Habermas J (1990) *Moral Consciousness and Communicative Action* (Trans: C Lenhardt and S W Nicholson) Cambridge: Polity Press.

Habermas J (1993) *Justification and Application – Remarks on Discourse Ethics* (Trans: C P Cronin) Cambridge: Polity Press.

Hagerty B (1986) A Second Look at Mentors. In *Nursing Outlook* Vol. 34 No 1 pp 16–24.

Hall B (1996) Adult Education and the Political Economy of Global Economic Change in P. Wangoola and F Youngman (eds) *Towards a Transformative Political Economy of Adult Education* Illinois: Northern Illinois University – LEPS Press

Hall S and Gieben S (eds) (1992) *Formations of Modernity* Cambridge: Polity

Hamilton P (1992) The Enlightenment and the Birth of Social Science in Hall S and Gieben B (eds) *op cit*

Hand S (ed) (1989) *The Levinas Reader* Oxford: Basil Blackwell

Hare R M (1956) *The Language of Morals* Oxford: Clarendon Press

Harrow A J (1972) *A Taxonomy of the Psychomotor Domain* New York: McKay

Harvey D (1990) *The Postmodern Condition* Oxford: Blackwell

Harvey D (1993) Class Relations, Social Justice and the Politics of Difference. In *Principled Positions* ed J Squires. London: Lawrence and Wishart

Heelas P, Lash S and Morris P (eds) (1996) *Detraditionalization* Oxford: Blackwell.

Heidegger M (1962) *Being and Time* London: SCM Press

Heller A (1984) *Everyday Life* London: Routledge and Kegan Paul

Heller A (1987) *Beyond Justice* Oxford: Blackwell

Heller A (1988) *General Ethics* Oxford: Basil Blackwell

Heller A (1990) *A Philosophy of Morals* Oxford: Basil Blackwell

Hiemstra R and Sisco B (1990) *Individualizing Instruction* San Francisco: Jossey Bass.

Hircsh R, Paolitto D and Reimer J (1979) *Promoting Moral Growth* New York: Longman.

Hirst P (1974) *Knowledge and the Curriculum* London: Routledge and Kegan Paul

Hirst P and Peters R (1970) *The Logic of Education* London: Routledge and Kegan Paul.

Hollins T (ed) (1964) *Aims in Education* Manchester: Manchester University Press

*Holy Bible*

Horton M (1990) *Myles Horton* New York: Anchor Books

Husserl E (1962) *Ideas: General Introduction to Pure Phenomenology* London: Collier MacMillan

Hutchins R (1970) *The Learning Society* Harmondsworth: Pelican

Illich I and Verne E (1976) *Imprisoned in a Global Classroom* London: Writers and Readers Publishing Corporation

Jameson F (1991) *Postmodernism* London: Verso

Jarvis P (1972) *Religious Socialisation in the Junior School* Birmingham: University of Birmingham (Unpublished M.Soc Sc thesis)

Jarvis P (1983a) *Professional Education* London: Croom Helm.

Jarvis P (1987) *Adult Learning in the Social Context* London: Croom Helm

Jarvis P (1991) Practical Knowledge and Theoretical Analyses in Adult and Continuing Education. In von Herausgegeben et al (eds) *Erwachsenenbilden im Kontext* Bad Heirbrunn: Klinkhardt.

Jarvis P (1992) *Paradoxes of Learning* San Francisco: Jossey Bass.

Jarvis P (1992b) Reflective Practice and Nursing *Nurse Education Today* Vol. 12 pp.174–181.

Jarvis P (1993) *Adult Education and the State* London: Routledge.

Jarvis P (1993a) Learning as a Religious Phenomenon In Jarvis and Walters (eds) *op cit*

Jarvis P (1994) Learning Practical Knowledge In *Journal of Further and Higher Education* Vol. 18. No 1 pp.31–43.

Jarvis P (1995) *Adult and Continuing Education: Theory and Practice* London: Routledge. (Revised Edition)

Jarvis P (1995a) Educating the Adult Educator in an Information Society: the Role of the University in M Collins (ed) *The Canmore Proceedings – International Conference on Educating the Adult Educator: the Role of the University* Saskatchewan: College of Education, University of Saskatchewan, pp.179–188

Jarvis P (1997) Self-Directed Learning – Self-Help or Self-Service? Paper presented to the International Conference on Self-Directed Learning. Florida, February.

Jarvis P and Dubelaar J (1997) *The Untapped Potential at Work: The Elder Mentor* Research Report, obtainable from: Department of Educational Studies, University of Surrey.

Jarvis P and Gibson S (1987) *The Teacher Practitioner in Nursing, Midwifery and Health Visiting* London: Croom Helm

Jarvis P and Walters N (eds) (1993) *Adult Education and Theological Interpretations* Malabar: Krieger

Jarvis P, Holford J, Griffin C and Dubelaar J (1997) *Learn More for Less* London: Corporation of London and the University of Surrey, Department of Educational Studies.

Kelly T (1970) *A History of Adult Education in Great Britain* Liverpool: Liverpool University Press (Second Edition)

Kidd J R (1973) *How Adults Learn* Chicago: Association Press. (Revised edition)

Knowles M S (1975) *Self-Directed Learning* Chicago: Follett

Knowles M S (1977) *The Adult Education Movement in the United States* New York: Krieger (Revised edition)

Knowles M S (1980) *The Modern Practice of Adult Education: From Pedagogy to Andragogy* Chicago: Association Press (Revised edition)

Knowles M S (1986) *Using Learning Contracts* San Francisco: Jossey Bass

Kohlberg L (1969) Stage and Sequence: The Cognitive Developmental Approach to Socialization. In *Handbook of Socialization Theory and Research.* (ed) D Goslin. Chicago: Rand McNally.

Kohlberg L (1976) Moral Stages and Moralization: The Cognitive-Developmental Approach. In *Theory, Research and Social Issues* (ed) T Lickona. New York: Holt, Rinehart and Winston.

Kohlberg L (1986) *The Philosophy of Moral Development* San Francisco: Harper and Row

Kohlberg L (1987) The Cognitive-Developmental Approach to Moral Education. In *Value Theory and Education* (ed) P Carbone Jr. Malabar: Krieger.

Krathwohl D, Bloom B and Masia B (1964) *Taxonomy of Educational Objectives, Book 2, Affective Domain* London: Longman

Kumar K (1987) *Utopia and Anti-Utopia* Oxford: Blackwell

Kyrö P (1995) *The Management Consulting Industry Modelled Through Profession* Helsinki: University of Helsinki PhD Thesis

Lawton D (1973) *Social Change, Educational Theory and Curriculum Planning* London: Hodder and Stoughton

Lengrand P (1975) *An Introduction to Lifelong Education* London: Croom Helm

Levinas E (1991) *Totality and Infinity* (Trans A Lingis) Dordrecht: Kluwer

Levinas E (1989) Martin Buber and the Theory of Knowledge in Hand S (ed) *op cit*

Levitas R (1990) *The Concept of Utopia* New York: Philip Allan

Lippett R and White R K (1958) An Experimental Study in Leadership and Group Life. In Maccoby *et al* (eds) *op cit*

Long H and associates (1990) *Advances in Research and Practice in Self-Directed Learning* University of Oklahoma: Research Center for Continuing and Professional Higher Education.

Longworth N and Davies W K (1996) *Lifelong Learning* London: Kogan Page.

Lukes S (1974) *Power: a Radical View* London: Macmillan

Lyotard J-F (1984) *The Post-Modern Condition* Manchester: Manchester University Press

Lyotard J-F (1992) *The Postmodern Explained to Children* London: Turnaround

Maccoby E, Hartley T and Hartley E (eds) (1958) *Readings in Social Psychology* New York: Holt

McGregor D (1960) *The Human Side of Enterprise* New York: McGraw Hill.

MacIntyre A (1985) *After Virtue: a study in moral theory* London: Duckworth (Second Edition)

MacIntyre A (1988) *Whose Justice? Whose Rationality?* London: Duckworth

MacMurray J (1961) *Persons in Relation* New Jersey: Humanities Press Ltd

McNair S (1993) *An Adult Higher Education: a Vision* Leicester, National Institute of Adult Continuing Education.

MacQuarrie J (1973) *Existentialism* Harmondsworth: Penguin

Mabbott J D (1966) *An Introduction to Ethics* London: Hutchinson

Marcel G (1976) *Being and Having* Gloucester, Mass: Peter Smith

Marsick V and Watkins K (1990) *Informal and Incidental Learning in the Workplace'* London: Routledge

Marton F and Saljö R (1984) Approaches to Learning in *The Experience of Learning* Edinburgh: Scottish Academic Press (Eds) F Marton, D Hounsell and N Entwistle

Maslow A (1968) *Towards a Psychology of Being* New York: Van Nostrand.

Mead H H (1964) *Mind, Self and Society* reprinted in Strauss *op cit*

Mehrens W and Lehmann I (1991) *Measurement and Evaluation in Education Psychology* Fort Worth: Holt, Rinehart and Winston. (Fourth Edition)

Melucci A ( 1989) *Nomads of the Present* London: Hutchinson Radius

Mill J S (1962) *Utilitarianism* Collins: Fontana Library

Miller R (1995) *Arguments Against Secular Culture* London: SCM Press

Moore G E (1902) *Principia Ethica* Cambridge: The University Press.

Murray M with Owen M (1991) *Beyond the Myths and Magic of Mentoring* San Francisco: Jossey Bass.

Nozick R (1993) *The Nature of Rationality* Princeton: Princeton University Press

Nyiri J (1988) Tradition and Practical Knowledge. In *Practical Knowledge* (ed) Nyiri J and Smith B London: Croom Helm.

Pastuović N (1995) The Science(s) of Adult Education. In *International Journal of Lifelong Education.* Vol. 14 No 4.

Paterson R.W.K. (1979) *Values, Education and the Adult* London: Routledge and Kegan Paul.

Peffer R G (1990) *Marxism, Morality and Social Justice* Princeton: Princeton University Press

Peters O (1984) Distance Teaching and Industrial Production: a comparative international outline. In D Stewart, D Keegan and B Holmberg (eds) *Distance Education: International Perspectives* London: Routledge

Peters R S (1965) Education as Initiation In R D Archambault (ed) *Philosophical Analysis and Education* London: Routledge and Kegan Paul

Peters R S (1966) *Ethics and Education* London. George Allen and Unwin

Peters R S (1970) Education and the Educated Man. In Peters R S (1977) *op cit*

Peters R S (1972) Education and Human Development. In Dearden R F, Hirst P H and Peters R S (eds) *op cit*

Peters R S (1977) *Education and the Education of Teachers* London: Routledge and Kegan Paul.

Phillips D L (1986) *Toward a Just Social Order* Princeton: Princeton University Press.

Piaget J (1929) *The Child's Conception of the World* London: Routledge and Kegan Paul

Piaget J (1955) *The Moral Judgment of the Child* New York: Free Press.

Polanyi M (1967) *The Tacit Dimension* London: Routledge and Kegan Paul

Poole R (1990) *Morality and Modernity* London: Routledge.

Pring R (1993) Liberal Education and Vocational Preparation in Barrow R and White P (eds) *Beyond Liberal Education* London: Routledge

Ranson S (1994) *Towards the Learning Society* London: Cassell

Rasmussen D M (1990) *Reading Habermas* Oxford: Basil Blackwell.

Rawls J (1971) *A Theory of Justice* Cambridge, Mass: Belknap Press of Harvard University Press

Reber A (1985) *Dictionary of Psychology* Harmondsworth: Penguin

Reich R (1991) *The Work of Nations* London: Simon and Schuster

Reischmann J (1986) *Learning en passant: The Forgotten Dimension* Unpublished paper, presented at the American Association of Adult and Continuing Education Conference: Florida

Ritzer G (1993) *The McDonaldization of Society* Thousand Oaks: Pine Forge Press

Robertson R (1992) *Globalisation* London: Sage

Robinson D and Robinson J (1989) *Training for Impact* San Francisco: Jossey Bass

Rogers C (1967) *On Becoming a Person* London: Constable

Rogers C (1969) *Freedom to Learn* Columbus, Ohio: Merrill

Rogers C (1983) *Freedom to Learn for the 80s* Toronto: Collier MacMillan (Revised Edition)

Rumble G (1995) Labour Market Theories and Distance Education In *Open Learning* Vol 10 Nos.1–3 (3 papers) London: Pitman Publishing

Ryle G (1949) *The Concept of Mind* London: Hutchinson reprinted as Ryle G (1963) *The Concept of Mind* Harmondsworth: Peregrine Books.

Scheler M (1980) *Problems of a Sociology of Knowledge* London: Routledge and Kegan Paul (ed Stikkers K)

Schon D (1987) *Educating the Reflective Practitioner* San Francisco: Jossey Bass.

Schumpeter J A (1976) *Capitalism, Socialism and Democracy* London: George Allen and Unwin.

Scott A (1992) Political Culture and Social Movements in *Political and Economic Forms of Society* (ed) J Allen, P Braham and P Lewis Cambridge: Polity Press in association with the Open University

Selman G (1991) *Citizenship and the Adult Education Movement in Canada* Vancouver: University of British Columbia in cooperation with ICAE

Simmel G (1903) *The Metropolis and Mental Life* Reprinted in *Sociological perspectives* (1971) ed K Thompson and J Tunstall. Harmondsworth: Penguin.

Simpson E J (1966) *The Classification of Educational Objectives: Psychomotor Domain* Urbana: University of Illinois Press

Sloan J and Slevin O (1991) *Teaching and Supervision of Student Nurses During Practice Placement* Belfast, The National Board

Smart B (1990) Modernity, Post-Modernity and the Present in Turner B (ed) *op cit*

Smiles S (1996) *Self Help* London: IEA Health and Welfare Unit

Smith A (1976) *The Theory of Moral Sentiments*-1759 reprinted in D Raphael and A Macfie (eds) *The Glasgow Edition of the Works and Correspondence of Adam Smith Vol 1* Oxford: Oxford University Press

Smith A (1976) *An Inquiry into the Nature and Causes of the Wealth of Nations* 1776, reprinted R Campbell and A Skinner (eds) in *The Glasgow Edition of the Works and Correspondence of Adam Smith Vol 2* Oxford: Oxford University Press

Snook I *Concepts of Indoctrination* London: Routledge

Speake J (ed) (1979) *A Dictionary of Philosophy* London: Pan Books.

Sprigge TLS (1988) *The Rational Foundation of Ethics* London: Routledge

Stanton H (1988) Independent Study: a Matter of Confidence? In Boud (ed) *(op cit)*

Steele T (1994) The Colonial Metaphor and the Mission of Englishness: Adult Education and the Origins of English Studies in Marriot S and Hake B (eds) *Cultural and Intercultural Experiences in European Adult Education* Leeds: Leeds Studies in Continuing Education

Stephens M and Roderick G (eds) (1983) *Samuel Smiles and Nineteenth Century Self-Help in Education* University of Nottingham: Department of Adult Education.

Stevenson C L (1944) *Ethics and Language* New Haven: Yale University Press

Strauss A (1964) (ed) *George Herbert Mead on Social Psychology: Selected Papers* Chicago: University of Chicago Press (Fifth Edition)

Svec S (1990) Gnoseological/Epistemological Profile of Didactics/Pedagogy In *Proceedings of the Xth Congress of the World Association for Educational Research* ed M Cipro. Prague: Charles University Press.

Taylor C (1991) *The Ethics of Authenticity* Cambridge. Mass: Harvard University Press.

Thompkins C and MacGraw M-J (1988) The Negotiated Learning Contract. In Boud D (ed) *op cit*

Thompson E P (1977) *William Morris: Romantic to Revolutionary* London: Merlin Press

Thornton A (1983) Introduction – The Smilesian Philosophy In Stephens M and Roderick G (eds) *(op cit)*

Tilly C (1984) Social Movements and National Politics in C Wright and S Harding (eds) *Statemaking and Social Movements* Ann Arbor: University of Michigan Press

Toennies F (1957) *Community and Society* New York: Harper and Row

Tough A (1971) *The Adult's Learning Projects* Toronto: Ontario Institute for Studies in Education. (Second Edition)

Turner B S (1990) *Theories of Modernity and Post-Modernity* London: Sage

United Nations (1948) *The Declaration of Human Rights*

Urmson J O (1968) *The Emotive Theory of Ethics* London: Hutchinson.

Usher R and Edwards R (1994) *Postmodernism and Education* London: Routledge

Vollmer H and Mills D (eds) (1966) *Professionalization* Englewood Cliffs: Prentice Hall.

Wallerstein I (1990) Culture as the Ideological Battleground of the Modern World System In *Theory, Culture and Society* Vol. 7 pp.31–55

Warnke G (1987) *Gadamer* Stanford: Stanford University Press

Weber M (1930) *The Protestant Ethic and the Spirit of Capitalism* London: Unwin University Books

Weber M (1947) *The Theory of Economic and Social Organisations* New York: Free Press.

Welsh National Board (1992) *Mentors, Preceptors and Supervisors: Their Place in Nursing, Midwifery and Health Visitor Education.* Cardiff.

Welton M (ed) (1987) *Knowledge for the People* Ontario: OISE

Williams B (1985) *Ethics and the Limits of Philosophy* London: Fontana Paperbacks

Williams G and Fry H (1994) *Longer Term Prospects for British Higher Education* London, Centre for Studies in Higher Education, University of London.

Wiltshire H (1966) The Nature and Uses of Adult Education. In Rogers A (ed) (1976) *The Spirit and the Form* Nottingham: Department of Adult Education, University of Nottingham.

Wolfe A (1989) *Whose Keeper?* Berkeley: University of California Press.

Yeaxlee B (1929) *Lifelong Education* London: Cassells

# Author Index

# Subject Index

**Globalization, adult education and training: Impacts and issues**
Shirley Walters (ed)
ISBN 1 86201 026 9 (pbk); 1 85649 511 6 (hbk)
1997, 256pp, £14.95 (pbk); £39.95 (hbk)

Globalization has become a key shorthand for the times we live in, summing up some of the important changes affecting life in all parts of the world. And adult educators are having to come to terms with the processes involved and the implications for their own work. This book looks at the impact of globalization on adult education and training generally and on women in particular, and draws the lessons for adult education trainers. It explores adult education and training strategies towards women, workplace training and participatory approaches in diverse contexts and countries. The contributors focus on the notion of lifelong learning, its meaning and how to go about implementing it.

This book is the first in a series co-published by NIACE and ZED BOOKS on global perspectives in adult education and training. It includes well-documented material on the effects of globalization from both North and South. Launched at the UNESCO World Conference on Adult Education in Hamburg in July 1997.

**SPECIAL OFFER** to NIACE readers only. NIACE has arranged a privilege price of £35.95 (normally £39.95) for the hardback version – a saving of 10 per cent. Order direct from NIACE to take advantage of this excellent offer.


**The learning divide: A study of participation in adult learning in the United Kingdom**
Naomi Sargant
with John Field, Hywel Francis, Tom Schuller and Alan Tuckett
ISBN 1 86201 016 1
1997, 144pp, £20.00

This publication reports on a survey carried out by the Gallup Organisation in 1996. It highlights the full scale of the challenge which the UK faces in involving all its people in the learning society, and shows that the learning divide between the learning-rich and the learning-poor is growing. It shows that 60% of adults have not taken part in adult learning in the last three years; more men than women are currently learning or have been recent learners; age is a barrier; social class is still the key discriminator; and length of initial education is still the best single predictor of participation in adult learning.

The report includes the first full study of participation in Northern Ireland, and, with studies from Scotland and Wales, gives the most comprehensive coverage of the United Kingdom. With over 60 tables of statistical information, this report will provide an invaluable resource for researchers, academics, media and information officers.

**Words in edgeways: Radical learning for social change**
Jane Thompson
ISBN 1 86201 013 7
1997, 160pp, £14.95

Jane Thompson's books and essays have inspired and validated the work of radical practitioners in adult and community education not only in Britain, but also overseas – particularly in Ireland, Australia, New Zealand, Canada and the United States.

This is a collection of extracts, essays and conference presentations, written over a 20-year period, on working class and women's education. This volume covers the application of Marxist, sociological and feminist analysis to adult education; connections between the women's movement and adult education, and a collection of writings by women learners whose lives were restricted by poverty and family violence.

This book will be useful to students on adult and continuing education courses at Diploma and Masters level. It will also be of relevance to staff development activity, conferences and workshops in which matters of curriculum, political education, participatory learning, citizenship and social change are being discussed. Practitioners in adult learning and community education who are concerned about disadvantage and issues of inclusion and exclusion will also find the book valuable.

**Electronic pathways: Adult learning and the new communication technologies**
Edited by Jane Field
ISBN 1 86201 008 0
1997, 176pp, £14.95

What does the information society really mean for adult learning? A rapidly-growing range of communications technologies is being developed to support the adult learner. Telematics applications can have an impact on education, leisure and work, but adult educators and others involved in working with adult learners need practical help if they are to make the most of the opportunities.

This is the first book to place the new information and communications technologies firmly in the context of adult learning. It is written by adult educators who have used the new technologies to widen access to learning and promote independent learning. They have seen that it is possible to offer different ways to communicate and support learning, whether in college, the home, the workplace or other settings.

Case studies provide examples of the pitfalls involved, good practice identified and the opportunities available. The book is an accessible, informative and practical resource for all who are professionally concerned with developing adult learning.

**Imagining tomorrow: Adult education for transformation**
Marjorie Mayo
ISBN 1 86201 006 4
Publication date: June 1997, 184pp, £14.95

This is a study of the increasing importance of community and workplace adult education in the First and Third worlds. Marjorie Mayo looks at the impact of globalisation, economic restructuring and the enhanced role of community and voluntary organisations in the provision of education. She presents the case for wider understanding of the context and possibilities for local development as part of longer-term strategies for transformation.

The author looks at the implications of adult learning for sustainable development for social justice, defined by local communities themselves. She takes case studies from Tanzania, Cuba, India and Nicaragua as well as from the industrialised 'North' to illustrate her themes. The book concludes by focussing on issues of culture, identity, diversity and changing consciousness; and the role of community education in strengthening collective confidence to effect social transformation.

**Adults count too: Mathematics for empowerment**
Roseanne Benn
ISBN 1 86201 007 2
1997, 224pp, £14.95

More and more adults are learning mathematics, either for work-related purposes, or as a qualification leading to a desired course of study. *Adults count too* examines the low level of numeracy in our society, the reasons why this is critical and the forces acting on adults which contribute to this state of affairs. Written to encourage the development of a curriculum which is tailored to the priorities and lives of individuals, Benn argues that mathematics is not a value-free construct, but is imbued with elitist notions which exclude and mystify. The book seeks alternative approaches to teaching mathematics which recognise the sophisticated mathematical techniques and ideas used in everyday work, domestic and leisure.

This book will be of interest to adult educators who teach mathematics or to mathematics educators who teach adults.

**Adults learning**

ISSN 0955 2308
Subscription rates:   £30 (institutions); extra copies @ £15 each
£17.50 (individuals)
£15 (concessions for part-time tutors and adult learners)

The need for a professional journal for those concerned with adult learning has never been greater than now. The majority of students in further and higher education in Britain are adults. More and more awareness of the importance of adults as learners is being shown by government, the media, employers and trade unions. In a quickly-changing environment it is vital to keep abreast of current issues and initiatives, debates and events.

*Adults learning* is the only UK-wide journal solely devoted to matters concerning adult learning. It carries the latest news on policy and practice, and is published ten times a year by NIACE. It is a forum for adult educators and trainers to exchange information, share practice, network and engage in dialogue with fellow professionals.

In-depth features, commentaries, reviews and case studies, together with news of courses, conferences and resources, make *Adults learning* essential reading for policy-makers and practitioners, tutors (both full-time and part-time) in universities and further education colleges, staff in voluntary organisations who are developing learning opportunities, and trainers in industry seeking advice on skills development.

**Studies in the education of adults**

ISSN 0266 0830

| Subscription rates: | UK £20 individual; | £30 institutional |
|---|---|---|
| Overseas surface mail: | £22/US$40 individual; | £33/US$59 institutional |
| Overseas airmail: | £25/US$45 individual; | £38/US$67 institutional |

An international refereed journal published twice a year (April and October) by NIACE. It is addressed to academic specialists, postgraduate students, practitioners and educational managers who wish to keep abreast of scholarship, theory-building and empirical research in the broad field of education and training for adults.

*Studies in the education of adults* publishes theroetical, empirical and historical studies from all sectors of post-initial education and training, and aims to provide a forum for debate and development of key concepts in education and training. With feature articles and book reviews, the journal provides indispensable analysis of current developments and thinking.

A full publications catalogue is available from NIACE at 21 De Montfort Street, Leicester, LE1 7GE, England. Alternatively visit our Web site on the Internet: **http://www.niace.org.uk**